FAR OUT

Also by Charlotte McDonald-Gibson

Cast Away: Stories of Survival from Europe's Refugee Crisis

Charlotte McDonald-Gibson

Far Out

Encounters with Extremists

GRANTA

Granta Publications, 12 Addison Avenue, London W11 4QR
First published in Great Britain by Granta Books, 2022

A CIP catalogue record for this book is available from the British Library.

1 3 5 7 9 10 8 6 4 2

ISBN 978 1 78378 646 6
eISBN 978 1 78378 648 0

Typeset in Bembo by Avon DataSet Ltd, Alcester, Warwickshire B49 6HN
Printed and bound by CPI Group (UK) Ltd, Croydon, CR0 4YY

www.granta.com

For Casper and Nathaniel

Contents

Prologue

Brussels, 22 March 2016. My taxi makes its way through the early-morning traffic, a touch lighter than it should be at this time on the airport route. It's the cusp of rush hour, but things are still not quite right. Not here, not in many big cities. It's a hazy feeling of mild fear, a needling, constant awareness that violence is possible. Because we have seen the kind of terror that can happen. Four months earlier, nine suicide bombers and gunmen launched an attack on Paris nightspots, killing 130 people. Now we no longer take our safety for granted, and we are slowly getting used to this new era of low-level fear and mistrust.

   The fear came quickly to Brussels, where I had been living for three years, reporting on the European Union (EU). Soon after the Paris attacks, the army took over the streets and we were ordered to avoid public spaces. There was intelligence about an imminent attack, and for a week in November 2015 we were told it was too dangerous to send our children to nursery or school. It was too dangerous to take the tram or the bus. We grumbled about having to find babysitters, about the cost of taxis, at the same time wondering whether it was safe to go shopping, to see friends, to leave our homes at all. The confinement ended, but the tanks and soldiers stayed, guarding synagogues, department stores, train stations. At first it was jarring seeing soldiers every-where in this European city, armoured vehicles on the pavements, guns guarding the suburban shopping centres. But it is amazing how quickly we adjust to the extreme.

A remnant of that fear flickers across people's faces as they pull their wheeled suitcases into Brussels Airport and notice the two soldiers standing guard at the entrance. Life still isn't back to normal, our expressions register, but that's OK, we are used to this. My mind plays the same trick as everyone else's – a brief acknowledgement of risk before returning to the comfort of the usual routine: check-in, security, breakfast.

About fifteen minutes later, three young men enter the airport, following the route I took from the taxi rank, past the two soldiers and into the departures hall: they are Ibrahim El Bakraoui, a 29-year-old with a doughy face and a conviction for shooting a police officer; Najim Laachraoui, a 24-year-old aspiring electrical engineer and brother of a Belgian taekwondo champion; and Mohamed Abrini, a 31-year-old former drug dealer with a rap for petty crimes. They each push a large suitcase on a trolley. The taxi driver who brought them to the airport later said that he wondered why those unusually heavy cases emitted a strange smell. It was because each one contained a lethal combination of combustible chemicals, explosives and nails.

At 7.58 a.m. the first bomb detonates near check-in row 11, followed seconds later by another at check-in row 2. Ibrahim El Bakraoui and Najim Laachraoui are dead. Mohamed Abrini's device fails to explode and he flees.

Just through security and having breakfast in the terminal building, I don't hear the explosions, but I hear the panic as an airport employee rushes into the restaurant and shouts, 'Get up, get out!' An evacuation order echoes over the loudspeakers. Then another, contradictory announcement: 'Stay in your terminals.' Which is it? Passengers pull their little suitcases back and forth across the terminal building, unsure where to go. News of the bombs reaches our smartphones, but still we can't grasp what has happened just a few hundred metres away. Eventually we are escorted out of Terminal 2, along the runway and into a cargo loading area.

A man with a bloodied sweatshirt sits on the ground and stares at nothing.

Snipers perch on the roofs.

We finally see the blown-out windows of the departure hall. Inside are seventeen bodies in a hell of dense smoke, overturned prams, broken glass and shattered lives.

I had been a foreign correspondent for nearly fifteen years by then, mostly in Asia. In 2010, I moved back to the continent of my birth and found it going through its most seismic upheaval since the fall of the Berlin Wall. An economic crisis had shattered faith in governments and state institutions, and a refugee crisis would soon paralyse the European Union. This new wave of terror would further unmoor Europeans from the principles of trust and security that were meant to hold us together.

By the end of 2016, we would understand that extremism didn't just refer to young men with bombs. A spectrum of political extremism would propel both the United Kingdom and the United States onto deeply divisive paths. On 23 June, Britain voted to leave the European Union after a campaign typified by a blurring of truth and lies and incendiary rhetoric. On 9 November, Donald Trump was elected President of the United States, ushering in one of the most polarizing periods in American history.

Throughout my career I had sought out the people cast as victims of the times in which they lived and tried to portray the complexities of their struggles: ordinary people suffering from austerity policies; refugees struggling to be recognized as human beings; minority communities targeted by hate crimes. But during that seismic year, I realised that to make sense of the extraordinary times in which we lived, I also needed to understand the other side. The victims give us part of the story, but without listening to the voices of the extremists themselves, we will never truly understand what drives people towards the hatred and fear that overshadow our lives today.

Five years on, and that worrying week I spent in Brussels following the terrorist attack in Paris, unable to leave my home, seems like a foreshadowing of the lockdowns that COVID-19 wrought upon us all. It is undoubtedly a new world, and one in which all the divisions that became painfully clear in 2016 are now embedded in our daily lives. The language of extremism permeates every debate, and the simplest gesture – such as wearing a face mask – becomes a battleground of ideologies. Coronavirus has intensified the divisions that were already so pronounced, and around the world people look ahead to an even more uncertain future. Britain struggles to forge a new identity as it pulls away from the European Union. The United States heads into a new presidency at a time when communities are locked in bitter dispute over differing views that seem intractable and disagreements that appear insurmountable. Dangerous conspiracy theories capture the imaginations of people around the globe and divisive language reaches ever deeper into our societies. In among all the hatred and fear, people become entrenched in their beliefs, perceiving theirs as the only truth, and we wonder whether our societies will ever be able to heal.

But hope hides in the strangest of places. When I started speaking to former extremists and to the families of extremists, I wanted to find the common threads that lead people down the path of radicalization, regardless of their ideology. Sure enough, a picture emerged of the complex web of hopes, grievances, fears, insecurities and disappointments that drives people towards adopting extreme beliefs. What is striking is how similar their stories are, regardless of when they were radicalised, where they hail from, or what belief systems they found themselves drawn to. And when we start to see the lines that connect these men and women, something powerful emerges: a blueprint to overcome the division and tribalism that are starting to define the times in which we live. The stories of the extremists reveal the possibility of a better future, one where human interaction and empathy are celebrated rather than mocked; where people can be flawed and make mistakes and disagree with each other but retain their humanity; and where people can focus on what connects us rather than on what tears us apart.

We don't listen to the stories of former extremists to judge them, to absolve them or to feel sorry for them. We don't listen because we think we can magically cure people drawn to extremist beliefs overnight. We listen because they are our stories too, and reflect the temptation we all have right now to fight the many injustices and inequalities around us by shouting louder, by getting angrier, by blaming others for everything that is wrong in the world. We listen because their stories speak to a universal experience and reveal truths that can help us connect to all the people in our lives, and because they might enable us to start the slow process of healing the divisions in our societies.

There are no easy answers, and things may get worse before they get better. But as the women and men in these pages know, sometimes you need to go all the way to the extreme to find your way back to a better place.

A Note to Readers

Writing about people who have made an informed choice to follow violent, hateful or polarizing ideologies is challenging and controversial. A headline a few years ago in a newspaper opinion piece read: 'We Need to Stop Humanising Neo-Nazis'. That headline was in response to a number of articles justly criticized for normalizing or even glamorizing extreme far-right groups and individuals, and the media – (and I include myself here) – has been on a steep learning curve in its reporting of extremism. Coverage of Islamist extremism has been more sensational than any exploration of the far-right threat, and the emergence of far-left violence has often been downplayed. In the aftermath of the 2016 election of Donald Trump as US president, many media organizations profiled Americans with white nationalist ideologies in an effort to understand the mainstreaming of racist beliefs. Often those pieces missed the mark, portraying the 'neo-Nazi next door' without offering much insight into the hugely complex and nuanced process by which someone becomes drawn to divisive ideas. Other articles, in trying to explain extreme views, unwittingly gave them a platform. We cannot, however, escape the truth that people who follow extreme beliefs are human, and have very human motives for their actions. Until we fully understand these motives, we cannot hope to find effective ways to combat extremism.

There can also be no overarching definition of extremism. It remains nebulous and open to many different interpretations. Some readers may not agree that all of the ideologies featured on these pages are extremist ideologies, because what you consider extreme depends on your own political leanings. The people featured in this book were chosen because they self-identify as having been members of an extremist group or followers of an extremist ideology. The idea that there is a 'typical extremist' is also a fallacy, as people are drawn to polarizing beliefs from across religious, political and socio-economic divides. There are some demographic similarities, with studies showing that men are more likely to be drawn into violent extremism than women. Another commonality is age, as we are particularly susceptible when we are young and searching for guidance on how to live our lives. But the most striking similarities go beyond the demographic and emerge when we explore the underlying insecurities and motivations of people drawn to extremism. That is what this book is about: listening to the voices of people who have previously been involved in extremist movements themselves, or who have lost family members to extremist movements, and learning from them. Interviews with people still actively involved in extremist movements have been omitted, as they lack the retrospective self-awareness to assess the factors that may have driven them to adopt such ideologies, and this book is not about broadcasting their views. Throughout the book I have tried to avoid describing the exact nature of extreme ideologies and their belief systems, again in an effort not to further disseminate those conspiracy theories and false narratives.

All eight protagonists in this book have allowed me to use their real names. Some other names and biographical details have been changed to protect the identities of other people involved in their lives, and there is more about this in the Sources section at the back of the book, which also details the interviews and supplementary sources I have used to corroborate these stories.

It is also important to note that I am making no moral equivalence between the people featured in these pages. Some have broken no laws, while others have committed violent crimes in pursuit of their ideological goals, and clearly the latter have a greater burden on their shoulders. Equally, the people featured in this book are in different stages of the deradicalization process, depending on how long ago they left the extreme movement and how much support they have since received. There is a chance that some could fall back into adopting the divisive narratives once again. But in telling their stories, I hope we can come to a better understanding of what drove their choices — and what helped them change. Ultimately, it is easy to condemn and judge people. That takes little effort and can seem appealing when the tragic consequences of extreme actions are so apparent throughout society today. It is much harder to try and understand where those extreme views came from. But if our goal is to combat hate speech, heal division and create more tolerant societies for all, then we must unpick how such beliefs took hold in the first place.

List of People

Cathrine Moestue: *Born into a wealthy Norwegian family in Oslo, Norway, in April 1965. One of five children, Cathrine longed to be an actress and travelled to Sweden to study at a performing arts academy.*

Peter Cytanovic: *Born in Reno, Nevada, USA, in August 1996. Peter's parents worked in a Reno casino, and he grew up in the nearby town of Stead.*

Hadiya Masieh: *Born in Yorkshire, England, in January 1978. Hadiya's mother came from Uganda and her father from Mauritius. Both were Hindus of Indian descent, and the family owned a number of small businesses.*

Ibrahim Kamara: *Born in Bo, Sierra Leone in October 1994. When he was five years old, Ibrahim relocated to the Netherlands, where his parents claimed refugee status. The family then moved to Brighton, England, in 2004.*

Mak Kapetanovic: *Born in Jacksonville, Florida, USA, in February 1997. Mak's parents had fled the ethnic cleansing of Bosnian Muslims in the 1990s, coming to America as refugees.*

Tom Olsen: *Born in December 1974 in the western Norwegian town of Haugesund to a Finnish mother and a Norwegian father. Tom's parents divorced when he was small.*

Shayne Hunter: *Born in Adelaide, Australia, in December 1988. Shayne dropped out of school and studied at community college before becoming a stand-up comedian.*

Toby Cook: *Born in New South Wales, Australia, in January 1998. During his childhood, Toby travelled around frequently with his mother, a teacher, but later settled in Sydney.*

Part One

Youth

1

Cathrine Moestue

Oslo, Norway, 1965–86

'The truth.' With those two intoxicating words, Cathrine Moestue felt her resolve slipping away. She was living in Oslo, and it was 1986. She was twenty-one years old and had just returned home after two years of study in Sweden. There she had come under the influence of a man unlike anyone she had ever known before, an English professor who had promised to reveal all the truths she had been seeking: the truth about herself; the truth about the world; the truth about all the suffering she felt powerless to stop. It had been exhilarating and revelatory. But it had also been stifling and frightening, and when Cathrine returned to her parents' home she thought perhaps she could leave that part of her behind. She had been on a journey that no one could have imagined the day she left the family home in summer 1984, curious about the future and excited to be heading to another country. Now she was changed. She could see the concern in her parents' eyes when they looked at her lean body, her sagging shoulders. It was all because of Cornel and the weight of knowledge he had placed on her. Did she really think she could escape from that? Another letter had arrived from him, and it was so familiar, so relevant to her deepest thoughts and feelings, that she could almost hear him speaking the words to her.

'When we fight against injustice, we've got to rise above

petty pleasure seeking,' he wrote. 'I say rise up, go above all the stupid, trivial, crazy ways society wants you to accept, and live for what's right, not for others' expectations of you. Of course it's up to you to decide. Where is the devil and where is the angel? Who has the truth? Are you really interested?'

Cathrine was interested. And he was right, wasn't he? She was back in the life of wealth and comfort her parents had created, surrounded by the pleasures Cornel said would distract her from the true path to meaning. What had Cornel called her father? A fascist pig. A monster. When she looked at her parents now, his words ran through her head. What did they care about the suffering on the other side of the world? How could she help fight anything from her cosseted existence in Oslo?

Cathrine hadn't always felt guilty about the comfortable life she had been born into. She had simply taken it for granted. Her mother's family had had land, wealth and privilege as far back as anyone could remember. Her great-great-grandfather had once owned most of downtown Oslo and books were written about his great deeds and philanthropic spirit. Her great-grandmother had been a lady-in-waiting to the Queen, and members of the royal family had attended Cathrine's mother's christening. Cathrine's maternal grandfather had made the most of his inheritance by investing in a large potato farm and processing plant just outside Oslo, and her mother was proud of the life they had lived in their sprawling country estate, with all the trappings of an aristocratic lifestyle – parties, yachts, hunts.

Her mother had inherited nothing herself – the land and money had been passed down to her brothers – so the expectation was that she would marry into wealth, before building a dream home and raising the perfect family. And while Cathrine's father didn't have the same privileged lineage – his own father had been a doctor – when he met her mother, then twenty-four, at a party, he was well on the way to making his own fortune as an insurance broker. They married after a short courtship, and Cathrine was born on 20 April 1965, two years after her older brother. A younger sister arrived thirteen months later, and the family moved into the house their father had built on a hillside overlooking Oslo. The house was on the outskirts of an affluent suburb, with the beautiful dense forests that envelop Oslo on the doorstep. Huge windows opened out onto views of the sea and let the bright Nordic light spill into rooms expertly decorated by her mother. Cathrine spent lots of time playing outdoors with siblings and friends. Even when the days became short and the long, cold winters arrived, she would remain outside in the snow well past sunset before hurrying inside to warm herself in front of the large open fire. Cathrine felt loved, and she felt safe.

In the late 1960s Norway was experiencing a golden era, having been rebuilt after Nazi occupation and then striking rich with oil and gas deposits discovered in its North Sea waters. The petroleum wealth wasn't squandered, but instead was used to fund a generous social welfare system and build a society that would be admired for its liberal and egalitarian outlook, albeit one which remained ethnically homogeneous. While other European nations such as Britain, France and Germany relied on a large influx of migrant labour to fuel the frantic post-war growth, Norway initially limited the number of work visas it issued, before imposing a ban on immigration in the early 1970s as the global oil crisis hit the economy. The faces at Cathrine's school were white faces, but at the time she accepted this as normal, in the same way that she accepted her life of comfort. Her father did a lot of business with Lloyd's of London and would often bring the family with him to the UK capital, putting them up at the Savoy and taking them for shopping trips at Harrods. He was a generous man, both with his money and with his love, and Cathrine felt happiest in his warm and vivacious company.

Relations with her mother were not so easy. From as early as

Cathrine could remember, she had fought against the identity she felt her mother was trying to mould for her – that of the pretty and proper eldest daughter. Cathrine had a round, cherubic face with a slightly upturned nose and expressive eyes, and when her thick blonde hair was scraped into high pigtails, she could just about pull off the look of an angelic schoolgirl. But it was a face better suited to cheeky grins, and Cathrine felt more like a polar bear than a dainty doll – all clumsy paws and lumbering gait. This contrast between expectation and reality seemed to bewilder her mother and caused the young girl to rebel in small ways. When Cathrine was about four years old, a photographer came to the house for a magazine story about friends of the royal family. Cathrine and her sister wore elaborate dresses matching their mother's gown, with black velvet bodices and pink silk skirts, to create the image of perfection and elegance that her mother so valued. Cathrine fumed with resentment as her mother dragged a brush through her hair. One of the photographs taken that day shows her immaculate mother beaming and seated by the grand fireplace, her son in a full suit and bow tie standing to her left, and her youngest daughter draping a leg affectionately over her mother's knee. On the periphery of the shot, facing the other way, is Cathrine, frowning under her pigtails, with her shoulders slumped in petulant rebellion.

Throughout her childhood, although Cathrine longed to please her mother, she found it so difficult to do. It seemed to come easily to her younger sister, but Cathrine did not have the patience to bake or do household tasks, and her efforts always seemed to miss the mark.

There is nothing I can do or say to make my mother happy, she thought.

As a coping mechanism, Cathrine frequently turned to humour, sharing inside jokes with her beloved older brother and watching British comedy on the television, enjoying shows such as *Fawlty Towers* and *Monty Python's Flying Circus*. It brought some light relief to the rules that governed her life. From the moment the children woke up, there was a strict schedule to the day, starting with breakfast and carrying on through until dinner, which had to be on the table at 6 p.m. ready for their father's return. There seemed to be little opportunity for a simple 'Good morning, darling', let alone any time for discussing Cathrine's inner thoughts and feelings.

Once she reached adolescence, Cathrine would have to contend with a whole new set of perceived failings. The softness that had given her a cherubic appearance during childhood had remained, and her body became athletic and curvy, rather than slim and dainty like her mother's. It was a healthy and growing teenage body, but Cathrine wasn't always made to feel that way. The family doctor would grab at her sides and explicitly tell her to lose weight. Even worse was the disapproval she felt from her mother. She didn't even need to say anything: it was clear from the small shake of her head and the tuts when she was measuring her daughter up for clothing and alterations.

'Oh, there is no waistline,' her mother would murmur as she busied herself with the tape measure. She was trying to help by adjusting the clothing to flatter Cathrine's figure, but Cathrine herself could only see the negative side of such alterations, and it hurt. She had defence mechanisms now, though, wearing her humour and defiance like a shell. She adopted a general attitude of adolescent insolence, sometimes stayed out late with friends, and experimented a little with alcohol and marijuana. One day, when she was thirteen, Cathrine came home with a love bite on her neck and her mother was furious. Not long after, her parents sat her down and told her she was to be sent to boarding school in England. At the Grove School in Surrey, they said, Cathrine would improve her English and better her prospects. Cathrine wasn't sure if there were other, unspoken reasons for her exile – was her behaviour too much to handle? A few years ago, her mother had given birth to twin girls, and she now seemed overwhelmed by the toddlers. But with muddled teenage logic, Cathrine interpreted her parents' decision to send her away as proof that they loved her.

They have been thinking about me and trying to find something I might like, she concluded.

She may have been excluded from that process, but for the first time in ages, Cathrine felt like she mattered. And her mother seemed so happy! If going away was what it took to please her, then Cathrine was willing to comply. And besides, she was excited about her trip. That excitement built through the summer and stayed with her on the journey to England, all the way up to the point at which her parents started to say their goodbyes as they left her at the Grove School. It was then that it hit her.

I'm going to be all alone.

For the first time in her life, Cathrine would be away from her family. She loved them dearly, and for all her confrontations with her mother, she knew they loved her back. She made her way to a quiet room and wept. In the months that followed, an intense loneliness and depression overcame Cathrine, a sadness so deep that she thought for the first time about suicide. The fact that death had slipped into her mind at all surprised and frightened her, and she tried to focus instead on what was good in her life. She genuinely liked her new school. Cathrine had always dreamed of adventure, and here she was in a new country surrounded by new and exciting people. These were not the little blonde heads and white faces of her classmates in Oslo, but girls from all over the world whose parents were able to pay for a traditional British education. The year was 1978, and while there was much talk of equal opportunities for women, the literature promoting her new school didn't dwell too much on that side of things. 'It is assumed that all girls will train for a career,' the Grove School leaflet simply said, without elaborating any further.

The other girls in Cathrine's class came from Nigeria, Greece, Iran. Then there was Lisa, with her Ghanaian mother and Danish father. Cathrine decided they would be friends and began trying to win Lisa over.

At first, Cathrine spoke only basic English, but she learned fast and soon picked up a useful phrase from the older girls.

'Who's going to stop me? You and whose army?' she would say with confidence and bravado when anyone challenged her, without fully understanding what it meant. However, it seemed to do the trick, and soon she and Lisa would walk the rhododendron path from the dormitories to the classes together, and her circle of friends expanded. To Lisa, Cathrine was hilarious, a breath of fresh air, someone who didn't take life seriously, and who had a laugh that lifted everyone's spirits. The girls shared a love of music and an affinity for mischief-making, and they would retreat to the attic together on Sundays to listen to the chart countdown. But Cathrine's bright personality and apparent self-assurance obscured the anxiety, self-doubt and loneliness to which Lisa and all her other friends were oblivious. She despaired that no one saw her true self, but then she wasn't sure whether even she knew who the real Cathrine was. By the time the first term was over, she had settled into school life, enjoying her new friendships, British food, and horse riding through the English countryside at weekends.

Her first trip back to Oslo for Christmas had been pleasant, but when she returned home in spring 1979, she found that her perfect family life was falling apart. A relative she was close to had fallen gravely ill. The illness had a huge impact on her extended family, and amid all the turmoil there was little time for Cathrine. She returned to England haunted by the memory of this person she loved dearly suffering so much.

Why is this happening to my family? How could a God allow such suffering? she wondered.

School seemed less important now too, and her rebellious

streak re-emerged. Afternoons would be spent surreptitiously smoking in the toilets. Cathrine had a creeping feeling that the world was somehow tilted against certain people – if a younger child was being picked on, she would step in and stop the bullying. But punishments seemed arbitrary to her. When Lisa got into an argument with a teacher, Cathrine – sensing that Lisa was being targeted because she was Black – struck the teacher. Her punishment was to be sent to the back of the class to copy out lines from a textbook, deepening her sense that it wasn't always the right people who got justice in the world.

As the months passed, Cathrine began to miss her family keenly. Her tight group of school friends was also dwindling. An Iranian friend disappeared from the school after the 1979 revolution in her home country. Another good British friend was also gone, having been expelled for smoking in the toilets. By the end of the year, Cathrine had had enough, and begged her parents to let her come home and finish her studies in Oslo. They agreed, and in early 1980, Cathrine said goodbye to Lisa and flew back to Oslo. All the Norwegian friends she had left behind were waiting at the airport to greet her. Cathrine returned to her old school to finish her last year of high school, before embarking on three years at the Gymnasium. She felt like a different person, however. While she settled back to life in Norway easily, she was more worldly, more attuned to the injustices happening around her and more aware of her inability to change anything.

One of Cathrine's favourite television programmes at the time was *Roots*, an American civil rights drama about the life of a Black slave named Kunta Kinte. The themes of bravery and injustice, of right and wrong, moved Cathrine deeply. Decades later, she would still get shivers watching the scene where Kunta Kinte, in chains and whipped on the orders of a slave owner, is forced to deny his identity.

'I want to hear you say your name. Your name is Toby. What's your name?'

'Kunta,' he moans, before he succumbs to the pain and accepts his fate.

One evening she was watching *Roots* with her mother. But while Cathrine felt consumed by the emotion on screen, by the injustices of the world, by her own impotence, her mother saw none of that – she simply made a flippant comment about her daughter having a crush, and Cathrine saw it as another example of how clueless her family were about what was going on inside her. School would be finishing soon, and she couldn't remember her parents ever having asked her what she wanted to do next. She was desperate for some independence, but it was difficult to make such an important decision alone, so she asked her father for his advice.

'Why don't you study law?' he asked her.

The words stung. Cathrine had the intelligence and ability to do so, but there was no way she had the confidence to read a competitive subject like law.

How can he not know that about me? she thought. *How can he not see my self-doubt?*

Even surrounded by friends, she felt alone. She never felt attractive and still worried about her weight. Since the incident with the love bite, she hadn't had many other experiences with boys. On the day of her graduation from the Gymnasium, she put on the traditional red clothing which marks the passage from childhood to adulthood in Norway and went out to celebrate. She smiled and laughed with the others, but she felt nothing.

In the end it was a schoolfriend who inspired Cathrine with a plan for her future.

'You are funny, you should be an actress,' the friend said.

Yes, thought Cathrine, *that makes sense!* She was social and liked to perform, and her step-grandmother had been one of Norway's most famous actresses. Here was something she could do, and the stars seemed to align to make it happen. Her mother had recently travelled to Stockholm, where she had seen a newspaper advert for a new performing arts school just west of the Swedish capital. Everyone agreed: Cathrine would go to Sweden to study acting.

It was the summer of 1984. News of a famine was seeping out of Ethiopia. Newspapers published photographs of suffering that affected Cathrine deeply. These were children, and they were dying by the hundreds, yet the people in power in the world seemed utterly incapable of stopping it. Cathrine was gripped by a sense of powerlessness and guilt. Here she was with more money than she needed, the best foods, the most comfortable life, and in another corner of the world children were just wasting away until their frail bodies gave up, simply because of where they had been born.

It was in this frame of mind – disillusioned and confused about a world which didn't seem to care, yet desperate to find her own place in it – that nineteen-year-old Cathrine Moestue packed up her green Ford Taunus and set off alone on the road to Sweden.

2

Peter Cytanovic

Reno, Nevada, USA, 1996–2015

Peter Cytanovic VI wanted to be great. Growing up in rural Nevada, he wasn't sure what form his greatness would take. He looked up to the presidents of the United States, the scientists, the academics whose achievements lived on long after they died, and believed he was destined for the same immortality. He wanted to be noteworthy – to go to the best schools, to get the highest grades, to excel at whatever he did. But there were not many role models for greatness in the community Peter grew up in. His lofty ambitions had taken root in modest surroundings, and in a family with its share of difficulties.

Peter was born on 21 August 1996. The most noteworthy thing about his baby photos is the shaved head of his mother, a deep cleft running across the top of her skull from ear to ear, a dark fuzz of hair struggling to grow back over the angry red scar. Underneath, dark eyes peer down at the tiny new life in her arms, bringing with it so much hope after so much hardship. Around five months earlier, the young woman had had a seizure, and the doctor delivered the bad news: she had brain cancer and she should abort her baby so she could start chemotherapy. If she did not follow that advice, there was a high chance that both mother and child would die. But she was already so attached to the child growing in her belly, so she decided to leave his fate in God's hands. The pregnant woman underwent extensive surgery to remove the tumour, then started radiation therapy. A team of doctors monitored the baby as the pregnancy progressed, eventually inducing labour a month before the due date. Peter was born in August, and when the baby and his mother finally came home from the hospital, it was uncertain what further challenges the family would face. Shortly after Peter's birth, his mother began chemotherapy. It worked and she went into complete remission, though the gruelling treatment would leave her with crippling headaches and lifelong memory problems.

Peter's mother was from Wisconsin, the same as those who came before her as far back as anyone could remember. His dad's family were more recent transplants, Peter's Croatian great-grandfather having escaped the depression in Europe by emigrating to America after the First World War. Peter's grandfather joined the US Army as a young man, and Peter's father spent much of his childhood in various military bases around the world. After high school, he travelled round the United States for a while, living a nomadic existence among the alternative communities of the California coast. 'A beach bum' was how he defined himself during those years of self-exploration. He ended up in Reno, which, like Las Vegas, takes advantage of Nevada's liberal gambling laws and is home to sprawling mega-casinos, albeit with slightly less glamour and glitz than Vegas. While the gaudy strip welcomes visitors to 'the Biggest Little City in the World', flashing in red and gold neon, you don't have to stray far from the main drag to find the pawn shops and cheap motels that are reminders of the destitution that failed dreams of winning big can bring. Peter's mother and father met in one of Reno's mega-casinos in 1989. She was making good money as a cocktail waitress, while his father worked as a cashier. They were both in their late twenties, and Peter's mother already had a son from a previous relationship. The couple would soon have their first child together, a daughter, followed a few years later by Peter.

The family home was in an area northwest of Reno called

Stead, a lower-middle-class suburban town surrounded by trailer parks, desert and sagebrush. There was a school, a small grocery store, a Walmart and a McDonald's, so it was as good a place as any for a young American family on a modest income to try and build a life. But there was a lot of poverty, and the area had problems with drugs and crime. It was the kind of place where being privileged meant having a car that didn't break down all the time. Peter's home life was stable and safe, however, and he enjoyed the freedom of being able to follow the railway tracks into the wild with some of the neighbourhood kids. There, they could make as much noise as they wanted and not be bothered by anyone. They didn't have the money to do much else, and the bus lines were so unreliable that they very rarely went into Reno.

But in a short space of time, Peter's family went from being a double-income household in an economically solid America to something much more splintered and precarious. The bills from his mother's cancer treatment came to more than two million dollars. The insurance covered a chunk of it, and fundraisers at his mother's workplace and in the local community raised more than 150,000 dollars. But there was still a huge outstanding debt that left the family permanently on the brink of bankruptcy. A glass-fitting business that Peter's father had set up went bust. He was able to find another job back in the casinos, but dealing with so many setbacks put a strain on the marriage. When Peter was eight, his parents divorced. It was an amicable arrangement, but for Peter it was still a slog travelling between his parents' homes. His mother had hung on to the family home in Stead, but his father had moved to the other side of Reno, to an area that was isolated and where public transport was non-existent. But Peter loved spending time with his father, an eccentric libertarian with unorthodox political views who defined himself as an anarchist – neither on the left nor on the right – although when Ron Paul ran for president on an anti-establishment platform, he was so enthused he put up signs in his front yard. Peter's dad had a fierce belief in the rights and responsibilities of the individual, and a deep distrust of the State. He just didn't understand why he should be forced to wear a seat belt. Those kinds of intrusions on his personal liberty infuriated him.

'There are only two things that matter in life,' Peter's dad would tell his children, 'religion and politics.' But he didn't want them to copy his political beliefs.

'If you think you are on your path, and I am there cheering, then you are probably not on your path, you are on my path,' he told them. 'You want to hear me give a "what the hell are you doing?" at least once.'

Books were considered a vital part of that learning process, but Peter struggled to get through novels. He had a condition called aphantasia – an inability to conjure up visual images in his head. If someone told Peter to picture a red star, he would know what they were talking about, but in his mind's eye he didn't see the red star. That made it difficult for him to leap into the shoes of a fictional character and imagine their reality, so after finishing *The Lord of the Rings* when he was sixteen, he never willingly opened another novel again. He devoured non-fiction, however, and was an avid student of his dad's life lessons. There was everything from *Mein Kampf* to *The Communist Manifesto* on his father's shelves, and Peter would listen intently as his father talked him through the political wrongs in the world. Sometimes their conversations would leave him incensed, overwhelmed with anger and emotion at the injustices he was told about, but with no idea how to express these strong feelings.

Peter's dad also liked to challenge taboos. When Peter was in his freshman year at high school, his father showed him some swastikas and explained the history of the symbol in Asian cultures. Peter promptly took those ideas and tried to start a class debate on reclaiming the Nazi symbol, causing great upset. But he discovered that he quite liked provoking reactions in that way. It was a way for him to show off his intellect in an educational environment he sometimes found tedious and unchallenging. Peter had the capability to excel academically, but he could also be lazy and complacent, with little regard for other people's feelings. The power to shock made school life a bit more interesting, so he would goof around and make offensive and occasionally racist comments, testing the boundaries of how far he could push people. His comments were not aimed at anyone in particular – he just wanted to piss off as many people as possible. And it worked: there was a lot of eye-rolling when Peter was around. But at a school where many families were struggling to make ends meet and had concerns beyond an emotionally immature teenager's clumsy attempts at attention-seeking, no one seemed to take his comments very seriously or make any effort to understand why he was provoking people. He did struggle to make friends though, and his father wondered if he might be lonely, but Peter remained focused on his visions of future greatness. His childhood had been spent surrounded by people from a similar background and he had rarely ventured further than the suburbs his parents lived in, which made him long to expand his own horizons.

I'm smart, he told himself, *and I can be whatever I want.*

Peter had a firm plan for where he needed to go to achieve his ambitions: first there would be Stanford to study history, then a Rhodes Scholarship to Oxford University. But when it came to making that dream come true, Peter was clueless. No one at his school talked him through the different colleges he could apply for; no one helped him write the application essays; no one told him about how competitive the college applications process was and that he should manage his expectations to be more realistic. Only around sixteen per cent of students attending the most prestigious Ivy League colleges came from a poor enough background to require financial assistance. Neither of Peter's parents had gone to college, and they could offer him little help, so Peter was on his own. When he graduated from high school in 2014 with a major GPA of 3.97 out of 4.00, he was so confident that he would be going to Stanford that he didn't bother to apply for any other colleges.

Why would I apply to other schools like Georgetown and Virginia? he wondered. *That's a waste of time. I am the perfect student for Stanford.*

The admissions board at Stanford, however, disagreed. The first communication he had from them was a rejection letter. There wasn't even an interview. Suddenly, Peter was unmoored from his dream of greatness. Part of him wanted to blame it on a system stacked against poor kids like himself.

It is unjust, it sucks, but there is nothing I can do about it, he thought.

There seemed to be a whole different set of rules for people born into money and privilege. He once saw a headline in *The Onion*, a satirical newspaper, that read: 'Harvard streamlines admission process by directly growing new students from DNA of top donors'. That absurd notion sounded about right to him, and it was a world away from his day-to-day life of watching his parents trying to keep afloat in an America that didn't seem to care much about them. But Peter knew he had to take responsibility for himself too. He had been overconfident, and perhaps had not put in the effort that was needed to beat all the other poor smart kids with big dreams. Now he didn't have many choices left. It was too late to apply to the other prestigious colleges, so he ended up putting in his papers to the University of Nevada – Reno (UNR).

I have just been rejected from Stanford – what the hell am I doing with my life? he wondered.

Peter's Stanford rejection coincided with another tough spell for his family. He had only been twelve when the 2008 financial crisis hit, and he was a little fuzzy on its origins, but several friends had lost their homes. Somehow his parents had both managed to weather that crisis and hold on to their homes. But although his family had been lucky that time, it all changed just as Peter was about to start college. His mother had exhausted her financial options, and having seen all her children through high school, she went to the bank and told them they could have the house. His maternal grandmother lost her house at around the same time, and mother and daughter were forced to live in a motel for a few months as they searched for a place where they could afford to live. Peter's dad was going through a difficult time too. The casino he was working at was bought by William Hill and his position eliminated. Technically he was not made redundant – his job just ceased to exist overnight – so he got no severance pay. He was in his early fifties and had years of experience in management, but there were no positions for someone of his age and skill set. So he took minimum-wage jobs, working the graveyard shift doing security at convenience stores and warehouses. He sold his car and had just about enough to cover the rent. Then life dealt him another blow when his landlord decided to evict him with thirty days' notice. He was forced to move, with little money to find anywhere decent to live.

When Peter packed for college, he wasn't just stuffing his suitcases with the essentials for dorm life. He had turned eighteen the week before college began, and he marked that milestone by packing away all his childhood things into storage boxes with an uncertain destination. When he moved into the college dorm and started his undergraduate degree in history at UNR in the autumn of 2014, it was with a sense of injustice at every-thing that had befallen him and his family that year.

College should have been an awakening for Peter, an exposure to new ideas and new people, an intellectual challenge. It didn't quite work out that way. The culture shock was immediate and intense. Peter thought he was worldly, but college made him realize how steeped he was in traditional small-town ways. In Stead, people were on the whole hard-working but poor, reasonably conservative and moderately religious. College was the first time he had met real rich people — not just people whose cars worked, but people who really had a lot of money — and he found them utterly mystifying. They didn't appear to have any interest in studying and seemed to take for granted the college education that Peter valued so highly. They were more interested in drinking, partying and sleeping around as much as possible, and Peter was shocked.

He retreated into the part of himself that brought him calm: his faith. As a child, he had been drawn to the old Bible stories, making his father read the tales of the prophets to him. He liked the idea of a higher purpose in life, and a shared sense of community. He discovered a beautiful Catholic cathedral a 20-minute walk from his dorm and started going regularly. He loved the building, and when he sat in the pews and listened to the priest and the music, it was as if all his troubles melted away. He would sit silently watching the other people pray, and everything stopped. It was an island from the world. But Peter had inherited his father's intellectual curiosity, so he decided to try out other religions too. He started going to a local mosque on Fridays, where the imam took him under his wing and gave him a copy of the Qur'an. He read the Book of Mormon too and spent a lot of time at the local Mormon church. He kept this up for about six months — reading everything and attending different places of worship every week, determined to find a calling — before realizing that in his heart he was a Catholic, Catholicism being the religion of his Croatian great-grandfather. It would take a couple of years before he was officially confirmed into the Catholic faith, but he had found his religious identity. He took comfort in the moral certainties the Church offered, and he now had a valid reason to take the stands he did. He had always been the most socially conservative member of his family. Perhaps it was because his own life had nearly been cut short by an abortion:

had his life meant that little? Or maybe it was a reaction against his eccentric father. While his dad had the air of a hippy, with scruffy T-shirts and wild, shoulder-length hair, Peter's dark brown hair was always meticulously gelled to one side, and he favoured preppy polo shirts and smart slacks. He had a lot in common with his father, but he did not share his affinity with alternative cultures. When they were kids, his dad had offered to take all the children to the Burning Man music festival. Peter had politely declined.

And now Peter had a framework for his conservative leanings. He could be opposed to same-sex marriage because his religion forbade it. He could be anti-abortion because his Church told him it was wrong. When there were so many uncertainties in the world – and about his own future – it was a relief to find something that gave him peace.

But these conservative religious beliefs did not help him fit in at college. He did not try and force his views on others, but if asked, he would, for example, say he was against an LGBTQ+ fundraiser at his dorm. This set him apart from the largely wealthy, liberal student body, and he felt his views were ridiculed and attacked. Peter often didn't help himself in this regard: he could be tone-deaf to other people's feelings, particularly when it came to sensitive issues like race. In his early freshman days at college, he attended a session on diversity. A Black student addressed the class, explaining the deep hurt caused by racist language. It was meant to be a learning experience for new students, but Peter assumed it was a class debate and pitched in.

'Why would you give some shithead racist that power over you?' he asked, in a misguided attempt to be supportive.

A few young men in the class – all of them white – took him to one side. He couldn't say things like that, they told him. He needed to think about his white privilege. It was the first time he had heard this term and he found it confusing. It did not speak to his personal experience. Suddenly he was hearing that white people owned America, but who would think that the people he grew up with had any power or owned anything worth having? He knew exactly what awaited many of his high school friends: shitty jobs, health problems, drug addictions, teenage pregnancies, large debts. Peter certainly didn't see many people like the ones he had grown up with when he turned on his television, nor in his dorms or in his classes. The median family income of a student at UNR was more than $100,000, and only four per cent of its intake were from the poorest percentile. It was a college that did little to narrow the gap between the haves and have-nots, with one of the lowest social mobility rates of colleges across the USA. When Peter's fellow students talked about white privilege, he figured they must have meant the rich white people in New York, the people who ended up in Harvard simply because of the family they were born into, rather than white working-class families like his own. People like himself. He could not get his head round the concept and became increasingly frustrated.

'Where I grew up, you had junk food because you couldn't afford anything else,' he would try and tell anyone who would listen. 'What did you have for dinner? McDonald's. What did you have for breakfast? McDonald's. Because you can't afford anything else.'

The more he tried to challenge and debate these ideas relating to white privilege, however, the worse it got.

They think I'm just this dumb, uneducated white trash racist, he thought.

In an effort to find somewhere his voice could be heard and taken seriously, he scoured the political clubs and joined a Marxist study group. He had always been attracted to socialism, especially left-wing economics, but its stance on social issues clashed with his own religious beliefs. So he ended up gravitating towards the closest political fit he could find: the college Republicans.

It should have been a good moment to be a combative young white man from one of America's forgotten communities with strong political leanings, as finally, Peter felt like there was someone out there speaking up for people like him and his family. When Donald Trump declared his run for the presidency in June 2015, Peter felt seen. He didn't like everything about Trump. He was put off by the reports of sexism and womanizing, and by his habit of making outrageous and unbelievable statements. But when it came to the message of making American great again, of economic nationalism that, had it come a few years earlier, may have prevented companies like the one his dad worked at being bought by foreign corporations – it made sense. Peter's family were the forgotten people that Trump was talking about – the ones Hillary Clinton had casually dismissed as 'deplorables'.

Peter's fellow college Republicans, however, did not share his enthusiasm for Trump, considering him a racist and a bigot. Peter was already feeling alienated and ostracized, and now he was angry too at the perceived moral superiority emanating from his peers and at the clear gulf between his background and theirs. The other college Republican kids were always insisting that they were not wealthy, while at the same time boasting of the cars they received as graduation gifts, the price tags on their homes, their plans for unpaid internships in DC funded by the Bank of Mom and Pop. They never asked about how Peter had got to college; they never asked about his weekend work and summer jobs cleaning floors, doing maintenance work. He couldn't afford to join them on their drinking binges – and besides, politics was meant to be about changing the world, not just an excuse to party. There were things going on in the world that Peter wanted to talk about: a refugee crisis in Europe; terrorist attacks. But unless the conversation stayed focused on narrow areas like economic policy and taxation, his fellow Republicans would shut any debate down. There was no way he could talk to these people about his place as a white working-class male in America – their experiences were so far removed from his own, and Peter couldn't shake the feeling that something important was under threat. Why was he always being made to feel bad about who he was? He didn't want to be racist, but he needed to talk through these issues, to help him make sense of his thoughts. But there was no one to talk to, and he felt utterly alone.

3

Hadiya Masieh

Yorkshire, England, 1978 to London, England, 1997

When Hadiya Masieh was seven years old, she turned on the television and wept. It was 13 July 1985, and Live Aid was being broadcast to 1.5 billion people in 150 countries. The fundraising concert for the victims of the Ethiopian famine was an unprecedented spectacle of globalized humanitarian unity that captured people's imaginations everywhere and galvanized millions into thinking they might be able to change the world, even just a little bit. It was a message that appealed to the little girl with long, glossy hair and chubby cheeks who cried as she watched the images of suffering unfolding before her. Hadiya's own mother had suffered hardship in sub-Saharan Africa, arriving in the United Kingdom in 1972 as a refugee following Ugandan dictator Idi Amin's expulsion of the country's Asian population. The 80,000-strong community had called Uganda home for more than 100 years, but Amin gave them just three months to pack up and leave, calling them 'bloodsuckers' in a thundering speech and claiming to be giving Uganda back to the Ugandans. Most of the Ugandan Asians held British passports as a legacy of colonial rule, yet the British government sought to absolve itself of responsibility. This was four years after Conservative populist politician Enoch Powell's famous speech warning about the 'rivers of blood' immigration would bring, and there was still a deep suspicion in some quarters. Government ministers tried to convince other countries to offer sanctuary to the displaced Ugandan Asians, and even considered resettling them on a remote Pacific island. In the end, Britain offered refuge to 25,000 of them, but as the planeloads of displaced men, women and children arrived in the country, many were greeted at the airport with signs reading 'Get Back to Where You Came From'.

This sudden uprooting from everything familiar had left its mark on Hadiya's mother, who was fourteen when she arrived in the United Kingdom. At school, she was chased by a group of boys shouting 'Paki' at her. It made her feel like the conditions were always ripe for another uprooting, for another opportunistic politician to come along and exploit the ethnicity of her family for political gain.

'We might get thrown out of the country – you don't know what is going to happen,' she would later tell her daughter.

Despite her mother's fears about the impermanence of everything, Hadiya's childhood was a comfortable one. Hadiya's father had left the island of Mauritius to seek prosperity in the United Kingdom, and he had been successful. He met Hadiya's mother and they settled in a village in West Yorkshire, where Hadiya was born in January 1978. Her father first worked as a nurse, but later the family branched out into business, buying the local sweet shop and several care homes for the elderly. The village where she was raised, however, was not exactly diverse. Racism was common, and her family's sweet shop was frequently targeted with racist graffiti, often by members of the local branch of the far-right National Front. Her parents tried to hide the hatred from Hadiya, who would see her mother scrubbing paint off the walls of Yorkshire stone without having any idea what the sprayed words had been, or what affect they had had on her mother. But no amount of scrubbing could clear up Hadiya's confusion about her identity. Her mother was an Indian from Uganda and her father was an Indian from

Mauritius, both communities having been removed from their original homelands, and now having been displaced once again to northern England.

What does that make me? she wondered.

The one constant was her family's Hindu faith, so she passionately embraced that religion and discovered that her exotic background could also be an asset. She was a confident and intelligent child and revelled in getting white friends to try on her saris, instructing them in the ways of Hinduism and introducing them to the exuberance of Bollywood. She became something of a chameleon, adapting herself to whatever environment she found herself in, whether that was the Christian Sunday school which she attended because her friends did, the convent preparatory school she went to for a while, or the private Quaker boarding school her parents sent her to when she was eleven. She always felt like she fitted in − except when she didn't. Once, at the prep school, she brought some sweets in for the class and held them out to share.

'I don't want sweets from your dirty hands,' the teacher said.

This wasn't as overt as the racism her mother had experienced when she had first arrived in England, but Hadiya saw such comments as clear evidence that she was different, making her long to be fully part of something rather than always on the margins of belonging.

It wasn't only the injustices against herself and her family that struck Hadiya. Live Aid and the Ethiopian famine were the first global issues to touch her heart, and as she grew into adolescence, her keen interest in politics and humanitarianism grew too. When Hadiya was sixteen, the genocide in Rwanda dominated the news, and she was horrified. In 100 days, nearly one million Rwandans were killed by members of the Hutu community, whose political leaders had co-opted local media outlets to condemn the minority Tutsi community as 'cockroaches' and 'snakes', unleashing unimaginable violence on these people. Hadiya didn't fully understand the politics behind the genocide, but she was aghast at the suffering.

Why isn't the world doing anything to stop this awful killing? she wondered.

At the age of eighteen she bought a subscription to the *Herald Tribune*, determined to educate herself on the world's troubles. Her interest wasn't purely altruistic – she also wanted to show how grown up and intellectual she was, and she was aware of the image she presented, of a beautiful teenage girl thumbing through a broadsheet newspaper. For all her intellectual pursuits, she had more teenage preoccupations too, and spent time and money caring for her long hair – a cascade of impossibly glossy thick black waves that she considered to be her best asset.

As she finished school, Hadiya's thoughts turned to the future. There was so much to ponder in the world, and she longed to encounter new ideas and discuss them with interesting people. She was drawn to anthropology and history as subjects to study at university. But when she passed her A levels with good grades, her parents urged her to choose something more practical instead – something that would solidify the family's status as prosperous and successful immigrants in thriving multi-cultural Britain. It was 1997 and it seemed that real change was in the air. Tony Blair had just swept Labour to power in a landslide election victory, bringing elation and hope to many. After the recession of the 1980s and the devastating unemployment it had wrought, the economy appeared to be booming. British culture and music were celebrated around the world. Many children – especially those from white, middle-class back-grounds – grew up thinking racism was a thing of the past. To this optimistic new generation, the ideological conflicts that had dominated the twentieth century already felt like something from a school history book, even though it had been less than a decade since the Berlin Wall had come down. But dangerous new chasms were forming. The western economies that had emerged from the wreckage of the recession would turn out to be stacked in favour of the wealthy. Tax rates were lowered for high earners, while social welfare remained stagnant. Traditional industry in many countries was dying and jobs were going overseas. Growth was coming from white-collar industries such as financial services, that were concentrated in the capitals of those countries and other large cities. The post-war ethics of countries working together for the greater good was being replaced by individualistic societies where the goal was to get rich, even at the expense of others around you. Many countries – especially the English-speaking ones – would see a huge rise in inequality.

But still, in the heady days of the 1990s, the future looked bright for many young people coming of age in the West. And Hadiya was among them. She had acquiesced to her parents' wishes and enrolled on a business management degree at Brunel University. But in doing so, she had felt conflicted. In her heart she wanted to find a path that gave some meaning to her life, but she knew how hard her parents had worked to forge a good future for her, and they had instilled the work ethic in her too, making sure she took weekend jobs and always knew the value of money. It was this side of her that finally made peace with the idea of studying for a less cerebral university degree.

What kind of future do I want? she wondered. *I want to be independent and not rely on anybody.*

Besides, Hadiya reasoned, if she managed to make lots of money, she could then devote her life to philanthropy and still make a difference. She set off for London in late summer 1997, the New Labour soundtrack of Things Can Only Get Better ringing in her ears.

4

Ibrahim Kamara

Bo Town, Sierra Leone, 1994 to Brighton, England, 2009

Ibrahim Kamara was six weeks old when he first felt the physical terror of war. He was in the arms of his fifteen-year-old mother Khadijah at their home in Bo Town, the second largest city in Sierra Leona. Suddenly gunfire rang out, and Khadijah froze. It was like her body belonged to someone else. At first she couldn't move, and then she began to shake violently. Khadijah's husband and parents-in-law wrenched tiny Ibrahim from her arms and ran. Eventually Khadijah's body released her and she too began to run, to follow her baby.

It was 1994 and Sierra Leone was three years into a civil war, with the Revolutionary United Front battling to overthrow the government. Many of those fighting were just boys themselves, traumatized children kidnapped by the rebel forces for a brutal indoctrination. Hardening children to the barbarity of war was terrifying in its simplicity: the guerrillas gave them alcohol and drugs – marijuana, crack cocaine, hallucinogenics – then forced them to kill over and over and over until murder became as normal as drinking a glass of water. Those malleable young minds were taught that they were the only ones who deserved to survive – the enemy were to be killed like animals.

Up until that rebel attack on Bo Town in late 1994, Ibrahim and his mother Khadijah had largely been spared the full horrors of the war. But the past year had been a terrible awakening for

Khadijah, and it was not just the rebels who were robbing her of every trace of her childhood. It was her own community too.

For much of her life, Khadijah had been happy and carefree, living with her extended family in a comfortable home in Bo Town. Her Muslim father had broken from tradition to marry her mother, a Christian from a tribe considered to be of lower status, and by the time Khadijah was born in March 1979, her parents were successful traders. Her early years were filled with prosperity, laughter and love. Gregarious and with an enormous heart, Khadijah wanted to make people feel good, even if her efforts didn't always please everyone, like the time she took her mum's clothes to the river to wash them, then gave them away to poorer villagers. It was this generosity of spirit that impressed her father's cousin, who had come to stay with them in Bo Town when Khadijah was around eight years old. Khadijah loved the attention of the twenty-year-old man, who seemed warm and friendly. She thought of him as her favourite 'uncle', so she was taken aback one day when he said to her, 'Will you accept that when you grow up you will marry me?'

Khadijah thought it was a joke, but it still made her feel uncomfortable and she became shy whenever he was around. Her thoughts were far from marriage, as she loved school and dreamed of becoming a doctor, an ambition supported by her father. But as Khadijah approached adolescence, life became more uncertain. Her father fell ill and moved some of the family to a village in the countryside. Khadijah was left in Bo Town, staying with a succession of relatives so that she could finish her schooling, but her position within each household always felt precarious. Then one day her father's cousin showed up again and told her that the time had come – she was grown now and must marry him. She was fourteen years old.

'I'm not ready to get married,' Khadijah retorted, 'I am going to school.'

That day, her father came to visit her too, and Khadijah showed him a recent test score: she had got ninety per cent and she was certain he would be proud of her. But this time, he hardly made any fuss. He just got back into his car and drove away. The next day, when Khadijah returned from school, she found a note from her father's cousin: 'You denied me, but you cannot deny the elders.'

Khadijah's fate had been decided, and there was nothing she could do to change it. Her life had been taken out of her hands before she even had a chance to try and make it her own. She cried all day and night up until the wedding, which passed in a blur, and then she moved in with her parents-in-law and the happy little girl was gone. Khadijah was unprepared for married life: she had no idea how to cook or keep a house, and she missed her parents so much. But there were other duties she had to submit to as well, and within a month of her wedding, Khadijah was pregnant. She felt a deep lethargy throughout her pregnancy, an unhappy tiredness that prevented her from getting out of bed. When the day of the birth finally arrived, she had a long and difficult labour, during which she screamed for her absent father. Eventually Ibrahim made it into the world and Khadijah collapsed into a long sleep. When she awoke to his cries, she looked at the tiny baby and could hardly believe he came from her body.

Khadijah struggled with those early days of motherhood. All she wanted to do was sleep, but Ibrahim was always crying. People came and went with food and gifts, each of them imparting advice on how long she should feed Ibrahim for, when she should wake him, when she should let him sleep. She felt completely overwhelmed. However, as the weeks passed, the fog of depression lifted and a deep maternal love blossomed. Holding this little boy, so small and soft, brought such comfort. Ibrahim was now the centre of her world, a tiny life to keep safe in an increasingly dangerous country. Each day there were new reports of gunfire outside the city, the rebel army getting closer. The horror finally caught up with them in late autumn 1994, when the shots rang out at the back of her house and the family was forced to flee. They joined the silent crowds on the road, everyone too frightened to scream, and just focused on making their legs move as fast as possible to get away from the violence. Along the road, Khadijah saw a rebel who had been captured by local militia. He was kneeling on the ground, a car tyre wedged around his shoulders. Then the soldiers poured petrol over him and set him ablaze. Khadijah would never forget the image of the man's face, terror in his eyes as he burned alive.

The family made it past the government barricades to the other end of Bo Town before embarking on a journey to the capital, Freetown, walking, taking taxis, trying to find a safe place. They spent a few months in Freetown before it became clear that the rebels didn't have the numbers to hold Bo Town, so Khadijah and Ibrahim went home. But it still wasn't safe, particularly for Khadijah's husband. He was in his late twenties – a dangerous age to be in a country in which all the warring sides were looking for more recruits. So when Ibrahim was three months old, his father left for Europe. The year that followed was filled with uncertainty: would the rebels come back? Khadijah never felt safe, and the constant worry affected her health. She stopped eating and became thin. She was consumed by the hopelessness of her situation. She had no say in what happened in her own life, and no say about the forces ripping her country apart. And in the end, she had no say about the most important thing in her life: she was told that she had to leave her beloved baby.

Khadijah's husband had been granted asylum in the Netherlands, and she was to leave Ibrahim with her parents-in-law and go and join him. It was May 1996, and Khadijah was seventeen years old. She did not understand why she had to leave Ibrahim behind, but she did not have the words to ask.

Just like when she was married off a few years earlier, the only thing she had the power to do was cry. And once again, her anguish changed nothing. When the time came to say goodbye, Khadijah could not do it. She knew if she kissed those soft cheeks and uttered that word, the tears would start flowing and never stop. It felt like every part of her was dying. She got in a car and left. Ibrahim was nineteen months old, and Khadijah didn't know when she would see her son again.

For his first few months without his mother, Ibrahim was safe in the care of his father's family. He knew the smell of his paternal grandmother, the sound of laughter from his grand-father and uncles, the layout of a house he happily toddled around. But the war never went away. A military coup in January 1996 was followed by elections and the promise of peace, but the ceasefires didn't hold. Sporadic attacks continued in Bo District throughout the year, intensifying in 1997 as another coup sent the country spiralling into a protracted war. Finally, in 1998, the rebels came back to Bo Town. The family packed up their belongings, and three-year-old Ibrahim joined 350,000 other Sierra Leoneans on the road to neighbouring Guinea. Ibrahim had his family with him, but many of the other children were orphans, and Ibrahim's dreams would always be haunted by the cries of these young victims of war.

Thousands of miles away in Europe, his mother was going through her own torment. Khadijah arrived in the Netherlands in the spring of 1996, but it wasn't like spring back home. There seemed to be no warmth – just damp, rain and relentless wind. Any hope of human warmth was dashed when Khadijah arrived in Rotterdam and her husband told her to go straight to the authorities and request asylum. Khadijah was shocked.

A refugee? she thought. *Refugees are the kind of people living in tents on the outskirts of towns, the ones with nothing at all who rely on handouts.*

But once again, she had no choice. Her husband drove her into the countryside and pointed to a building in the distance.

'That's where you should go,' he said.

As the terrified seventeen-year-old presented herself at the reception desk and was taken to temporary accommodation, she had no idea that it would be four years before the bureaucratic Dutch asylum system would finally approve her request. When she arrived in the asylum processing centre, she was simply exhausted and spent her first two months battling a succession of colds and fevers. She cried all day, thinking of the warmth of her baby. At night, she would dream of Ibrahim, sometimes sleepwalking into other rooms as if searching for him in the dark. She treasured her small photo album. Back home, it had been her little indulgence to dress Ibrahim in wonderful outfits and then get a professional photographer to capture his beauty. Now the well-thumbed album was the piece of hope she clung on to for the day when they would be reunited.

Nine months later, Khadijah was moved to new accommodation, which meant she could spend weekends with her husband. Not that she particularly enjoyed his company. She felt that the beloved 'uncle' from her childhood had become a sullen man who was always snapping at her. But she was still expected to fulfil her duties as a wife, and soon became pregnant again, giving birth to her second son in 1998. This new little life brought rare happiness in those long years, but it did nothing to diminish the longing she felt for Ibrahim. Every few weeks she begged her husband, 'Let's bring him!' But he told her she had to wait for her papers to come through. When Khadijah's asylum request was eventually approved in early 2000, she was twenty-one years old, heavily pregnant again and in a marriage that was now deeply unhappy. But she could finally send for her first-born son.

On the day her husband drove to Paris to pick Ibrahim up from the airport, Khadijah stood by the window at home, willing the hours to pass so they could be together as quickly as possible. When he finally arrived, she let out a scream. Her little baby was a boy of five now, dressed in a brown pinstripe suit which was too large for him, the arms and legs rolled up like some sort of premonition of the tall and gangly teenager he would become. Seized with pure joy, she fell upon the overwhelmed child, bundling him up in her arms, squeezing him tight, tears rolling down her cheeks, determined to never let go of him again.

But Khadijah's euphoria at having Ibrahim back could only sustain her for so long. It didn't change the fundamental misery that her life had become. Soon after Ibrahim returned, her third son was born, and now she was responsible for raising three small boys and looking after her husband. The Dutch government set her up with a nice house in a small town right on the polders in the south of the country. But she never felt at home in the Netherlands. The Dutch seemed friendly on the surface, but she always had a sense that she wasn't quite welcome there. She struggled with the language. She missed her mum and dad. She missed the sunshine and the warmth of the sky back home. Here the sky was the colour of nothing. And she had nothing to do but have babies, work erratic cleaning jobs, and keep the house for a husband she felt no love for. Sometimes, when she had a rare moment to herself, she would stand in the kitchen and look out the window. But she didn't see the grey skies and the drab municipal housing. She would see the life she would be living if she hadn't been forced into marriage at the age of fourteen – a life in which she had continued at school, studied abroad, and was now on her way to becoming a doctor.

Khadijah tried to stay upbeat for her children and desperately wanted to provide a haven in which Ibrahim could heal. She could tell that his experiences of war had affected him. Whenever he heard another child cry, he would look distraught and ask if they had lost their parents. But she was so busy with his younger brothers that there wasn't much time for her to spend on this withdrawn five-year-old. He seemed so listless, lacking the boyish energy she imagined a child of his age should have. School was also a problem. Ibrahim was one of just a handful of black faces in a school that was ninety-five per cent white, and he didn't speak a word of Dutch. His misbehaviour was a cry for attention, but Khadijah was too overwhelmed to hear it. Instead, she scolded him and punished him. The problems with school continued over the years, and by the time Khadijah's fourth son arrived in 2003, she was barely holding her life together. Something had to change.

In 2004, Khadijah made a decision. She had visited a cousin in London and liked it there. That was where they must go. Everything was going to be better in England, she could feel it.

Feeling safe and secure in your childhood home is one of the essential building blocks for a successful and happy life. Ibrahim could rely on the unconditional love of his devoted mother, but her ability to provide that crucial sense of stability would be tested by the shortcomings of Britain's crumbling social welfare system. While government spending on public services increased under the Labour government during the boom years of the late 1990s and early 2000s, Ibrahim arrived when investment was starting on its downward trajectory as the global economic crisis brought in a decade of austerity. In the coming years, Ibrahim would interact with all the state instruments that were meant to protect him and better his prospects: education, social services, housing, policing. Each time, he would be let down. And it all happened in Brighton & Hove, a seaside city on the south coast of England that revels in its liberal and cosmopolitan reputation. It is known as 'London-on-Sea' because of its popularity with commuters and weekenders seeking respite from the capital. But another characteristic it shares with London is the enormous gulf between the haves and have-nots. While certain areas in Hove are the most desirable and least deprived communities in England, you don't have to go far from the commuter flats, the well-tended seafront and the craft ale pubs to plummet to the other end of the scale. Areas like Moulsecoomb and Whitehawk languish in the bottom two per cent of the most deprived areas in Britain.

The problems for Ibrahim and his family began as soon as they arrived. His dad found a job in security, but when he went to the social welfare office to request housing, he was unable to answer basic questions about his children and their education. Khadijah ran the household, but her husband hadn't asked her to go with him. The social services decided there was not enough evidence to prove the children were his and ordered Khadijah and the four boys to return to the Netherlands. If they didn't comply, the children would be taken into care. They were given a lawyer and a chance to appeal, but while they waited, they had to stay in a dingy bed and breakfast far too small for a family of six. Khadijah decided it was time to take charge. Despite the early setback, she liked Brighton and felt the return of her old tenacity. She found her own work, which meant she could now apply independently for housing. It wasn't easy: it was an hour-long walk to the office where she cleaned, so she had to leave home at 4 a.m., when there were no buses running, and dodge the drunks returning from a night out. When she finished at 8 a.m., she had to rush home to get her four children up and ready for school, and then she had a second job in the evenings. But now she could stay in the UK, and after three difficult and cramped months in the bed and breakfast, the family was given a small flat overlooking Brighton's main cemetery in the east of the city.

Ibrahim started at Fairlight Primary School, rated as just 'satisfactory' by Ofsted, the school inspection board, which had raised concerns about poor attendance and a lack of focus. Most pupils came from socially disadvantaged backgrounds, with nearly a third having special educational needs. The Ofsted report claimed the students were from 'a fairly wide range of minority ethnic backgrounds'. Of the 350 pupils, four were black, while twenty were from other ethnic minority backgrounds. In Brighton, that counted as diverse.

Khadijah liked the school, however, and it was only a short walk from home. But less than a year after settling in, the family had to move. Their social worker decided their flat was too small and unhygienic, so in 2005 they relocated to a house that was bigger but that was all the way across town in Hove. Now it was a long and tiring bus journey to and from Fairlight every morning, so after a year, the council decided to move them again, this time back to the east of the city. All this upheaval came just as Ibrahim was preparing to start at Varndean School for his secondary education. Varndean had fared better than Fairlight in its assessment by Ofsted, but more than ninety per cent of the pupils were white, and it wasn't long before Khadijah started to suspect that Ibrahim's race might be affecting his schooling. There were complaints that he was being disruptive. At the time, Khadijah was going through a rough time in her marriage and the darkness of depression overwhelmed her again, so she lost patience with Ibrahim.

'The last thing I need is for you to go to school and not concentrate,' she snapped.

Then one day, Ibrahim came home with a scrape near his eye. Another child had thrown a pencil at him.

'Did you tell the teacher?' Khadijah asked.

Ibrahim said he had, but the teacher hadn't done anything. It seemed so unjust: whenever he did something wrong, he was hauled up and punished. But the white kids didn't seem to be treated in the same way.

'If you had fought back, they would have called me,' Khadijah said. 'You are not going to school until they do something about that.'

Ibrahim's teachers called a meeting, and Khadijah stood

her ground, explaining how the sense of injustice was causing Ibrahim to act up.

'I want him to see that something has been done,' she said.

The teachers were sympathetic, and even offered him counselling. Khadijah was satisfied and went home to speak to Ibrahim.

'All this trouble you are causing, it's not going to make people understand you and your problems,' she said. 'You have to speak. When something is bothering you, you have to say it. I want you to know, no matter what you do, whatever happens, I love you.'

The words were like a balm to Ibrahim. The calls from the school stopped. Home life was improving too. In 2008, Khadijah finally found the strength to ask her husband for a divorce, and that strength had come from an unexpected place. Khadijah had never practised Islam, blaming her father's religion for her unhappy childhood marriage. But one day, she switched on the Islam Channel. The presenter talked in a calm and confident voice about the rights of women and the ease with which you could divorce. Khadijah was astonished. Women were respected in Islam after all! Ibrahim seemed drawn to the teachings too. The cartoons aimed at youngsters were about being respectful and having good manners. Ibrahim seemed soothed by the messages of peace and tolerance. And he was changing as he entered his teenage years. Those little limbs of a decade ago that had been swamped by that brown pinstripe suit were stretching out as he grew into a tall and lanky adolescent. Despite his early sullenness, he was now acquiring a certain goofiness, a cheeky grin that lit up his face, and an infectious laugh. A congenital eye defect meant that he always had to wear thick glasses, and while this and his Blackness made him stand out at school, he found that clowning around was a way to fit in. The family was forced to move again after the divorce, but Ibrahim had begun to make friends at school and Khadijah dared to hope once again: perhaps this was finally the fresh start she had always dreamed of.

5

Mak Kapetanovic

Jacksonville, Florida, USA, 1997–2013

Mak Kapetanovic spent much of his childhood avoiding asking difficult questions. He didn't ask much about his parents' life back in Bosnia before they fled the war. You had to be a pretty brave kid to ask your dad if he ever had to kill anyone. So Mak learned to skirt around the subject of the past. He didn't even ask how his parents met. All he knew was that his mother and father were Bosnian Muslims from different towns in the south of the country, and that they came to America as refugees from the ethnic cleansing in the former Yugoslavia. But for all the silence, the past was always with them. Sometimes when trains would rattle by their house, his dad would roll off the bed, as if taking cover from gunfire. In the rare times his father did talk about the six months he spent in a concentration camp, he would focus on the miracle stories, like the time he felt thirsty and saw a cucumber growing in the ground. When he bent down to pick it up, gunshots rang out over his head. That cucumber saved his life. That was the kind of story Mak's dad liked to tell.

It was easy to understand his parents' reluctance to dwell on their lives before they came to America. Their childhoods had been tough. Mak's mum had lost her own mother to cancer when she was fourteen, watching her slowly deteriorate in the hospital. His dad lost his father when he was around the same age. Then in 1991 a war began that brought genocide back to Europe. The ultra-nationalist Serb leader Slobodan Milošević turned the might of the army and the paramilitary forces on former Yugoslav republics battling for independence, backing up his campaigns with exclusionary rhetoric calling on Serbs to reclaim an imagined historical glory. All other ethnic groups became the enemy in this violent quest for Serb supremacy, and it was the Bosnian Muslims who suffered the most, labelled as invaders, aliens and terrorists. Scholars linked to the regime gave interviews to the state-owned press in which they claimed that Bosnian Muslims were genetically inferior to Serbs, and that they were plotting a 'demographic jihad', threatening the very existence of the Serb people. The lies laid the groundwork for crimes against humanity on a scale unprecedented in Europe since the end of the Second World War. More than 23,000 people were violently expelled from their homes as Milošević attempted to rid the territory of Bosnian Muslims and Croats. In July 1995, around 8,000 Muslim men and boys were killed by Serb forces in Srebrenica.

Mak's mother and father were offered sanctuary in America, and they embarked on building a new life in Jacksonville, Florida, in 1995. Two years later, Mak was born. Home was a modest one-storey house with a small backyard in a suburb in the north of Jacksonville. There wasn't much to differentiate it from any other suburbs of the sprawling city: a few gas stations and a corner store, that was it. There was nothing resembling a local community in his immediate suburb, and no extended family or brothers and sisters for Mak to play with, so it was a lonely childhood. When Mak did hang out with other kids, there wasn't much to do apart from walk to the gas station and back again. Public transport was so poor that they rarely used it. It was the same in many cities across America. The 1990s and early 2000s had seemed stable and prosperous for many Americans, but it was an illusory prosperity underpinned by reckless banking practices and risky lending. This had fuelled an unsustainable property boom, which led to poorly planned urban sprawl and shoddy developments with little grounding in existing communities and without the transport infrastructure to support them. In this isolated suburbia, Mak spent most of his free time at home with his mother while his dad caught up on sleep from working night shifts as a line manager in a factory.

Mak's mother worked too, first as a translator for immigration services, then helping with an after-school club for the kids of poorer families. That was just the way she was, always finding something to do that helped other people. If Mak ever brought friends home, no matter what time, she was always there, ready to make sure everyone had something to eat and felt at home. When Mak was younger, she would often bake a traditional Balkan pita. It seemed to take the whole day, and Mak would watch as his mother stretched the dough paper-thin over the kitchen table, and then moulded it into intricate rolls. He enjoyed the ritual. It was a connection to the land of his parents – a country and heritage that started to confuse him as he grew into a teenager and learned about its history.

Why did my family get hurt supposedly for being Muslim when they are not really Muslim? he wondered.

His parents never went to the mosque. There were some Islamic holidays that they celebrated when Mak was younger, but in the same way that many other people who aren't religious observe Christmas. His dad called himself an atheist. His mother was a bit more spiritual.

'I believe in an energy,' was the way she put it.

Mak didn't know what he believed, or what identity to call his own. This was particularly pronounced at school, where he felt that he didn't have the same experience as the other regular American kids. At home, he spoke a different language. His parents had accents. He didn't eat the same foods. But while he didn't feel like an American kid, he didn't feel like a Bosnian one either. The family went back to Bosnia for a month every year, and were in touch with the Bosnian community in the wider community of Jacksonville, but he never felt terribly close to them. Mak felt stuck between two identities, though this tension was invisible to his peers. They assumed he was a normal white kid with a hard-to-pronounce last name, not unusual in a country built on waves of foreign immigration. No one knew that any of his people were Muslims unless he explicitly told them. Other Muslim kids from Middle Eastern or Pakistani backgrounds seemed to have a much harder time.

Why are Muslims that don't look like me treated in a different way? he wondered.

It wasn't just religion. People seemed so keen to push an identity on you, to fit you into a little box that then defined everything about you. But Mak didn't feel like he fitted into any of the stereotypes that American high school life offered: the jocks, the nerds, the kooks, all the different tropes from the movies. Pale and skinny with straight hair falling over his eyes, he could easily have been pegged as a grungy band kid. But Mak himself didn't feel defined by anything, and that deepened his sense of loneliness and alienation. He went to a magnet school – an establishment that was meant to provide a higher level of education, and where places were allocated on a lottery system. But the school was not in his neighbourhood – it was a half-hour drive there and back every day – so although there were a few kids there who Mak liked to hang out with, it was difficult to see them outside of school hours. So he spent a lot of his free time at home, most of it in front of a computer screen.

School was difficult in other ways too. Mak had an intellectual curiosity and a passion for learning, but what they did in the classroom didn't feel like learning to him. It felt like the students were on some sort of educational conveyor belt churning out college-ready kids without making any effort to understand who they were or what they wanted from life.

They are just trying to work me to death instead of trying to teach me stuff, he thought.

He would flip from feeling bored and unmotivated by his studies to being completely overwhelmed by the amount of work he was expected to do. He didn't know what he wanted to do with his life, and felt lost. The pressures of school were compounded by feelings of listlessness and lethargy that started when he was around thirteen. When friends called and tried to get him to come out, he would refuse.

'No, I want to be at home not doing anything,' he would tell them.

He wasn't familiar with words like 'depression' and 'mental health' – even if he had been, he would not have known what to do about them, or how to link them to his general malaise. And there were things that he did enjoy doing. He loved to play video games. Through online gaming he could hang out with his friends without having to go anywhere.

He also loved music, being drawn particularly to the drums. He felt soothed by the methodical beat, the repetition, and he could go into a trance-like state for hours. His passion for music was inherited from his mother, who had piles of old CDs and cassette tapes around the house. She had eclectic tastes, playing everything from classic rock to old Balkan music. Mak and his mother had a strong bond, but he was a teenager, and acted like one. Because his dad was always working, his mother was the one pushing him to do his schoolwork, to do his chores. There always seemed to be an argument about something.

Then she got sick. It was early 2013, just before Mak turned seventeen. She had been suffering from a fever for about a week, but it didn't seem serious. Then one afternoon Mak's dad asked for his assistance.

'I need to move your mom to the bed, she can't move by herself,' he said.

Mak was shocked. He had spoken to his mother that

morning, but when he looked at her now, he could see she was transformed. Yellow foam gathered around her mouth. She was totally unresponsive. It was like it had happened in a flash: one moment she was fine, then this. Mak called the police, and an ambulance came and took her to the hospital. At first, the doctors thought she had meningitis. But after a few tests, they came back with bad news: it was a stroke. They explained it to Mak carefully: the part of her brain that was still functioning was the area controlling auto-response actions like breathing. Anything to do with memory or speech was gone. She was effectively brain dead. Mak and his father had to decide whether to turn off the life-support system. For all the pain of the moment, at least this was a decision she had made for them ahead of time. When she was young, she had seen her own mother slowly deteriorate from lung cancer, so the family had already had the difficult conversation about end-of-life care. His mother had always been clear: to her, the way her mother ended up was no way to live. They told the doctors to turn off the life support.

Mak insisted on staying in the room when the machine was turned off. His dad was reluctant, but being outside waiting as the woman who had raised him slipped away just didn't sit right with Mak. He needed to see her while she was still alive.

Towards the end, as Mak watched his mother take her final breaths, it seemed like she was trying to say something. Mak knew that couldn't be true, that it wasn't possible, but she really seemed to be trying to get some words out. Then that was it. Something turned off in her eyes. He was sixteen years old, and now he knew what death looked like.

The next few weeks and months were a painful exercise in father and son learning to live with their grief and without the kind-hearted woman who had held the family together. They ate nothing but junk food; the laundry piled up; they sat on the back porch smoking cigarettes. Mak's dad was still working night shifts, so the teenager was mostly alone with his grief. People didn't know what to say. When members of the local Bosnian Muslim community came round, he felt that they wanted to use him as a crutch for their own grief, crying on his shoulder and acting like his life was over too.

'Oh poor Mak,' they would say. 'Things are going to be so hard for you now. I'm so sorry.'

That just wasn't what he needed. Some of his school friends were cooler about it. They reminded him of all the lovely, positive memories he had of his mother. That was how he liked to remember her, not the image of her dying in her hospital bed, head half-shaved and tubes in her mouth. The school arranged some counselling, but Mak didn't feel like it helped.

I guess I'll vent for a bit, but I'm still going to feel bad about it, he thought.

Mak withdrew further into himself. He didn't care about school any more, and hardly ever turned up for class. There were two more years left until he graduated from high school, but now he had no motivation. When he did go to school, he would either sit in a corner staring at his phone or go outside and wander round the school grounds playing a marching drum, desperate to lose himself in the rhythm. No one said or did anything.

Part Two

Education

6

Cathrine Moestue

Eskilstuna, Sweden, 1984–86

Cathrine Moestue had watched the movie *Fame* so many times that she practically knew it by heart, and it was how she imagined her life at the performing arts academy would be. But as her green Ford Taunus rounded the final bends of the Swedish countryside and she peered through her frizz of bobbed blonde hair at Eskilstuna, with its folksy town centre and sea of white faces, she felt quietly devastated. This was not New York City. This small town about 100 kilometres west of Stockholm did not strike her as the kind of cosmopolitan metropolis where she was going to find herself.

But soon she had moved into a small studio apartment, and the simple act of having a space to call her own reinvigorated her sense of purpose. She covered her walls with black-and-white photographs of the actress Greta Garbo, drawn to the maudlin eyes which spoke of great inner depths. Questions about her future looped around in her head, an adolescent cacophony of the banal and the profound.

Am I good enough? Can I master my emotions? How can the mystery of this life be unravelled? Will I ever be thin enough? How can I make an impact in the world?

The year 1984 was marked by suffering, with a famine devastating Ethiopia and killing hundreds of thousands of people. It was a humanitarian catastrophe with complicated political origins, but while the television crews from western news organizations broadcast the suffering in full colour, their interpretation of events was strikingly black and white: the rains failed, the world did nothing, and people died. Beaming into living rooms night after night were haunting images of the apparently mute victims of a natural disaster, their accusatory eyes looking into the camera from emaciated bodies. Cathrine would stare at the images, overcome by guilt and a sense of powerlessness, with no one offering any hope for a solution. Three decades later, the intense suffering in the Syrian war would have the same effect, as images of children dying in chemical attacks or being pulled, terrified and bloodied, from the rubble of buildings would flood the Internet. These images elicited overwhelming emotional responses in people who felt they had no power or voice to make a difference.

Cathrine did what she could about the Ethiopian famine. She donated some money and old clothing, even though it felt futile. Later in the year she would buy the charity song *Do They Know It's Christmas?*, playing it over and over and trying to find some hope in the soaring chords and lyrics promising to feed the world.

In among the guilt and anguish, however, there was also an irrepressible feeling of being young, alive and full of potential. It turned out that there were like-minded people at the Charlie Rivel Entertainer Art School, and Cathrine settled in quickly. The school had only recently opened, and classes were small and intimate. There were just ten other young men and women training with Cathrine, and she got on well with everyone, striking up a strong friendship with a girl called Christina. Together they would practise singing, dancing, circus skills and acting, and Cathrine was happy to forget her existential dilemmas and allow herself to be in the moment.

One autumnal evening soon after she arrived, Cathrine joined Christina at a shopping centre across the road from the school.

Some students from the academy were putting on a show there, and Cathrine whooped enthusiastically after each performance, making her voice heard above all the others. During a break in the performance, Cathrine noticed a man weaving through the throng from the other side of the stage. He was short and rather plain with well-cut black hair and dark skin, and probably in his early thirties. She wouldn't even have registered his presence had he not been in a crowd of mostly blond heads and white faces. Then she realized that he was headed straight for her. By the time he was next to her, learning close to her ear, it was too late to do anything.

'I could use someone like you on my team,' he whispered in perfect English. Then he turned on his heel and walked off.

Has he been watching me this whole time? she wondered. *Who is he? Why has he chosen me?*

It was such a strange experience that goose pimples rose on her flesh. As soon as the show was finished, she rushed over to Christina to ask her who he was.

'Oh, he's an English teacher at the school, you will meet him soon,' Christina told her.

Over the next few weeks, Cathrine kept catching glimpses of the man in the school corridors. She discovered that his name was Cornel, and that he and his wife had relocated from the United Kingdom to teach English to students and to employees of local businesses in Eskilstuna. And while she was quietly impressed with his smart appearance – his shirt, tie and glasses conjured up images of classic English charm and reminded her of her time at boarding school – she still felt a deep disquiet. Then, a few weeks later, Cornel invited all the students in her class to his home.

'Do you really think we should go?' Cathrine asked Christina.

Her friend understood her concerns – Cornel seemed a bit creepy to her too. But everyone else in the class was going, so they decided they should too. It was a crisp evening and the air was beginning to chill as Cathrine found herself on the doorstep of Cornel's apartment, feeling a nervous mix of wariness and curiosity. His wife opened the door. Cornel was out for a run, she said. Would they like to wait in the living room? Cathrine and Christina shuffled into the small, dark apartment, its walls bare and the furnishings sparse. Cathrine thought it looked more like a student flat than a teacher's home, but the presence of Cornel's wife reassured her. This petite Englishwoman seemed warm and genuine, and, with her little round glasses and simple, elegant clothing, was dressed like a glamorous left-wing intellectual.

When Cornel finally swept through the front door, Cathrine was stunned. He was dressed in running clothes, his ruffled black hair framing a face that was flushed from rigorous exercise. He seemed possessed with an intense energy which immediately captivated Cathrine. The students watched as he made his way to the shower. A short time later he emerged from the bathroom naked except for a towel around his waist. Bathed in the light from the bathroom and a cloud of steam from the shower, this man had an otherworldly quality to him, and Cathrine was transfixed as he moved to the bedroom to dress. When he finally sat down with his guests, Cornel singled Cathrine out, asking her questions, praising her observations and flattering her intelligence with comments about her command of English. No mention was made of their fleeting meeting a few weeks earlier, but a familiar feeling of guilt crept over Cathrine.

Why did I judge this man so harshly? Was I racist? she wondered.

This man was clearly British of Indian extraction – one of her teachers at the Grove School had a similar background, so she recognized the ethnicity. Horrified by her assumptions about Cornel, she now felt determined to impress him, to show him that she was not racist. The other students started to drift off, and Christina wanted to leave too, bored by Cornel's lofty talk. Cathrine, however, was gripped, and could not tear herself away from his intense gaze, his eyes dark and wide like Bambi and impossible to ignore.

'Cathrine,' he asked, 'can you think clearly?'

'Yes, I can,' Cathrine replied with the brash candour of a teenager.

Cornel pointed to a crystal on the table.

'You see that crystal? How do you know that it exists?'

'I can see it!'

'How do you know you are not dreaming?'

Cornel talked to Cathrine for a long time about reality, perceptions, feelings, truth and the meaning of existence. By the time he was finally silent again, Cathrine's head was spinning. How could she prove she wasn't dreaming? It was impossible! The whole evening had a hallucinatory quality, and Cathrine's mind was ablaze. The surreal feeling frightened and fascinated her at the same time.

Has someone finally seen me? Cathrine wondered.

She hoped so with all her heart.

That dreamy autumn evening was the start of an awakening for Cathrine, a golden year in which it felt like someone special was giving her the tools she needed to make the transition to adulthood. Cornel suggested she join his English evening classes to improve her already excellent grasp of the language. After a few sessions, he told her she was so good that she should start her own English-language group. The feeling of confidence he gave her was a refreshing change from the endless self-doubt and internal questioning that had tormented her back home, and soon Cathrine was running her own conversation class and had helped set up a kids' theatre class. She felt she could talk to Cornel about anything: politics, family, her childhood, her mother, the African famines, the illness of her relative, her loneliness at boarding school, her mixture of pride and guilt at her background, her shame about her weight. The two of them would meet in a little café in the basement of a hat shop where, hidden away from the rest of the world, nothing went unsaid. Cornel listened

with complete absorption, asking questions, empathizing, prob-
ing, and offering insightful thoughts and observations. He shared
his own story too, confiding in Cathrine details about an abusive
relative, an unhappy childhood, his escape into the world of
books that had led to a career in academia. No adult had ever
spoken to her like this before, not patronizing her and speaking
down to her, but treating her as an equal, making her feel smart.

Cathrine rarely thought about their eerie first encounter at
the shopping centre now. She could hardly reconcile that small,
plain man with the charismatic professor who was transforming
her life. She could see now that, with his thick hair, those soulful
eyes, and that impossibly fit body, Cornel was attractive. She
started going running with him and was delighted to find he
could help her control her body as well as her mind. Despite this
closeness, Cathrine felt no sexual attraction. He was a teacher,
and he was married. She didn't want to sleep with him. It was
something else; something much more meaningful.

The politics came slowly at first. Most of their conversations
were personal, but when they drifted into world affairs, she was
impressed with how much he knew. He spoke about the left-
wing intellectual circles he frequented back in England. They
could talk for hours about all the injustices in the world, the
failure of the people in power to come up with any solutions.

Cathrine was so intoxicated with this new friendship that
she wanted to share the positive feelings it brought her, and
whenever she spoke to friends back in Oslo she gushed about
the course and the teachers. Her close friend Lise was so
seduced by her accounts of life in Eskilstuna that she too
decided to study at the academy, and moved into Cathrine's
small apartment in 1985. Cathrine introduced her to Cornel,
who suggested they start their own study circle at the university,
meeting once a week with a few other students to listen to and
discuss his moral puzzles.

Everything was finally coming together for Cathrine. She had a strong group of friends; she felt stimulated and empowered; and her weight was dropping with all the running. She still worried about the starving children whom she could not save, but at least she was with people who shared her concerns. Life felt so perfect that when the cracks started to appear, her first reaction was to blame herself. Cornel had told her that her childhood had been impossibly bourgeois, and that she faced a huge challenge to overcome the effects of such a privileged upbringing. The slights against her and her family were small at first – a chiding when she didn't have enough money left over at the end of the month to go out, a throwaway comment about her messy apartment.

'You don't have any life skills,' he would say. 'What did your parents actually teach you?'

Then the snubs started happening in front of others. During one of their moral philosophy discussions, Cornel posed a typical conundrum, asking what items they would bring if the world ended and they had to head into space to save mankind. Cathrine replied that she would take a gun. His put-down was immediate.

'A gun?' Cornel snorted. 'Are you a complete idiot? Do you think the Martians will come and get you?'

He had never spoken to her like that before. Cathrine felt humiliated and confused. In the weeks that followed, the digs kept coming.

What have I done to anger him? she wondered, as she desperately tried to work out what would please him. That feeling of being included had been so powerful and intoxicating, and she would do anything to get it back. Sometimes they would revert to their old ways, the guru and his apprentice sharing their secrets and figuring out how to right the world's wrongs. But then he would turn on her, using her insecurities against her. She was a fat, lazy slob; she needed to exercise more; she didn't know how to be a grown-up and organize her life. All the insecurities that had haunted her adolescence had suddenly been weaponized against her, and she was completely bewildered.

Cathrine was also aware that the further she drifted from Cornel's affections, the closer her friend Lise seemed to get to him. One weekend in late 1985, Cornel and Lise disappeared off to Copenhagen. While Cathrine had never fully accepted it, a part of her knew that their relationship was no longer one of student and teacher. Lise was a beautiful woman – she had the classic blonde Scandinavian radiance and modelled in her spare time – and Cathrine felt a jumble of emotions: confusion, jealousy, disgust, shock. When Cornel's wife called her, demanding to know where her husband was, Cathrine was furious that her two friends had put her in this position.

'I think he is in Copenhagen with Lise,' she replied.

Cathrine stewed for a few days, trying to reconcile this behaviour with the lofty ideals Cornel preached, and was determined to confront the pair when they returned from their tryst. However, one afternoon when she returned home from class, she opened the door to such a strange scene that any thoughts of challenging her friends vanished. Cornel was sitting on one of the sofa beds, stripped to the waist. Lise was beside him, her arms wrapped awkwardly around his waist, as if the two of them were locked in an artificial pose, waiting for an artist to come and paint them. And then Cathrine noticed that he was crying. She had never seen a grown man cry before, and it was deeply affecting.

'Why are you crying?' Cathrine asked.

'You would never believe me if I told you,' Cornel said.

'Of course I would.'

Cathrine was desperate to understand everything, to know the truth and share in this secret. Cornel turned his tear-filled eyes towards her. She must never tell anyone, he said gravely. Cathrine promised she wouldn't.

'I am not who you think I am,' he told her. 'I am living undercover in Sweden. My real name is Raoul Zindig. I am a guerrilla leader.'

It was the moment that would change Cathrine's life. He told her he was a Marxist–Leninist revolutionary with a Paraguayan guerrilla group dedicated to bringing justice and equality to the world. He was undercover in Sweden to find recruits in the final battle for a better world. One of their key missions was to fight against the capitalist regimes that were causing the starvation of children in sub-Saharan Africa. If a second's doubt entered Cathrine's mind, it was immediately swept away by the feeling of privilege that she had a friend who was so noble, so pure of heart, and that now she was part of his struggle too. She had been asking for the truth, and here it was.

Cathrine stared, utterly mesmerized, as Cornel talked her through his life, pointing out marks on his torso where bullets had penetrated his skin. It was like Jesus with his stigmata.

He is sacrificing himself to save the starving children, she thought.

'I feel safe with you,' Cornel finally said. 'You are such good people.'

Never had Cathrine felt so important. Finally, someone was giving her the power to change the world. How could she say no?

Following Cornel's extraordinary revelation, the speed with which Cathrine's world shrank was bewildering. A few months earlier, she had been enjoying her intellectual awakening and had been growing in confidence. Now she viewed anyone outside their small group as a potential enemy. The young man looking at her in the university hallway; the other teachers; even her family – they could be spies trying to kill her mentor, and the vital work they were doing to save the starving children would be over. Details about the exact nature of this vital work came slowly, drip-fed by Cornel on the rare occasions he deemed Cathrine worthy enough to receive such information. Cornel had made it clear that Cathrine had twenty years of indoctrination to overcome, and that she had a long path ahead of her before she could find her place at the heart of the revolution. His mild disapproval of her beloved father had now turned into explicit hate: he was a fascist pig, a monster, Cornel told her. She was so lucky, he said, that he, Cornel, had come along to redeem her from her past.

Cathrine was determined to prove her worth. She started working her way through Cornel's reading lists, slogging through the dense philosophy of the controversial British philosopher Peter Singer in his book *Practical Ethics*, but enjoying the diaries of Che Guevara. Having had little concrete detail from Cornel on the nature of his band of left-wing revolutionaries, she let her mind run wild with fantasies of romantic struggles in warm and exotic corners of the world – struggles that she soon would be a crucial part of. The revolution was coming, Cornel promised, and they had to be ready. The current capitalist world order was created to serve the white men in power, he said, and it was causing suffering and starvation. The people in power were fascists, capitalist pigs, Nazis, racists – and most of all, they were liars. Cornel told her how the societies that ran the world were built on the blood of slaves. Hadn't they taught her that in school? he asked. Cathrine vaguely remembered some classes on colonial history during her time in boarding school in England, but now it felt like her eyes were being opened to the real story of the world. Taking these kernels of truth, Cornel then spun them into intricate conspiracies. He told Cathrine how governments tried to control people through their food, subduing populations by encouraging them to consume meat and milk, which he claimed were harmful. Only his group had the answers to overcoming injustice and making the world a better place. On the rare occasions that Cathrine questioned his views or theories, Cornel would look at her with an intensity that made her tremble.

'I am reality,' he would say.

The bending of a person or a whole group of people to believe an inexplicable lie can take many forms. In recent years, thousands of people across the world have come to believe in the far-right QAnon conspiracy theory, which posits that Satan-worshipping Democrats, Hollywood stars and billionaires run the world while engaging in paedophilia, human trafficking and the harvesting of blood of abused children. Leading political figures have convinced sections of the population to believe their far-fetched claims and conspiracy theories, while dismissing the facts as fake news. Conspiracy theories about coronavirus, for example, have been shared far and wide. In many cases, the power to be believed is held by the person or group with the ability to convey their 'truth' with the most conviction and the strongest emotional connection. Once that alternative reality has been planted, anything outside it can be disproved and discredited with ease. Throughout history, leaders of cults and extremist groups have manipulated people to jettison their lives in favour of an imagined utopia. These recruiters are experts at homing in on people's vulnerabilities and luring them with flattery, empathy, a sense of belonging and the promise of a life of meaning. They identify commonalities with the potential recruits, gaining their trust by sharing their own experiences with them. The emotional connection comes first, followed by the ideology. Then the narratives so familiar in the world today begin – the 'othering' of people who hold different beliefs; the idea that only the members of the select group are privy to the truth, and that those outside are to be hated or feared. Some of the recruiters and leaders are highly manipulative individuals with narcissistic or even psychopathic characteristics. But they can be ordinary people too, and often it is the idealists who become the most valued recruiters, their purity of vision enthralling other people just like themselves, people searching for a black-and-white truth in a complicated world.

7

Hadiya Masieh

London, England, 1997–2003

After the limitations of the little Yorkshire village where she had grown up, Hadiya Masieh was struck by the wealth of possibilities offered by confident, multicultural London when she arrived at Brunel University in autumn 1997. She couldn't muster much enthusiasm for her business management course, but there were so many other opportunities. First, Hadiya joined her university's Asian Society, but she didn't like to feel defined solely by the ethnic heritage of her parents, so she searched elsewhere for the sense of belonging she craved. The swimming club that she then joined was fun, but it didn't offer her much spiritual fulfilment, so she turned back to the religion of her parents.

Trips to visit her father's family in Mauritius had already introduced Hadiya to more militant religious ideas. Some of her Mauritian relatives followed an austere version of Hinduism, and Hadiya was drawn to the intensity of their faith. She became vegetarian and searched for more information about her Indian heritage. Although she had never set foot in India, she felt drawn to its culture and politics. Just before she left for university, Hadiya's parents had installed cable TV – a relatively new technology for most British homes in the 1990s, where just four or five television channels were the norm – and Hadiya found herself glued to Indian television shows. Once, she heard a woman arguing that India should be exclusively for the Hindus, given that the Muslims had Bangladesh and Pakistan. Hadiya had little knowledge about the trauma of partition or the ethnic make-up of India, but she was impressed by the emotion of the argument and felt excited to find a cause she could throw her own passion behind.

For Hadiya, it was just one extra step from her new-found Hindu nationalism to feeling antipathy towards Muslim communities. And it wasn't just historical animosities that influenced her. The media fuelled her mistrust. It was the late 1990s, before the September 11 attacks unleashed a global distrust in Islam, but already there was a negative tone to a lot of the media coverage of the Islamic world, an othering of people who followed the Muslim faith. A magazine article about the situation for women in Pakistan – which strongly suggested that Islam was the reason for their oppression – had a profound impact on Hadiya, and she came to believe that Islam was a religion that subjugated women and caused conflict in many corners of the world.

But for all her youthful zeal, Hadiya prided herself on her sense of fairness, and she wanted to find intellectual justification for her hatred of Islam. So she went to the library and took out some books by Islamic scholars, looking for proof to back up the stories she was reading in the media. She struggled to find it. The books she read gave the opposite view of everything she had been led to believe about Islam. They were about peace, kindness and a better world. The words touched her and brought peace to a mind that often raced like a rollercoaster. At first she was shocked, but then she experienced a most extraordinary feeling, like a gravitational force pulling her towards something unknown but enticing.

Why has this faith entered my heart? she wondered. *Why do I want to be a Muslim?*

She tried to fight the feeling, knowing what a devastating impact her conversion would have on her family. Her first term at university was dominated by this internal struggle, as she grappled with the theological, existential and practical challenges of embracing a new faith. As autumn turned to winter, Hadiya prepared to head home for the Christmas holidays. She covered her Islamic books with wrapping paper so that her parents would not see the covers, and acted as if nothing were amiss. When she returned to university for the new term, the tug of war in her soul continued.

Then Hadiya had the dream.

She was in a body of water when a huge wave appeared. She dived down, before emerging in a chaotic scene back on land, with panicked people running around as though in the aftermath of a disaster. Hadiya approached a person holding a clipboard.

'Can you tell me which is the right one?' she asked.

'The one with the rhyming book,' the person answered.

Hadiya woke up. She had been given the sign she was looking for, and converted to Islam in early spring 1998. For months, her parents refused to speak to her. While she now had purpose and energy, she had no one to talk to about her faith. She didn't even know how to speak to God properly, and was desperate for guidance. She was too shy to go to a mosque alone, so she summoned the courage to enter the university prayer room, tucked inconspicuously between the library and the campus laundrette. Pulling back an old curtain, she found the women's area, a cosy space that reminded her of the dens she used to make from sheets and pillows when she was a child. Sitting in the centre of the room on a tattered red Persian rug was a young woman wearing a simple headscarf. She turned towards Hadiya, who was immediately struck by the beautiful eyes shining out from the austere outfit. They were pale and mesmerizing, like a cat's.

'As-Salaam-Alaikum,' the woman whispered.

'Wa-Alaikum-Salaam,' Hadiya replied nervously.

The enigmatic young woman placed her finger to her lips

and gestured to Hadiya to sit next to her. When the prayers were over, the woman broke into a grin.

'What is your name, sister? I am Sister Zeba.'

Just like that, Hadiya had found her spiritual guide. Every day the pair would meet at the prayer room, where Zeba would share her knowledge about Islam with patience and warmth, prompting questions about faith, belonging and her place in the world. Hadiya was thrilled to learn that Islam didn't just have to be about faith: Zeba was passionate about politics too. Hadiya had loved history and philosophy during her A levels, and her reading of John Stuart Mill and Thomas Hobbes had convinced her that society needed to reform economically and politically to bring about change that reached all levels of the population. Zeba was speaking to exactly those themes. It was as if she could read her mind and pre-empt the questions before Hadiya even spoke. She asked Hadiya for her thoughts about world affairs too, flattering her with the attention she paid to what she said.

Hadiya and Zeba would talk into the night about the injustices against Muslims in Bosnia, Kosovo, Palestine and other corners of the world. Zeba told Hadiya about the British and US foreign policies that left many Muslims at risk of poverty, terrorism and war. Hadiya's mind was aflame with all the injustices Zeba told her about, and she became addicted to the feelings elicited by those intense and intimate conversations, the two young women taking on the world from their cosy prayer room. Hadiya had thought she was well informed about current affairs, but the injustices Zeba told her about hadn't appeared in the pages of the *Herald Tribune*. It was like her eyes were finally open to the workings of the world. This new-found knowledge provoked an indignant rage – but there was also the promise of answers.

These answers came from friends of Zeba – other Muslims, she told Hadiya, who were determined to build a better society and who could use someone with Hadiya's purity and zeal. The group they belonged to was called Hizb ut-Tahrir. Hadiya had never heard of it before, but she was just pleased to have found other people who shared her passion. Although Hadiya knew none of this at the time, Hizb ut-Tahrir is a hard-line Islamist group that advocates for the establishment of a caliphate to unite the Muslim world. It is non-violent but controversial, and is considered extremist in its aims to abolish democracy and install Sharia law. It does not represent mainstream Islamic thinking, and some countries have banned it. Some of Hadiya's friends did try to warn her about the group, a fellow member of a human rights group taking her to one side and saying to her, 'It is really good you converted, but you shouldn't be hanging around with these people, they are dangerous. Don't go down that route.'

'But what they are saying makes sense,' Hadiya replied indignantly, and seeing that this woman could provide no further evidence of her claims, dismissed her concerns.

Hadiya felt that she had found somewhere to belong, and soon she came to believe in Hizb ut-Tahrir's singular vision of how to build a better and more peaceful world. The arguments its adherents used were persuasive. They took a truth, then followed it in a direction which to Hadiya seemed completely logical: hadn't politicians from the world's democracies created so much suffering in the world? So it was best to get rid of them and revert to the purity of faith. Hadiya herself used to hate Islam, didn't she? That was proof that there was a conspiracy to destroy her faith. Cut off from her family, she fell further under the spell of this insular group that had a concrete plan to bring about change, winning over the hearts and minds of the people in a way that reminded her of the thrilling tales of the French revolutionaries.

That's how you create a revolution, and I'm going to be part of one, Hadiya thought.

I'm not confused any more. I know what life is about. I know why I am in this world.

Her education intensified, with lessons about the covert Islamophobia that existed in western culture, about the lies perpetrated by the media, and about the true nature of God's will. Then there were the reading lists: *Milestones* by Sayyid Qutb, *Arabic Thought in the Liberal Age, 1798–1939* by Albert Hourani, *The Clash of Civilizations and the Remaking of World Order* by Samuel P. Huntington. Her new mentors would chide her too. If she made a joke or a light remark, she would be criticized, told that she must focus and stop being so frivolous.

They are only correcting my behaviour for my own good, she told herself, more determined than ever to please them and prove herself worthy of a place in the utopian Islamic homeland.

In a matter of months, under the tutelage of Zeba and her friends, Hadiya transformed from a glamorous, spiritually curious student into a dogmatic follower of an extreme Islamist group. She covered the long brown hair she had cared for so meticulously in a drab headscarf and donned the shapeless robes that the group said God wanted her to wear. Recognizing Hadiya's irrepressible sociability, the group soon put her skills to use, sending her out to spread the message. Sure enough, Hadiya turned out to be an excellent recruiter, easily infecting others with her enthusiasm and passion. She seemed to have a knack for finding other people who were looking for answers or seeking solace from life's hardships. Hadiya would take her message to mother-and-baby groups, diabetic clinics, university clubs. It was easy for her to make other people feel that their voices mattered and that they were being heard. She instinctively knew how to hook people in with a lot of attention and a little bit of love, before appealing to their feelings of injustice and oppression.

Hadiya continued studying, but her education wasn't so important now. After she graduated, she found a good job but quit after a short time because she wanted to apply herself full time to the cause. She married another member of Hizb ut-Tahrir, and was soon the mother to two children. This was her life, spreading the word and raising her family. Hadiya didn't spend any time with non-Muslims. They were *kafir*, non-believers, part of the problem, not the solution. It was an insular world, and for a long time, that felt good. When the two aircraft hit the Twin Towers in New York City on 11 September 2001, Hadiya didn't feel horror and terror at the deaths of thousands of people. She just felt a numb hopefulness that maybe now things would be different.

Now will you listen? she thought. *Now will you stop with your interference? Now will you understand the plight of the innocent who you inflict war upon? Will this be the change we were waiting for and tirelessly working for?*

But the 9/11 attacks led to even more military intervention in Muslim lands – the so-called war on terror – and suddenly Islamophobia was everywhere, in the mouths of politicians, on the pages of newspapers, in the portrayal of people of Islamic backgrounds in films and television. This enmity spread onto the streets, with hate crimes against Muslims soaring. Across Europe, a growing suspicion of the Muslim faith translated into hostile government policies: burka bans, debates about the wearing of full-face veils, rows over the provision of halal food in schools. It wasn't a climate that made people feel like they belonged, and this rising tide of hatred gave Hadiya even more material to help draw potential members to the cause. Prior to 9/11, when Hadiya tried to talk about a war on Muslims, most people would look at her as if she were a madwoman peddling conspiracy theories. But the war on terror made it a lot easier to convince people that the world of non-believers was conspiring against the Islamic faith.

First, a coalition force invaded Afghanistan. Then, a few years later, another war began that still reverberates across the world today. It was a war based on a lie that would shatter trust in world powers for generations to come. On 5 February 2003, Colin Powell, then US Secretary of State, stood before the assembled world leaders at the United Nations in New York and talked them through Saddam Hussein's covert nuclear weapons programme, which he asserted was a threat to the world. The British government led by Tony Blair had its own dossier of evidence purporting to show that the Iraqi dictator's weapons of mass destruction could attack British targets within forty-five minutes. Despite the confidence both of Powell's delivery and of the British government in the evidence it claimed to have, not everyone was convinced, and the UN Security Council failed to agree on military action. It wasn't just national leaders who were sceptical. Across the world, citizens were rising up to voice their opposition to another war. Soon after Powell's UN speech, up to 10 million people around the world marched against the invasion of Iraq. It was one of the biggest gestures of direct action ever undertaken – and one of the most futile. The opposition of two million people in London, three million in Rome and hundreds of thousands in the United States did nothing to sway the parliaments, presidents, lawmakers and leaders. Less than a month later, the Iraq War began. It was a turning point in which the gulf between the rulers and the ruled became painfully clear, with a crushing of people's belief that their voices mattered. Britain, Spain and the USA headed into an intractable war that would claim hundreds of thousands of lives, sow unrest across the Middle East and help spawn the Islamic State. The British dossier and the US presentation would prove to be based on flawed intelligence, and no weapons of mass destruction were ever found. That governments and politicians could manipulate information was not a huge revelation to anyone who followed world affairs. But throughout the Cold War, the western narrative had been one of moral authority, the noble truth-seekers overcoming the Soviet machine that was riddled with lies and propaganda. Now that narrative was broken. The scale and audacity of the misinformation over Iraq was shocking, and the boundary between truth and lies began to blur, laying the groundwork for the collapse in trust that would in the coming decade herald a new era of conspiracy and deceit.

For Hadiya in 2003, the war on terror simply gave her more grist for her recruitment. It took time and energy to find suitably vulnerable people, ingratiate herself into their lives, then slowly use that emotional connection to plant her 'truth' as their own. She didn't know that she was probably the last generation of recruiters operating in this way, and that one day soon, it would be possible to draw people towards an alternative 'truth' without even turning away from the computer screen.

8

Tom Olsen

Haugesund, Norway, 1974–97

In 1989, in the Norwegian port town of Haugesund, an enthusiastic media studies teacher showed a class of teenagers *The Birth of a Nation*, the 1915 American propaganda film considered as technically groundbreaking as it was grossly racist in its portrayal of slavery, the Ku Klux Klan and the American Civil War. The teacher wanted his students to appreciate the early film-making techniques, but he didn't understand how impressionable some of his young charges were. Among them was Tom Olsen, a fifteen-year-old boy already romanticizing rebellion and on the radar of the local police. Tom didn't pay attention to the camera angles and artistry: as he watched a distorted version of history being portrayed as fact and delivered with such an emotional punch, he saw the heroes he wanted to emulate.

Ever since he was small, Tom had dreamed of adventure and excitement. He had inherited his spontaneous streak from his mother, who, at the age of sixteen, had abruptly left her hometown of Oulu in Finland and jumped aboard a ship with a Norwegian sailor. She sailed down the Scandinavian Peninsula with her new love, making land in Haugesund. The young couple married shortly after, and Tom arrived a year later, in 1974. This whirlwind teen romance was short-lived, however, and Tom's parents divorced when he was small. His mother remarried when Tom was six – a happy marriage that gave Tom a loving stepfather, a new baby sister and a stable home – and the family moved to a house beside a lake just outside Haugesund. It was perfect for a boisterous child like Tom. He and his friends would build rafts using old barrels, hoisting a makeshift sail and floating out into the open water, with a taste for freedom and adventure. Forts were fashioned from old tree branches, and battles waged between warring knights armed with cardboard swords and shields.

Tom's parents would have been content for his wholesome existence to continue unchanged. But he was growing up, and that isn't the way teenagers work. He was looking to forge his own path in life, but in Haugesund, the options were limited. The town owed its existence to the abundant herring which swam in the calm waters, and it conformed to many of the stereotypes of a provincial fishing town. As a community, it was socially conservative, religious and close-knit. When Tom was young, his grandfather would recount tales of the brawls he and his friends had with boys who came over from the island of Karmøy. These interlopers were considered hillbillies from the countryside, and when they tried to make advances on the local girls at the village dance, fists flew. Loyalty to the tribe still ran deep among the working-class kids Tom grew up with, and outsiders – even those from a few kilometres away – were treated with deep suspicion. A sense of bitterness also pervaded the town. The people in the settlements along the west coast worked hard in the industries that made Norway rich – first fishing, then shipping and oil – but the wealth went to Oslo, and never seemed to come back. In Haugesund, the infrastructure was creaking. Tom's mother and stepfather were always muttering about the general state of disrepair of the permanently potholed road in front of their house.

We are only left with the scraps, Tom thought. *The government couldn't care less.*

The lack of investment meant there wasn't much for a teenager to do in Haugesund, so Tom and his friends hung out at each other's houses and in parks and the local forest, drinking beer and talking about nothing much. Sometimes Tom would go to the harbour and earn a few extra kroner by helping ships dock and unload their cargo. He watched the sailors coming and going, wondering about an outside world that seemed tantalizingly close, but also so far removed from the clannish antics of his group of rowdy friends. Tom's parents were determined to keep him busy, however, even if it meant forcing him into activities in which he had no interest. They enrolled him in a folk-dancing club, which Tom didn't think was a fitting pastime for a teenager. Then there was a sailing course, but the boat flipped Tom into the icy water. At basketball, all the other players were imposingly tall. With his round, soft face and close-cropped fair hair, Tom did not stand out as a particularly sporty type, and was never picked for teams. When he finally found a sport he wanted to do – jiu-jitsu – his parents said it was too violent. Tom felt frustrated: the more he tried to forge his own path, the harder his parents would push back, grounding him for the smallest infractions of their strict rules. He was doing fine in school, so why couldn't they give him a break?

Tom didn't understand that his parents were trying to protect him from the more unsavoury elements of Haugesund. With ships coming from all over the world, the town had become an entry point for illegal drugs in Norway, and with those narcotics came all the associated petty crime and social ills. Quite a few of Tom's friends had connections to the local underworld, and there was always some trouble going on. One evening, Tom and his friends were hanging out in a house listening to music and lamenting the fact they had no money to buy alcohol. Then they heard police sirens, and a car screeched to a stop outside. An older man got out, a notorious bootlegger who dealt in moonshine. He was carrying two 25-litre bottles filled with his finest liquor.

'Watch these, boys,' he shouted, before speeding off.

The teenagers now had two barrels of moonshine, and what promised to be a fun night ahead.

Alcohol was playing an increasingly important part in Tom's life. He was fourteen when he first tried beer, and he liked the way it made him feel – pumped up, confident, invincible.

Nobody can stop me, I can do whatever I want, he thought.

Each weekend, he would drink more, heading out at midday, starting the drinking binges early, and only going home when he had already started to sober up. The more Tom and his friends drank, the more trouble they got into. One evening Tom was getting a hamburger when he noticed a beautiful girl outside the restaurant. He kicked in the window, stepped over the glass, and gathered the girl up in his arms for a kiss. Tom thought it was a grand romantic gesture. The police, who arrived soon after, thought otherwise. At fourteen, Tom had his first experience of being behind bars. He was also regularly brawling with the various local gangs who ruled different turfs around Haugesund. There were potential enemies on every corner: skinheads who came over from Karmøy island; anarchists who had moved into a squat; refugee kids from a new centre in town.

It was around this time that Tom's teacher showed his class *The Birth of a Nation*. Tom had not been taught the real history of slavery or the American Civil War, so he had no reason to doubt this racist retelling of the past. He was captivated by the KKK Knights in their white sheets, their antics bringing back childhood memories of playing with his friends in their forts in the forest, and he responded to the simplistic narrative depicting noble saviours protecting a nation from savages.

Tom's first brush with white supremacist propaganda coincided with a growing anti-immigrant feeling in Haugesund. After decades of controlling immigration, Norway was becoming more diverse, with larger numbers of refugees being allowed to enter the country and the immigration policy being liberalized. Not everyone was supportive of this move. A new far-right political group was forming, called Folkebevegelsen mot innvandring (FMI), or the People's Movement Against Immigration. With a rabble-rousing populist at its helm, the party proved popular with many people in Haugesund who were already disillusioned with perceived government failings in their community. The FMI's message was a simple, jingoistic one that would be mined for votes by populists for decades to come: it gave disenfranchised people an enemy to blame for their problems, while encouraging their pride in an exclusive vision of what it meant to be Norwegian. The message even infiltrated Tom's school, as the FMI was allowed to put forward candidates to run in the high school elections, and swept the board, capitalizing on an animosity felt by many of the Norwegian pupils towards a tiny contingent of Asian kids. Suddenly dozens of students were turning up to classes wearing badges reading 'Norway for the Norwegians'. The school took no action. Not once did Tom hear a teacher speak out against the group or offer a defence of the ethnic minorities that the FMI was demonizing. Having this openly xenophobic rhetoric accepted by people in authority normalized such language for Tom, and his us-and-them mentality hardened.

Beyond the school, there were some voices speaking out against the FMI, and these came from the opposite end of the political spectrum. The 1970s and '80s were a time of deep ideological divides reflecting the opposing sides in the Cold War, and far-left extremism caused more deaths in the world than any other ideology. Communist and Marxist groups and cults were responsible for bombing and terror campaigns in all parts of the globe, and some incidents – like the 1974 kidnapping of American heiress Patty Hearst by the Symbionese Liberation Army – captured headlines worldwide. By the late 1980s, with Cold War tensions abating and far-left groups losing their relevance, anarchist subcultures began to flourish. In Norway, an anarchist collective called Blitz took over a building in Oslo, and members of a splinter group called Acid set themselves up in a squat in Haugesund. They described themselves as anti-fascist and held noisy protests against the FMI, sparking violent clashes between the two groups.

Tom had his own reasons for hating the anarchists. They had spray-painted slogans on the building they took over, and one in particular caused his chest to swell with rage: 'Free Marijuana'. For all his teenage rebellion, Tom had never dabbled in narcotics. A friend's life had been ruined by drug addiction, and now here was a group glibly glorifying the drugs that he had seen cause such harm. Tom didn't only blame the anarchists – he held the authorities responsible too: Haugesund had serious problems with drugs and gang violence, but the cops spent all their time chasing down a bunch of teenagers for drinking a few beers, rather than trying to catch the drug dealers who had destroyed his friend's life.

Tom's enemies were crystalizing: the police and the anarchists. And when your enemies crystalize, so do your allies.

At first Tom saw the skinheads from Karmøy in the same way his grandfather had done two generations earlier – as outsiders to be chased off the home turf. But soon Tom and his friends found themselves engaged in street battles against the anarchists, and running alongside them were the skinheads. Tom was drawn closer into their circle, a bond forged in battle. They were welcoming and friendly, and always happy to share their alcohol. After one particularly brutal street battle, they invited him back to their base to celebrate. When Tom walked through the door, he felt an instinctive jolt of shock at the sight of the huge swastika flag hanging in the room. He knew the history of the Nazis, and knew too about their brutal occupation of his home country during the Second World War. But he had not yet connected all the threads running through his head – his admiration for the KKK; his support for an anti-immigration party; his battles against the anarchists. Up until then, as far as he was concerned they were unrelated – separate crusades, each of which appealed to his misguided sense of justice. Now he was being indoctrinated into a group that would bring it all together. The groundwork had been laid: his own growing feelings of frustration, anger and alienation from the state; mistakes by a school that had failed to guide an impressionable pupil; the normalization of hateful language in the mainstream political process. Tom's drinking and dabbling in petty crime escalated. He was spending more time locked up at the police station for violence and disorderly behaviour and had started dressing in the bomber jackets and high boots favoured by his new skinhead friends. But the police never told his parents that he was involved with an organized neo-Nazi gang, nor did they refer him to child protective services or social services to try and examine the causes of his behaviour. So Tom fell ever deeper into the neo-Nazi ideology.

At the age of seventeen, Tom dropped out of school and asked to be formally initiated into the skinhead group. He wasn't completely convinced by their philosophy, but it was something to do in a place where he didn't feel like he had much future. First, he had to make a public declaration of support. As night fell, Tom and a friend took a couple of cans of spray paint and daubed swastikas on public buildings all over Haugesund. They even targeted the police station. It didn't take long for officers to track the inept teenagers down, and Tom was hauled in front of a judge.

'I don't want neo-Nazis in my town,' the judge told the boys, 'so I'm going to be very, very strict.'

Tom was ordered to stay in solitary confinement as he awaited trial. For a month, he sat in an empty cell with nothing but a bed and a bucket. He was not allowed TV, radio, books or magazines. He ate his meals in his cell, and never interacted with other detainees. As he stared at the wall with nothing but his own thoughts for company, Tom's anger built. His lawyer managed to get his conditions slightly relaxed. He was to remain in solitary confinement but was allowed reading materials. So Tom sent a letter to his new friends with his requests. Soon the packages arrived: Hitler's *Mein Kampf*; the nineteenth-century racist manifesto *Might is Right*; and writings by jailed anti-Semitic terrorist David Lane. With nothing else to do and no one to talk to, Tom devoured the material. Every waking minute was spent poring over the hateful texts, imbibing all the messages. Alone with all the conspiracy theories, he absorbed them into every pore, and they transported him from his cell into another world of alternative truths.

My whole life I have been living inside a small box and fed only what the authorities want me to know, he thought.

Now it felt like he had jumped out of the box and could see reality. This 'reality' consisted of age-old anti-Semitic conspiracy theories and long-discredited ideas linking race and intelligence. He read that the United Nations was about to occupy Norway and that they would then all be put in concentration camps as part of a global plot to carry out a demographic genocide. Tom was locked up in a cell on his own and thus physically prevented from hearing any voices that might have countered those narratives, so the force of the emotion they provoked cemented them at the very centre of his being. They gave him a purpose. For what could be more intoxicating to a teenager struggling to have power over his life than to be at the very heart of a revolution to transform the world?

Tom was released from solitary confinement a month later, after his lawyer struck a deal with the judge. It was 1991. The boy who had entered jail a troubled teenager just starting to dabble in far-right ideology had emerged a committed neo-Nazi, convinced that the world was under threat and that it was his destiny to lead a race war.

For the next few years of his life, Tom lived for the cause he believed he was fighting for. The deal with the judge stipulated that Tom had to join the army, so he did, reasoning that he could use the weapons training and combat skills in the coming race war. But the police were keeping an eye on him, and when they saw he was spending his leave with white supremacist organizations, they ensured that he was discharged. That meant, however, that Tom could now devote himself full time to his imaginary rebellion, and he gathered a growing number of disciples. He became a skilled recruiter, showing up at the youth disco where he had hung out as a kid and visiting children's care homes, using the same tactics that the Karmøy neo-Nazis had lured him in with. He found the vulnerable kids, gave them alcohol and a sense of belonging, then filled their heads with promises of truth and meaning. He had a formula for the new recruits: after warming them up, he would take them to see a former member of the SS, the military wing of the Nazi Party. This old man would tell them his 'truth' about the Second World War – about the bombing of Dresden by the allied forces, the raping of German women, all the atrocities committed by the allies that were never mentioned in school history classes. They would watch VHS cassettes filled with old Nazi propaganda, and Tom would tell the youngsters to ask their teachers about it. The simplistic good-versus-evil version of history taught in schools across Europe worked in Tom's favour. Uncomfortable facts were simply airbrushed out, so once you could disprove one version of events that had previously been presented as the absolute truth, then it became easier to cast doubt on everything else.

Spreading the word wasn't Tom's only role. Violence was also a daily part of the struggle. As well as engaging in frequent clashes with anti-fascist groups, Tom and his gang of neo-Nazis would randomly target those they considered traitors and enemies, people he now believed were less than human. Inter-racial couples, Black people, migrants – Tom saw them all as fair targets. When he came to town, dressed in his boots and his bomber jacket covered in swastikas, people would look at him and cower.

He was addicted to that sense of power. He didn't care that his family was suffering as a result. His aunt lost her job and his grandfather's business went bust because his customers saw the company as having links to a neo-Nazi, so boycotted it. But in Tom's mind, it was all for a just cause.

It was inevitable, however, that Tom's 'just cause' would land him in prison again, and his second incarceration began in 1992, when he was jailed for two years for around ten separate cases related to white supremacist violence. He served one year before returning to the streets. Tom had only been out a few months when he became convinced by events around the world that powerful forces were coming together: the 1993 siege at Waco, Texas; news reports about police exercises in Norway aimed at battling civil disobedience. Was the invasion coming? There was no logic or reason in Tom's thought process any more, just a jumble of anger, paranoia and egotism – shards of his alternative reality creating increasingly illogical scenarios. He and his dozen or so cohorts discussed their options. They needed weapons for the coming revolution, and one guy mentioned a local gun store.

'I saw they had guns with silencers in the window,' he said.

Five of them went to the store, armed with knives and pepper spray. As soon as they were through the door, one of them sprayed the store owner in the face, expecting him to reel back and let them take what they wanted. But instead he fought back. There was a scuffle, and suddenly a knife was sticking in the man's chest. Tom and his gang fled for the Swedish border. Soon after crossing into Sweden, they were arrested and escorted back to Norway. The store owner had survived – the knife had just missed a vital artery. Tom was jailed for armed robbery.

Prison was tough. As soon as Tom made any friends, the authorities would move him to another jail across the country, determined to prevent him converting other prisoners to his ideology. But Tom had a lifeline, and it came enclosed in envelopes sent from the other side of the world, from an enigmatic woman. Christine was the daughter of a prominent member of the Afrikaner Resistance Movement (AWB), a white supremacist group in South Africa fighting a violent battle against the presidency of Nelson Mandela. Tom had long been in awe of the AWB – its large membership, its organized structure, the glossy magazine it distributed to its supporters. It offered a sharp contrast to his ragtag group and the disarray that existed among the Scandinavian neo-Nazi outfits. Back when Christine's father was in jail for his violence against the South African state, Tom had written to him. The man had since been released, and now his daughter was returning the favour, writing letters to Tom that were full of stories about the threat she and her family were facing in the new South Africa. 'Mandela has become President and they will kill us all,' she wrote. The letters had a romantic undertone, and Tom was entranced by the damsel-in-distress depiction, which played straight into his desire to feel important, his longing for adventure, his old fantasies of knights and warriors. Christine said she needed him to save her. How could he say no? It was time to finally put his ideology into practice.

Men and women have been leaving their home countries and volunteering to fight in foreign wars for centuries – and history has been inconsistent in its judgement of them. Military figures from France, Germany and Poland crossed the Atlantic to join the fight for American independence in the eighteenth century. Around 32,000 foreigners took part in the Spanish Civil War that began in 1936, and those who fought against the fascist dictator Franco were hailed as heroes. Che Guevara was born in Argentina, but brought his Marxist revolutionary battle to Cuba, Congo and Bolivia. Many Muslims from other parts of the world travelled to fight alongside the Afghan Mujahideen, who were receiving US support to battle the Soviet occupation of Afghanistan in the 1980s. In most of those cases, the media and politicians cast them as heroes. But then there were those who chose the wrong side of history. The AWB actively recruited from white supremacist ranks in other countries, and dozens of men from Germany, the Netherlands, England, Norway and elsewhere in Europe answered the call.

When Tom was released from jail in 1997, he went to visit his parents to tell them that they might never see him again. He was leaving for South Africa. His mother wept and begged him to stay, but Tom was unmoved. He told them about the revolution, about the civil war that was coming. They looked at him as if he were crazy.

They are brainwashed, they don't understand, Tom thought.

He bought a one-way ticket to Johannesburg.

9

Mak Kapetanovic

Jacksonville, Florida, USA, 2013–15

Sometimes it felt good to be angry. Seventeen years old and grieving his mother, Mak Kapetanovic needed an outlet for all the loss, rage, confusion and loneliness inside. He needed something or someone to blame. It didn't take long for him to find what he was looking for. It was there on his phone, wherever and whenever he needed it.

Throughout his life, Mak had been passionate about video games, and a few months before his mother died a friend told him to check out the gaming boards on 4chan, an anarchic online forum where anybody can post threads for discussion on topics ranging from politics to pets. Mak could come across as an intense youth. He had a hawkish face, a lanky frame and a wary demeanour, but he had his own anarchic streak and a love of the irreverent and ironic. The tone of the talk boards appealed to his sense of humour – sarcastic, a little bit absurd, some edgy jokes that could be really funny. There were some more crazy comments – a lot of misogyny and casual racism. But Mak didn't take it very seriously. He just enjoyed the banter and liked the frisson of being part of a community that skirted the edges of what was socially acceptable.

It's just trash talking or whatever, he thought. *This is the wild, wild west of the internet. Everyone says crazy shit.*

After Mak's mother died, however, he started to take it all a lot more seriously. There was not much else in his life at the time. He went to school but didn't attend any classes, and the teachers didn't seem to care. It was as if because his mum had died, he had a free pass to screw up his life. When he returned home in the evenings, his father would be working, so he would get a takeaway and eat alone. The only places he found solace were in his music and in 4chan. The phone in his hand became a portal to somewhere else — a place where anger was allowed and where people were offered reasons to be mad.

Mak's immersion into 4chan coincided with a brewing storm of outrage on the platform. It began with a female developer creating a game addressing her experiences with depression. Soon, 4chan's games and politics boards were buzzing with misogynistic insults and conspiracy theories, slamming the developer for deviating from the ubiquitous violence and mindless entertainment that typified the average computer game. The viciousness of the backlash prompted soul-searching in some quarters about the portrayal of women in computer games — a debate which further infuriated some of the male purists who felt that their private world was being invaded by destructive interlopers. Mak was vulnerable to such suggestions, affronted by the idea that the one place he found solace from his dark thoughts was now becoming a political space.

I don't want to think about whether or not I'm a good or bad person when I'm playing video games, he thought.

What became known as the Gamergate controversy of 2013–14 was a vicious, targeted and organized campaign, a forerunner of the culture wars that would define political debates in the years to come. From the anonymous realms of 4chan, it spread onto Twitter and other social media platforms, with online provocateurs validating and then amplifying feelings of victimhood and offering up enemies to unload that anger on. Female gamers, developers and critics were hounded with online harassment and subjected to threats of death, rape or the publication of personal information. When the media started to report on the abuse, the Gamergate supporters claimed that the harassment victims were lying or exaggerating to push their politically correct agenda on the rest of the world. The tactics employed by the Gamergate attackers – the trolling of people they disagreed with, the discrediting of opinions through the spread of lies, the accusations of political correctness to hide a tide of hate – would soon become standard operating procedure for the alt-right, a blueprint for how to harmonize and mobilize the frustrations of a community around a common enemy.

Mak was hooked on this intoxicating stream of conspiracy and blame. It wasn't only the video games boards that he participated in now – he was also a regular consumer of 4chan's notorious politically incorrect board, following the threads on race and religion. Although the combative tone of the Gamergate debates had desensitized him to openly offensive content, at first Mak was taken aback by the extremity of some of the racist views espoused on the threads. He was, after all, the son of Bosnian Muslim refugees. But what could he do? If he put his phone down, he would have to re-engage with the painful realities of his life. So he chose to stay in the one space where he felt less alone. Everyone on 4chan seemed to feel as angry as he did, and he found it increasingly difficult to separate their pain from his own. It was like he was addicted to being outraged. Sometimes he would spend six straight hours refreshing 4chan over and over, rechecking the catalogues of different threads, making sure he hadn't missed anything. Even as he sat there all by himself, he felt like he was at the centre of a vital community.

Here are the reasons why I feel so bad, he thought.

To the uninitiated, the chat boards like 4chan, 8chan and Reddit which emerged in the early 2000s seem impenetrable, a mess of chaotically organized threads on disparate subjects with no coherent means of navigating around them. Threads seem to appear and disappear at random. This apparently anarchic structure is part of the attraction – an interface that takes time and effort to master adds to the feeling of being in on a joke that most of the world doesn't get. But its most compelling feature is its anonymity. People don't need to give any identifying personal information to start a thread. The founder of 4chan claimed that this anonymity would allow people to vent their feelings without fear of censure – it was supposedly a way of letting off steam that would, he suggested, be a positive release for its largely young male userbase. He underestimated quite how dangerous it could be to let people reveal the darkest sides of themselves without the constraints of normal social interaction or accountability. 4chan was becoming a dumping ground for weird, wacky and offensive ideas, and this online free-for-all was also a petri dish for memes and narratives that would migrate into more mainstream social media spaces. A lot of the migrating content consisted of juvenile pranks, like the 2014 hoax advising people to charge their iPhone in the microwave. But members of the far right seemed particularly adept at harnessing this unmoderated online world to spread their conspiracy theories. The extent of organized involvement of white supremacist and neo-Nazi groups on such chat boards was unclear given the impossibility of tracking who was posting what. But they were able to spread and grow confusion and misinformation remarkably quickly.

Whoever was behind the posts Mak was devouring in 2013 and '14 seemed to have an uncanny ability to identify genuine concerns affecting young people, then twist them to suit their own goals. They would talk about the crisis of loneliness affecting a generation of young men, then blame it on women. Postings went on at length about the failure of globalization to bring prosperity to all and about the greed of corporate America, and then say that these problems were the fault of Jewish people. If people complained about feeling alienated, they were told it was because multicultural societies didn't work.

It was a repeated pattern of first stoking outrage and then pointing the finger of blame.

It left Mak buzzing with the intoxicating feeling of being smarter than everyone around him. There was even a whole meme around it: red pilling, just like in the film *The Matrix*, where the protagonist is offered a red pill that will show him the reality of the fake world which has been created around him. If he takes the blue one, he gets returned to the zombie-like state of oblivion. So many of the threads Mak devoured started with the enticing phrase, 'I'm going to red-pill you about...' What followed 'about' could be anything: women, Black people, the white replacement genocide theory. The crazier the theory, the more intensely Mak felt that rush of exclusive knowledge. There were images, graphs, figures, statistics – for a teenager who wanted to be intellectually challenged but found school unstimulating, it was like a treasure trove of learning. Most of the ideas moulding Mak's thinking didn't come from school anyway. He had read Ayn Rand's 1957 novel *Atlas Shrugged*, and his politics were now taking a libertarian bent. In his search for a religious identity to craft from his confused cultural heritage, he had come across anti-theist videos on YouTube. They convinced him that religion was to blame for the violence in the world, and that chimed with a lot of the Islamophobic and anti-Semitic comments he was seeing on 4chan. All these new 'truths' were unravelling like the layers of an onion, bringing Mak ever closer to what he believed to be the hidden reality.

In fact, most of the revelations Mak devoured were a rehash of old anti-Semitic conspiracy theories. Propaganda and lies targeting people from other backgrounds have been around for hundreds of years, with the original blood libel conspiracy against Jewish people emerging in the twelfth century. And cults, gangs and extreme religious communities have long sucked people in with their promises of imagined utopias built on exclusive visions of paradise. But while in the past such groups had to physically find their recruits, and then indoctrinate them with group meetings, pamphlets and reading lists, today information is everywhere, to be dangled and manipulated at will. A solitary and angry young man like Mak with his eyes locked on a screen filled with racist hate was not so different from an angry young man locked in a jail cell with neo-Nazi propaganda. It's just that Mak built his own walls. Nobody – neither his friends, nor his father, nor his girlfriends – had any idea what Mak was looking at on his phone, or what was going on inside his head. It didn't matter that he had crafted his own cell himself – it had the same cumulative effect. The more time he spent online, the more disconnected he became from the world around him. All alone as he consumed reams of misinformation and racist rhetoric, he started to believe all these alternative truths. Mak Kapetanovic, the son of Muslim refugees who had fled the hatred of ethnic nationalism in Bosnia, had turned himself into a white supremacist without uttering a word about it to anyone.

10

Ibrahim Kamara

Brighton, England, 2009–14

The Kamara family's latest home on the eastern side of Brighton wasn't perfect. It was on the borders of Moulsecoomb, one of the more downtrodden areas of the seaside city, hidden away from the day trippers and the well-heeled commuters. And the house itself was a little run-down. But for fourteen-year-old Ibrahim Kamara, it had one huge draw: in front of the house was a long stretch of green space where he and his three younger brothers could play football for hours. Ibrahim was a Manchester United supporter through and through, and as he dribbled the ball round his siblings, he would imagine he was talented midfielder Paul Scholes, about to score the goal that would win his team the Premier League title once again.

The kids had taken their parents' divorce in their stride – Ibrahim's early traumas had somewhat hardened him in particular to life's blows – and they could see the difference in their mother, Khadijah. Once again, she was smiling, happy, playful – not always crying and shouting like a crazy woman. She was still young – not yet thirty – and suddenly had lots of energy to run around with her sons, playing chase and leapfrog, and dancing in the kitchen. At night, even though the children were now aged between six and fourteen, they would all end up in her bedroom. Khadijah's smallest son would sleep on her chest, while the other younger boys would fight over who got to snuggle up to her right side. Ibrahim would pull up a blanket and sleep on the floor.

Now in a position where she was providing for herself for the first time, Khadijah was optimistic about the future. Ibrahim felt the same way. School life was improving, and his interest in Islam was helping with his mental well-being. But it wasn't long before Khadijah began to worry about the company her boys were keeping. The other kids in the new neighbourhood could be badly behaved, using foul language and being disrespectful. She had taught her boys differently and didn't want them to be around anyone who would be a bad influence. She told Ibrahim and his brothers to play by themselves and keep away from the local gangs. That was when the trouble started.

In early 2009, soon after the family moved to their new home, unexpected snow fell across the country, and the green that ran alongside their road was blanketed in white. Snowballs started regularly hitting the windows of the family's home. At first they dismissed them as childish pranks, but when the snow cleared, the pelting at the windows didn't stop. Now it was stones that the neighbourhood kids had started throwing at the windows and the shed. Then the insults began. When Ibrahim and his brothers walked home from school, local boys would yell racist and Islamophobic abuse at them. On a few occasions, Khadijah allowed herself to see the black humour in her situation. Some of the kids would yell 'Paki' at her, presumably because of her headscarf, and she chuckled at their pathetic grasp of geography. Then there were the people who insisted on calling them refugees. Being labelled a refugee was not particularly desirable in a country where the term 'asylum seeker' was now a slur. The Kamara family were not claiming asylum in Britain. Yes, Khadijah had once been forced to seek refuge from a terrible war in Sierra Leone, but she and her family had arrived in the United Kingdom as European Union citizens, able to legally live and work there as part of the freedom of movement allowed across the bloc. Unfortunately, however, that could have made them vulnerable to abuse too, as the open borders of the EU had long been an issue of contention in Britain, with concern in less privileged areas of the country that increased migration from poorer EU nations would push down wages and overwhelm already stretched government services like healthcare and education. Certain newspapers, as well as nationalist parties such as the UK Independence Party, which was campaigning for Britain to leave the EU, fostered the misleading impression that people coming from overseas were being given preferential treatment, and the cycle of resentment grew.

For Ibrahim and his family, the abuse from the neighbourhood kids was becoming intolerable. They would circle around him and his brothers on their bikes, threatening them and screaming racist slurs. Khadijah called the police. An officer came round to the house and sat in their living room, listening to the details, taking notes, nodding in all the right places and promising to speak to the boys. Khadijah was satisfied with this. But the abuse continued. One morning, Khadijah found human faeces in the front garden. Again she called the police. A different police officer came round this time, one who appeared to have no knowledge of her previous complaint and who asked her all the same questions. Patiently, Khadijah explained everything. The officer promised to do something. Once again, nothing changed. This pattern was repeated every few weeks. The family never saw the same police officer twice, there seemed to be no detailed record of Khadijah's previous complaints, and no action ever seemed to be taken. Each time they filed another complaint, Ibrahim would earnestly quiz his mother.

'What did the police say?' he would ask her.

'They will do something,' Khadijah reassured her eldest son.

Ibrahim always seemed so disappointed when nothing then changed. He was acutely attuned to injustice, and it seemed obvious to him that his family was being treated unfairly. And the abuse was getting physical. One day some of the local kids came and asked Ibrahim if he wanted to play football. He wasn't sure if he should: he had just been released from hospital a week earlier after having his appendix removed. He was still feeling tender, but was moved by this gesture of conciliation, and headed outside with them. It didn't take long before the boys jumped on him, kicking and hitting him. Khadijah rushed him to their doctor, terrified the beating had set back his recovery. The doctor reassured her that he would be OK, and this time the police seemed to take the abuse more seriously. Ibrahim identified the ringleader of the gang that had beaten him, and the police promised to arrest him. But the next day, the boy was playing on the green in front of their house as if nothing had happened. Khadijah was incredulous. Not long after, Ibrahim's eleven-year-old brother came home terrified. An older boy had threatened his life.

'Mum, do you really think they are going to kill me?' he asked.

Enough was enough. Khadijah went to the housing agency and begged to be given another home. They had endured the abuse for more than a year, and no one had helped them. The family were given emergency accommodation in the town of Seaford, twenty miles to the east and nearly an hour's journey to the kids' school. There was no kitchen, and no fridge. The children ate junk food because there was no other choice. Khadijah lost her cleaning job because she couldn't travel to and from Brighton every day. Eventually the council found the family another house, this time in Hangleton, in the far west of the city. Khadijah visited her new neighbours when she arrived, determined to start off on a positive footing. One of the men seemed friendly and chatty. But when she told him about the problems the family had suffered in their previous home, his demeanour changed.

'They are going to hate you here just as they hated you there,' he said in a manner that felt threatening to Khadijah.

He was right: the abuse wasn't quite as blatant as before, but they were not made to feel welcome. The neighbours were always complaining about the boys playing football, while the other white kids played without censure. One woman would park her car right in front of their house and then tell Khadijah that meant the kids couldn't play there. A local man parked his motorcycle in front of the house and revved it loudly in front of the children. It was such a threatening gesture that Khadijah decided to try the police one more time. A female officer sat her down. 'It's better for you not to say anything because that will aggravate things,' she told Khadijah, who went home and wept. She decided that night that she would not waste another second of her life speaking to such a useless bunch of people.

But Khadijah was worried about Ibrahim. He didn't seem angry or indignant now. He simply seemed resigned to the fact that he would always be treated like he didn't belong. He stopped talking about it. He stopped asking if anything would be done.

Ibrahim did a good job of hiding his feelings at school. To the other kids, he was a jovial presence, making the class – although not always the teachers – laugh with his quips, his funny expressions and his outrageous dance moves. At 6 feet 2 inches tall and with long limbs, he was good at sports, and he had a passion for music, especially American rap. But the place he found most relief from the stresses of the racist abuse at home was the mosque. Khadijah had sent all her boys to the Al-Quds Mosque in Hove for Qur'an classes. The mosque was in a converted detached house along the prosperous Dyke Road, where the large family homes hidden behind high fences and electric gates offered a stark contrast to the dingy council houses Ibrahim was growing up in. It was at Al-Quds that Ibrahim met a like-minded teenager called Amer Deghayes. Amer was born the same year as Ibrahim and had suffered many of the same hardships. He grew up in a large family, his parents having fled the regime of Muammar Gaddafi in Libya. His uncle was Omar Deghayes, who had achieved notoriety as one of the Britons in Guantanamo Bay. Omar had been arrested in Pakistan in 2002 as the war on terror rounded up potential enemies with no regard for due process or human rights. His arrest appeared to be a case of mistaken identity, but there was no lawyer or trial for him to prove it. He endured years of abuse in the extrajudicial prison, losing an eye during a beating by camp guards. Omar was released in 2007 with no explanation or apology, and his return to Brighton prompted a wave of far-right hatred toward the whole family. By 2009, the Islamophobic and racist abuse directed at the Deghayes family was relentless and appeared organized: 'Behead All Muslims' was daubed on beach huts near the Deghayes family home; stones and bottles were flung at their windows; the car windscreen was smashed; death threats were made on public transport and social media; and there were brutal beatings. As with Ibrahim and his family, the police appeared uninterested in stopping it. Nobody was ever prosecuted. Amer's younger brothers – subjected to cries of 'Terrorist!' in the school playground – began to defend themselves. They were soon expelled, and with no coherent support plan from social services, the education system or the police, they turned to delinquency and crime as an outlet for their frustrations. They banded together with some other local youths who felt excluded from Brighton's liberal utopia and formed a street gang.

Ibrahim's friend Amer was different from the rest of the Deghayes family. He was always considered the sensible one: bright, engaged in the world, doing well at school. Soon after meeting at the mosque, the pair became inseparable, bonding over their determination to channel their negative experiences into something positive. A local youth group helped guide their creative impulses, and the duo wrote rap music and lyrics and produced plays and film scripts challenging stereotypes. Amer was more intellectually confident than Ibrahim, writing and producing a film called *Don't Judge Me* which challenged media portrayal of teenagers from deprived backgrounds. Ibrahim was in awe of his friend's articulacy, but he had his own projects too. He helped produce an anti-bullying film at school, making Khadijah so proud. It reflected the qualities she had raised her boys to have: to be respectful, and to intervene in the face of injustice.

In summer 2011, Ibrahim graduated from secondary school with passable grades, and after a faltering year at sixth form college, where he struggled with the more rigorous academic pace, he decided to follow Amer and enrol in City College, where he would do computer studies. Now Ibrahim was constantly with his best friend: at college, in the youth club, at the mosque. Increasingly, their attention was turning away from the injustices they had experienced first-hand and towards world events.

In December 2010, a fruit seller had burned himself to death in a remote Tunisian town to protest against state corruption and police brutality. Within weeks, in early 2011, the Tunisian president had been ousted and the Arab Spring had begun. Egypt's President Hosni Mubarak was the next to fall, and soon Libya's Gaddafi was in protesters' sights. Ibrahim would listen rapt as Amer chronicled the advance of the rebel forces closing on the Libyan dictator. Amer's own grandfather had been killed in one of Gaddafi's purges of the opposition, so his hatred for the dictator was intense. But it wasn't only teenage boys with a horse in the race who lionized the rebel army. Western reporters would embed themselves with the ragtag militias in their flips-flops and sunglasses, sending back breathless reports of the Kalashnikov-wielding revolutionaries marching across the desert to vanquish a monstrous foe. In March, the UN Security Council authorized military action, and on 20 October 2011, Gaddafi was dragged from a storm drain and executed by the rebels, a cause for jubilation for Ibrahim and Amer. By this time, however, the

Arab Spring was entering its autumnal phase, and the simplistic narrative of noble rebels battling evil dictators – a narrative which had dominated much of the media coverage and political debate – would soon become twisted and murkier. Libya would unravel into a prolonged civil war between the various factions as the NATO powers withdrew with little thought as to how the country would rebuild itself.

At first, the Syrian conflict mirrored this narrative. In February 2011, a group of schoolchildren in Daraa spray-painted graffiti calling for the end of the regime of President Bashar al-Assad, an authoritarian leader who ruled through violence, fear and corruption. The protest movement spread from the cities to the rural areas, and soon a Free Syrian Army emerged, to be feted like the Libyan rebels had been, as crusading saviours battling a corrupt oppressor. But there was to be no swift resolution to this war. The European powers and the US government gave diplomatic and financial support to the rebels but avoided direct military action, concerned about the political ramifications in the broader Middle East. Emboldened, Assad intensified his onslaught. In August 2012, the first barrel bombs fell on Aleppo. The metal containers were stuffed with explosives, and shrapnel tore through the flesh of anyone who happened to be nearby.

Having been born into war, Ibrahim found it traumatic to see other children go through the same ordeal. But he was sure that the world would act soon. In Iraq there had been no weapons of mass destruction, and the US-led coalition invaded anyway. In Libya, NATO intervened to help topple Gaddafi. US President Barack Obama said that if Assad used chemical weapons, that would be the red line that would provoke military action. A year after Obama made that promise, on the morning of 21 August 2013, rockets carrying the sarin nerve agent landed in neighbourhoods on the outskirts of Damascus. The horrific images flooded Ibrahim's Facebook timeline.

Children convulsing in their beds; tiny lifeless bodies laid out on hospital floors; people struggling to breathe as foam bubbled from their mouths.

Ibrahim and Amer waited for the West to intervene. But Obama went back on his word. The British Parliament too voted against military action. It was just like the police in Brighton, who promised they would act to stop the racist abuse endured by Ibrahim's family, then did nothing. Now the injustices in Ibrahim's own life were becoming intertwined with the injustices in the world, and Ibrahim couldn't turn away. On the nightly news, on social media, in the newspapers, he was transfixed by the images of bombed buildings, bloodied civilians, bereaved parents. It was the sight of suffering children that hurt Ibrahim the most. In all the anguished faces, he was reminded of the children he had heard crying throughout the night in the refugee camps in Guinea. Exactly as had happened with the Ethiopian famine and the Rwandan genocide a few decades earlier, Ibrahim was being bombarded with images of the most gut-wrenching suffering, while being told that the world was doing nothing. But as Ibrahim and Amer followed events in Syria, they were forming a plan. Maybe they did have the power to make a difference after all.

By the middle of 2013, the war in Syria had strayed far from the simple narrative of good guys versus bad guys. The opposition had broken into dozens of armed factions fighting for various goals. Shaky video footage emerged on YouTube and on Islamist extremist websites showing atrocities committed by anti-Assad forces, including beheadings, mutilations and the desecration of corpses. The al-Qaeda-linked al-Nusra Front was already active, and now another shadowy organization, the Islamic State in Iraq and Syria, otherwise known as ISIS, was emerging. Slowly the fight for freedom and democracy had for some people become a violent battle for an Islamic caliphate. But it took a while for the complexities of the battlefield to filter through into the media coverage. Ibrahim and Amer had become fascinated by a Channel 4 News film about Ibrahim al-Mazwagi, a twenty-one-year-old British Muslim who travelled to Syria to join one of the Islamist militias. Al-Mazwagi joked and smiled for the camera as he did target practice, chased a sheep for his wedding banquet, wandered through bombed-out buildings lit by moody sunsets, and went shopping with a Kalashnikov slung across his back. With his shoulder-length hair and unshaven face he was the Che Guevara of the Syrian conflict.

'A Muslim is a Muslim,' he intoned to the camera. 'Is he in need of protection? OK, I'm there.'

In the whole thirteen-minute documentary, only one sentence was devoted to reports of brutalities carried out by the Islamist forces, and no detail was given. Overall, the tone was one of a Boys' Own adventure with a noble cause. The film ended with al-Mazwagi's wedding, as he was embraced by a brotherhood of fellow fighters singing together and hoisting him aloft: a scene of belonging. Now here was something that Ibrahim and Amer could aspire to. Amer's father had already been to Syria, travelling as part of a 2012 aid convoy bringing supplies to the rebel forces. Again, the media coverage of such convoys was overwhelmingly positive, portraying them as much-needed humanitarian missions to a population abandoned by the world.

Khadijah didn't watch the news, and she found the Internet overwhelming, so she had no idea what was going on in Syria – or in her son's head. She was also busy with her new venture: a charity shop she had opened in January 2013 to raise money for orphans in Sierra Leone. The shop was doing well, and Khadijah was enjoying a renewed sense of purpose. So when Ibrahim finally confided in her, she was taken aback.

'I want to go to Syria to help,' he told her one evening in summer 2013 as they drove home from her charity shop. 'The government there is harming its people.'

Khadijah was furious.

'What are you going to do? You haven't finished your education and you don't have any money,' she screamed at him. She hadn't come across words like 'brainwashed' or 'radicalized', but something told her he was not acting alone.

'You are listening to somebody,' she told him.

Ibrahim insisted he just wanted to offer humanitarian assistance to those who were suffering. So Khadijah tried a different approach, telling him that Islamic scholars were the ones who decided what was a just cause, and that he should be guided by them.

'You can't just get up individually and say you are going to war,' she told him. 'That country has to ask you for help.'

But Ibrahim would not be dissuaded, and began to distance himself from his mother. He would leave the house in the evening and not return until well into the night, and Khadijah had no idea who he was with or what he was doing. He would spend hours behind closed doors on his computer. Now he wasn't only watching mainstream media reports about the war, but was heading deeper into dogmatic territory. First there were the prayer videos on YouTube. Then he found the sermons of Anwar al-Awlaki, a charismatic America-born preacher who had become a key propagandist for al-Qaeda, and whose words lived on in thousands of YouTube videos even after he was killed in a US drone strike in Yemen. It was Islamist extremist groups like al-Qaeda and its offshoots which first harnessed the power of the Internet and social media as a tool for recruitment, flooding the then-unregulated spaces with propaganda videos and training materials and reaching disparate groups via Facebook and Twitter. And al-Awlaki was something of a prototype for the YouTube gurus of every ideological stripe who would thrive in the coming years. He had a natural ability to home in on genuine concerns, and then manipulate them to fit his own agenda. He had an easy way in front of the camera and a resonant message for Muslims: namely, that they would never be accepted in the West. Faced with this onslaught of news from Syria, with his own experience of injustice, and with what he saw as the moral failure of the West to act, Ibrahim gravitated towards the anti-western conspiracy theories and the beguiling messages of extremist recruiters. It all confirmed that it was his duty as a Muslim to travel to Syria to fight for the oppressed.

As his resolve hardened, his adherence to his faith became more rigid. At the mosque, he was prone to outbursts and would argue with the imam about the duties of Muslims, and be dismissive of anyone who tried to question his hardening beliefs. At home, he started to chide Khadijah.

'Mum, you pray too fast,' he would tell her angrily.

Then Khadijah learned that Ibrahim had talked to one of his brothers about Syria. She decided she needed to protect the younger boys. She made sure Ibrahim's passport was not renewed, so he couldn't leave the country, and then in October 2013, to teach him a lesson, she asked him to leave the family home. Ibrahim moved into a bedsit but in many ways he remained the same kind-hearted, helpful young man she had raised. He would still pop round for cups of tea, and Khadijah thought it was only a matter of time before he came to his senses.

One morning in January 2014, Ibrahim came to Khadijah's charity shop carrying some personal items.

'Hi Mum,' he said.

Khadijah was busy with a customer so just gave him a wave, then handed over the keys to the house. She assumed he was carrying the extra bags because he had decided to move back home, and her heart surged.

Instead, Ibrahim went to the family home and told his brothers that he was leaving to attend university. While he was in the house, he rummaged round and found what he was looking for:

the passport of his fifteen-year-old brother. Soon he was on his way to Luton Airport. It was early 2014. Millions of Syrians were fleeing a war that was devastating their country. Ibrahim was heading in the other direction.

11

Peter Cytanovic

Reno, Nevada, USA, 2015 to Charlottesville, Virginia, USA, 2017

Peter Cytanovic's great-grandfather was one of around two million Europeans who had fled the Great Depression in the 1930s and travelled across the Atlantic to seek a new life in the United States, heading to New Jersey to join the existing Croatian diaspora. But in 2015, when about one million people embarked on a similar exodus from Syria towards Europe – a movement sparked by the devastating war in their country – Peter felt no affinity with the men, women and children seeking a safe place. Instead, he felt overcome with an inexplicable rage at something happening on a continent he had never even visited. To him, they were not fellow human beings with similar motives to his great-grandfather's; rather, they were invaders threatening Europe's way of life. He would look at his phone and read the news and just feel angry that no one was doing anything to stop them.

By the time he started his second year at the University of Nevada, Peter felt so alienated from the other students that he had started to retreat online, where he quickly discovered plenty of people who knew exactly how to speak to his deepest insecurities. They went by many names – alt-right; alt-lite; identarian; populist; nationalist – and had found their perfect home on YouTube, where they were unconstrained by the editorial boards and codes of conduct associated with the traditional media. The prototype of the shouty everyman spouting his 'truths' and smashing the mainstream narrative was Alex Jones, whose InfoWars website pushing far-right conspiracy theories grew out of his radio talk show. His heirs were Andrew Breitbart and Steve Bannon of Breitbart News, which in 2007 promised a legitimate conservative alternative to what it claimed was a largely biased liberal media space. There was the need for a genuine discussion about political diversity in the mainstream media, but Breitbart frequently ended up in the same conspiratorial quagmire as InfoWars, with poorly sourced far-right commentary that masqueraded as news.

But it was in the booming and unregulated world of YouTube that these alt-right voices really flourished. Political commentators who would have struggled to get their views aired on established channels spun a mix of conspiracy-laced bombast, using the formula familiar from the forums like 4chan of first identifying a problem, and then offering up an enemy. But while those anarchic online chat boards appealed to a young and technically minded userbase, the new YouTube gurus had a veneer of sophistication that brought their divisive messages to a wider audience.

And the 2015 refugee crisis propelled these provocative talking heads from the fringe to the mainstream. Here was a visible enemy they could unite their disparate followers against, helped along by an inept and confused response from world leaders. As Europe oscillated between compassion and condemnation and failed to come up with a coordinated and humane response to the crisis, the far right seized the narrative. The chaotic scenes at borders caused by squabbling European leaders provided the images to fuel their scaremongering, and suddenly the de-humanizing terms that had been used during the genocides of Rwanda and Yugoslavia were once again appearing in print and on the airwaves: the refugees were 'cockroaches'; 'aliens';

'rabid dogs'. This language had spread from YouTube and other under-regulated social media spaces to the pages of newspapers, and came out of the mouths of politicians from far-right and nationalist movements across the world. Rather than challenge this hateful rhetoric, more mainstream politicians shifted their own towards the far right, and suddenly what was once unsayable became commonplace.

The wave of terror attacks in Europe in 2015 and '16 provided more material for the far right's grand narrative of us versus them, and Peter was hooked. This all coincided with the approaching US presidential election in November 2016 and the excitement Peter was feeling about it. The Republican candidates had not shied away from exploiting Europe's turmoil for their own political gain. Hatred and fear were well and truly back as legitimate political tools, having been normalized by politicians around the world. So when Peter watched videos put up on YouTube by far-right commentators, it seemed to him that their words were not that far removed from those coming from the mouth of the man striving to be president of the United States, and they seemed all the more acceptable as a result.

The more of these videos Peter watched, the more he heard the same stories: these people were not real refugees, they were just young men trying their luck at getting better-paid jobs in another country; they raped women; they were a threat to European culture. Peter only spent a fraction of his time looking at what had now become derisively known in some circles as 'MSM': mainstream media. And he knew better than to try to discuss the refugee crisis with people in his college, so there was no one to challenge his increasingly distorted perspective. Instead, he spent more and more time online in the company of far-right YouTube personalities like James Allsup, Lauren Southern, Nathan Damigo, Paul Joseph Watson and Stefan Molyneux. They posted videos with provocative titles like 'White Privilege is a Dangerous Myth' and 'The Death of Europe'. As soon as

Peter watched one video, a link would appear to another, then another, then another, each one often more extreme than the last. YouTube's algorithms are designed to make people spend as much time as possible on the site in order to drive up advertising revenues, and over time the developers realized that offering people more of what they had watched already − or slight variations of it − kept people hooked. Facebook, Twitter and other social media platforms use algorithms with a similar effect. Soon these sites were inadvertently sending people like Peter deeper down a rabbit hole of their own biased views, amplifying and distorting them even further. In this way, radicalization had become automated, with people falling into those narratives of us and them, hate and fear, truth and lies without ever looking up from their screens.

It didn't take long before Peter was convinced that people on the left wanted him dead. It wasn't just because of the divisive narratives on YouTube: a very real sense of hatred was solidifying on both sides of the political spectrum. In June 2016, Trump supporters were pelted with eggs in angry scenes in San Jose, California.

They would probably line me up against a wall and shoot me, he thought. *They hate me, they hate America, and they are my enemy.*

In this online echo chamber of his own fears and doubts, Peter's perception of what was racist also shifted. In this new community he had found on YouTube and Facebook, he was coddled and told how people on the left of the political spectrum used the terms 'racist' and 'Nazi' about anyone who disagreed with them. With so many competing versions of the truth, Peter chose to believe the far-right groups when they said they were not racist and chose not to believe more established media sources when they said those groups were fronts for white supremacists. Over the space of about a year, Peter became convinced that it wasn't racist to believe that the white race should be protected; that it wasn't racist to believe the races should be separated; that it wasn't racist to be against people from different races getting married. He didn't think it was racist to believe that Islam was a violent ideology, or to believe that migrants should be forcibly deported.

Now there was no one there in the real world to tell him that he had turned into exactly the kind of racist that he claimed he didn't want to be.

By the summer of 2017, Peter had spiralled into far-right extremism, tumbling from the YouTube vlogs of provocative but reasonably mainstream right-wing commentators down into the realms of fully white supremacist content, albeit in some cases wrapped up in more presentable packaging. He finally landed in the arms of Identity Evropa, one of the new far-right groups masquerading as something much more benign. No longer was white nationalism the preserve of hooded Ku Klux Klan members and skinheads with swastika tattoos and high boots. By 2017 a new breed of white extremism had emerged, socially acceptable in trainers and sharp haircuts, polished to have an appeal that went beyond the traditional far-right recruiting grounds to make its way into colleges, businesses and sports clubs. A similar outfit in Europe – Generation Identity – was even profiled in the mainstream *Sunday Times* magazine, which ran a light-hearted piece entitled 'Heil hipsters' telling readers to 'forget bomber jackets and beer bellies: Britain's far right is rebranding with skinny jeans, trainers and honeyed words'. This normalization of the far right was aimed at people exactly like Peter: alienated young men and women seeking answers in a confusing world, but nervous about associating with openly neo-Nazi groups. The membership of Identity Evropa was steeped in racist and anti-Semitic beliefs, but these were soft-pedalled for the white college boys, veiled in diaphanous patriotic language about national pride, culture and heritage. Peter had seen overt racism and anti-Semitism on some of the alt-right Facebook pages and it made him uncomfortable. But he was convinced the guys at Identity Evropa weren't extremists – they were just people who cared about protecting European culture and heritage. They were authentic, unlike all the noisy frat boys who belonged to the college Republicans, who were just into girls and good times.

That same summer, Peter applied for membership of Identity Evropa and underwent a two-hour Skype interview. He was asked for his views on immigration and race, and there were personal questions too. Did he have any tattoos? Any drug convictions? Towards the end of the interview the questions veered off into territory Peter was uncomfortable with.

'What do you think about the Jews?' the man asked.

That's not right, Peter thought. While he had seen anti-Semitic conspiracy theories doing the rounds, he didn't relate to them.

'I don't think the Jews are causing any problems,' Peter answered.

His interviewer seemed satisfied and Peter's membership was approved. Peter didn't give any further thought to the undertones of the question about Jewish people – he was just glad he had been accepted, and excited to finally meet some like-minded people.

Identity Evropa was helping to organize a rally in Charlottesville, Virginia called Unite the Right, and Peter was keen to go. The stated aim was to protest against the planned removal of a statue of Robert E. Lee, a Confederate-era general who had held slaves. A shocking act of violence two years earlier had prompted nationwide soul-searching about the links between Confederacy nostalgia and racism. On 17 June 2015, a twenty-one-year-old white supremacist named Dylann Roof walked into a church in Charleston frequented by African Americans and shot nine people dead. Roof had been photographed posing with the Confederate flag, prompting South Carolina's government headquarters to remove the one flying outside their building. Across the South, states grappled with how to address the feelings of racism and exclusion such historical symbols provoked. In Charlottesville, the city council had voted to sell the statue of General Lee. It was a controversial decision that a judge had temporarily blocked, and a public consultation was ongoing about the pros and cons of removing the statue. But for the far right, the possibility of the statue being removed provided a convenient flashpoint for disparate groups that were capitalizing on the divisive rhetoric of Donald Trump's election campaign, and that were keen to mobilize their new recruits.

Peter flew down to Charlottesville on the morning of 11 August 2017 and spent a pleasant day in the grounds of the University of Virginia campus, a light breeze cutting through the oppressive southern summer heat. In the afternoon, he went to a motel to meet up with two other young men he had met online. They were going to share a room, and decided to go out and get some fried chicken before heading back to the university campus for an impromptu night-time rally ahead of the main protest at the Robert E. Lee statue on Saturday. Peter had heard rumours that openly fascist and neo-Nazi groups like Vanguard America and the Ku Klux Klan were going to be there that evening. He chose not to believe those rumours. It was another truth that he dismissed as a lie in a world where the difference between the two was blurring. Besides, if there were full-on neo-Nazis there, he would simply keep his distance.

If I just interact with the moderates, I'll be fine, he thought.

When Peter arrived on campus at sundown, the atmosphere was one of mild disorganization. Only a handful of people were there, and Peter and his friends waited at the front of the small crowd. Many people were wearing the same outfit: polo shirts and khaki trousers, the new preppy uniform of the American far right. Peter was dressed the same, proud of his Identity Evropa white polo complete with the group's triangle 'dragon's eye' symbol. Eventually someone came over and handed him a tiki torch – a bamboo-mounted flame intended for lighting gardens at night. A crowd of one hundred white men carrying open flames against a dark night held much more frightening connotations in the South, recalling the terror of the burning crosses of the Ku Klux Klan. Peter took the torch and waited. News crews were starting to arrive, and Peter watched as an openly racist member of Vanguard America started talking to the media. There could be no doubt now that the rally was more than just a gathering of Trump supporters expressing their love of American history and culture. It was something much more sinister. Yet Peter stayed. More people were arriving, and a buzz was growing. Then the instruction came: *Light your torches, line up, let's start moving.* Peter set his flame alight. He knew what it meant, and at that moment he no longer cared. He had heard there were counter-protesters on the campus, and he was ready to let out all the rage that had been building up over the past two years.

Let's go and show these fuckers what's up! he thought as he set off into the dark night.

The torches were held aloft at the front of the crowd, and a chorus of voices rose around him. The atmosphere was unlike anything he had ever experienced before: the torchlight, the heat, the smell of the burning kerosene, the energy of the crowd of mostly young white men. They were marching together now, screaming in unison: 'You will not replace us!' For some groups, this morphed into 'Jews will not replace us!' Elsewhere, cries of 'Blood and soil!', a phrase used in Nazi Germany to link white ethnicity to the land, rose from the crowd. Peter heard the chants about the Jews, and there was a flash of discomfort, but it was not nearly strong enough for him to put his torch down and walk away. Instead, he bellowed, 'You will not replace us!' with increasing ferocity. Not for a moment did he consider what kind of fear that phrase – shouted with such anger and vitriol under burning torches at night in the American South – might evoke in people from different ethnic backgrounds. He was too overcome with his own feelings to think about anyone else, and there was a frustration bubbling under his skin, ready to be unleashed.

The crowd moved through the campus and towards a statue of Thomas Jefferson. A few dozen counter-protesters had linked arms around the statue and were chanting, 'Black lives matter!' They were mostly student peace activists, but Peter did not see them that way. To him, they were the physical manifestation of the people he had come to see as the enemy, the ones out to destroy everything he held dear. Peter's blood was boiling. All around him there were shouts, chants. He was now at the front of the crowd of white nationalists who had encircled the much smaller group of counter-protesters. Peter screamed louder and louder.

'You will not replace us! You will not replace us!'

Around him camera flashes went off, photographers capturing this extraordinary moment when the new face of far-right America had finally emerged, unashamed and emboldened, in this latest era of hatred and fear.

There was a photographer just on Peter's left – Samuel Corum, who was working with the Turkish press agency Anadolu. He caught Peter's eye and trained his lens on the group. He wouldn't usually hold a shot for so long – it stopped him from being able to assess the danger in situations on the brink of violence – but there was something in the rage and energy of the moment. It was almost as if Peter wanted him to take his photo. His camera flashed a few more times, and then he ran for cover.

Peter too was braced for violence. He felt it in the air. Then suddenly torches were swinging, fists were flying. Peter tried to move away from the fray, but he backed into one of his fellow protesters, who shoved him forward, straight into a counter-protester, who landed a blow squarely on Peter's nose. The pain was intense and blood spurted forth. Then came a blast of pepper spray, sending Peter reeling, unable to see, unable to breathe. Some hands pulled him from the crowd; he was in pain, disorientated, the adrenaline still coursing. Then there was someone helping to clean the blood from his face, to soothe the stinging from the pepper spray. It could have been anyone, Peter didn't know. He accepted the help. His vision started to return. His senses sharpened. It was all over. Peter and a few other guys walked back to the motel together. They stopped by a store to get some milk to soothe their irritated eyes. When Peter returned to his room, he didn't spend too long reflecting on what had happened. Instead, he spent two hours in front of the mirror trying to get his contact lenses out. Every time he touched his eyes, the pepper spray would cause an unbearable stinging sensation and he would have to start all over again. Finally, the lenses removed, he went to sleep.

The next day was meant to be the main event, the protest at the Robert E. Lee statue, but it didn't have the same intensity. The bright Virginia day had a different feeling from the electric night of torchlight, and someone said the police were in the process of disbanding the rally. Peter and some of the guys he had met tried to find their way back to their motel around the endless roadblocks and diversions. It was then they heard the news: someone had driven a car into a crowd of anti-racism protesters. A young woman had been killed. Heather Heyer was a thirty-two-year-old paralegal who had been deeply affected by the hate speech she had heard in the run-up to the rally in her hometown. Her life was ended by James Fields, a white supremacist who espoused pro-Nazi, racist and anti-Semitic views on his social media. He would be sentenced to life imprisonment for murder and hate crimes.

No one was meant to die, Peter thought.

He was still reeling from the news when one of the men he was with handed him a phone: 'You are in the *Guardian*.'

Peter took the phone and felt a jolt when he saw the photograph. It was from the night before. There he was in his white polo shirt and with his slicked-back hair, a torch in his hand, his face contorted in a scream of hatred. His eyes were wide open but blank, his mouth frozen in mid-shout, his upper lip curled, his teeth bared in fury. The photo had gone viral; it was on the Twitter feeds of the major news outlets, on the front pages of their websites. The next day, it would be in print as well, forever etched into the lore of those dark few days in America's new history. This was the image of the Charlottesville protests, a face that told you everything you needed to know about what was wrong in America today. Peter was now the embodiment of the white supremacy entering the mainstream. His head wasn't shaved; there were no swastikas on his arms. He was your clean-cut college roommate, your overachieving son, your churchgoing neighbour. Entire narratives would be forged around that one image: people thought they knew exactly who Peter was, what he believed, what his fate deserved to be. In that moment, Peter should have realized what it meant to have your entire existence reduced to a stereotype; to have people make judgements based on your appearance alone. But it would take a while before he made that leap. For now, he just knew one thing: life would never be the same again.

Peter Cytanovic VI had always wanted to be noteworthy. Now he was the face of white supremacy.

12

Shayne Hunter and Toby Cook

Adelaide, Australia, 1988 to Sydney, Australia, 2015

It was 2015 and the height of summer, and Sydney's Cronulla Beach looked exactly as it should on a day when the waves were good and the sun shone brightly on the white sand packed with sunbathers, surfers and swimmers. Cronulla was named after the Aboriginal word for the unique pink shells that used to be found in the area. But while it looked like the kind of Australian beach that holidaymakers dream of, Cronulla had a dark history. And it was about to cast its violent shadow over the sunseekers that day.

A decade earlier, on Sunday, 11 December 2005, Cronulla had been the scene of ugly race riots, as thousands of white Australians – many drunk and draped in the national flag – screamed racist insults and rampaged through the streets, hunting down and assaulting anyone with darker skin. It was a mob event cheered on by a presenter on a local radio station, who let callers refer to 'lebs' and 'wogs' without reproach. The DJ demanded a 'community show of force' after an altercation took place on the beach between groups from different ethnic backgrounds, and thousands of people answered the call. Images of drunken white youths hounding people from minority backgrounds were beamed all over the world, the ugly face of Australian racism there for all to see.

It was an episode that many in Cronulla were keen to put

behind them. But ten years later, two very different groups were
ready to remind everyone of that tumultuous day. Dressed all
in black, his face covered with a black mask, twenty-seven-
year-old Shayne Hunter was at the front of a group of around a
hundred people who advanced down the beach carrying a huge
banner proclaiming 'The Only Good Fascist is a Dead One'.
They went by the name Antifa, a loose term referring to myriad
activist groups on the far left that claim violence is justified in
the fight against fascism. The Antifa movement has its roots in
the 1920s and '30s, when fascism spread in Europe, and such
movements would periodically swell and shrink in response to
similar ebbs on the far right. In the 1980s and '90s, anti-fascist
and anarchist groups across Europe would get into running
street battles with skinheads. By the late 1990s, the anti-fascist
movements were largely dormant again, with issues like nuclear
power, environmentalism and anti-capitalism dominating the
far-left agenda. However, the symbiotic relationship between
the political extremes would blossom in the economic, social
and political turmoil of the late 2000s and '10s, and this time
politicians would be fanning the flames. Antifa would become
an all-encompassing bogeyman for US President Donald Trump,
and the hatred between the far left and far right would spread
well beyond the fringes of society.

   That day in 2015 on Cronulla Beach, Shayne knew exactly
who his enemies were. They were at the far end of the beach – a
collection of far-right and white supremacist activists who had
gathered to celebrate the tenth anniversary of the 2005 race riots.
That celebration was a provocative act, and the New South Wales
Supreme Court had banned a full rally. Instead, a small event had
been allowed to take place on an isolated stretch of beach and
with a heavy police presence. That wasn't enough for Shayne.
He wanted to teach the right a lesson. As he and his black-clad
gang marched past, people on the beach looked wary. Shayne
didn't care. He was pumped with adrenaline, high on the idea

of righteousness and fighting for a cause that had given him the sense of purpose he had been craving since childhood.

Shayne was born in 1988 in the city of Adelaide to parents whose own difficult pasts made it hard for them to provide the emotional support and structure their son needed. The one stable presence in Shayne's life was his maternal grandmother. She stepped in where she saw her daughter struggling, and became Shayne's primary carer. When he was around six, money problems forced his parents to leave Adelaide and relocate to Brisbane. The move coincided with his grandmother's divorce, and she used the money from the settlement to set the family up in a middle-class home in a safe suburb. But it would prove impossible to iron out all the troubles in the fractious family unit. Shayne was the middle child of three, but there was an eight-year age difference between him and each of his siblings, and they had a rancorous relationship. Problems spilled over at school too. Shayne was intellectually curious and enjoyed the kind of mental conundrums posed by philosophy and chess, but he struggled to keep up with reading and writing in class – difficulties he later realized were due to undiagnosed dyslexia. At the time, Shayne just felt like he had been unfairly dumped in the 'bad kid' pile, ending up in classes with some of the most troubled pupils in the school. He compensated for his learning difficulties by clowning around and making his school friends laugh, but it wasn't enough to make the whole experience bearable. In his final year of secondary school in 2004, he dropped out without any qualifications. For the next two years he attended various community colleges, getting certificates in IT and fine arts, which looked nice on paper but never actually led to any jobs. It was in stand-up comedy that Shayne found something that suited him. When he made people laugh, he was getting the positive feedback he had lacked at school.

Shayne was soon making enough money from gigs to move

on to the semi-professional circuit, and in his early twenties he started touring, performing at a different comedy club in a different city each night. He took his inspiration from edgy, anti-establishment comedians like Bill Hicks and George Carlin. Their mission of telling the truth to power appealed to Shayne, especially when he looked around and was troubled by an uneasy feeling that things were not quite as they seemed in the world. He had followed the debacle over the Iraq War, the scandal over abuse at Abu Ghraib prison, and the charade involving the missing weapons of mass destruction. Now he was sucked into the WikiLeaks stories, as the whistleblowing platform released hacked and leaked information that showed, among other things, the killing and torture of civilians by the US military in Iraq and Afghanistan.

Then the global financial crisis hit, and Shayne became even more distrustful of governments and the media. He started investigating online and found enticing videos on YouTube which promised to 'connect the dots' between disparate events to create an overarching narrative of a population under the control of nefarious forces. There were slick videos in which images of nuclear explosions were juxtaposed with complicated economic graphs, with urgent voice-overs calling on viewers to revolt against the corrupt financial elite. These YouTube channels claimed to be independent media but were in fact fabrications easily concocted on video editing software available to anyone with a phone, and then uploaded on to a platform which made no distinction between fact and fiction.

By 2013, these videos were fuelling a growing anxiety about the prospect of another military intervention in the Middle East. The newspapers were saying that President Bashar al-Assad had used chemical weapons against his people in Syria.

This is just bullshit to invade, Shayne thought. *Half a million people died in Iraq. Enough money was spent to build a Mars colony. And you are doing this shit again?*

The video channels on YouTube backed up what he was thinking. Any military action in Syria could be devastating, they said, starting a chain reaction involving Russia which could lead to full-out nuclear war. A new fear started to creep into Shayne's life – and a desire to try and have some influence in the unravelling of the world that he saw happening before him.

My career seems meaningless in comparison to these grand events, he thought.

Around the same time, a former analyst for the US National Security Agency, Edward Snowden, leaked classified documents showing how governments had accessed troves of personal data and information from global tech and telecoms firms. Now Snowden's revelations appeared to confirm many of the conspiratorial narratives Shayne had been consuming online. Shayne felt like the true extent of this alternative universe had finally been laid bare.

The media is controlling everyone, he decided. *Everyone is corrupt.*

Shayne made up his mind: it was time to share some of the 'truths' he had uncovered in his quest to make sense of the world. He scrawled 'Edward Snowden is a Whistle-Blower not a Spy' in marker pen on a piece of cardboard and went down to a local television station. He stood outside the window and held up his sign, making the evening news.

See, I do have the power to change the world, he thought.

And Shayne was beginning to find allies in his grand quest for revolution. He had joined a few protests against western military action in Syria and enjoyed mixing with like-minded people. He was shocked at the indifference and apathy he felt among many of his old friends and couldn't understand why they failed to see the truth that seemed so obvious to him. It was at one of these protests that Shayne heard about an anarchist collective in downtown Sydney, and he was curious. One afternoon, he entered the collective's library. A man he assumed worked there was sitting reading a book.

'Hey, can I put my bag here?' Shayne asked.

'I don't care, man,' came the reply.

It was a throwaway remark, but to Shayne it was loaded with so much more, a hidden meaning which told him everything he needed to know about the new world he was entering. It wasn't that this man didn't care – it was as if the members of this group had freed themselves from all ideas of ownership and from the societal constraints that Shayne believed were part of a grand conspiracy to keep everyone docile and obedient. There was no hierarchy – it was like a utopia free of the capitalism and authoritarianism which had caused all the problems in the world. Shayne was hooked, and soon the collective became his second home. Everyone there seemed to have a shared purpose: they were all political, they all wanted to make a difference. They would organize protests on so many issues – Palestine, LGBTQ+ rights, women's rights, public housing. There was always a cause that required his energy, and increasingly life outside the collective faded way. He didn't see his old friends very much now, or his family. He moved in with other anarchists, squatting in vacant buildings. He adopted their uniform, donning the all-black clothing known as black bloc, an aesthetic which signified membership of the tribe and made it more difficult to be identified by police. Shayne stopped working and survived on social welfare.

It was around a year after he had joined the collective that Shayne first heard the term Antifa. Someone from their squat had travelled to Europe and told them about the emerging movement, which was dedicated to fighting the fascists. Many of the countries where Antifa's spiritual forebears had fought fascist forces in the early twentieth century – France, Britain, Germany, Italy – were experiencing a re-emergence of nationalist and far-right political parties. Australia had already experienced the shock that opportunistic populists could have on the whole political system when, in the late 1990s, a former fish and chip shop owner, Pauline Hanson, founded the far-right One Nation Party and made derogatory comments about Asians, migrants from sub-Saharan Africa, Aboriginal people and Muslims. Her rhetoric was a transparent bid to appeal to disaffected white voters and give them an enemy to pin their frustrations on. But politicians from the established parties on the right took the nativist bait, and successive liberal governments adopted toned-down versions of Hanson's incendiary language and implemented ever-stricter policies on refugees and migration. It was people like Hanson, coupled with the failure of politicians to challenge her hatred and examine the real roots of white disaffection, that galvanized the openly neo-Nazi and white supremacist groups, which in turn gave Shayne and his friends plenty of enemies to fight. Soon they were organizing most of their action under the Antifa banner. This largely involved heading to places where far-right groups were meeting and shouting 'Racist!' at them. Sometimes the confrontations ended in scuffles, and the police got involved. At one such melee at a Halal festival, Shayne parked his van so as to block far-right protesters who were harassing Muslim participants in the event, and ended up in custody charged with failure to assist a police officer. All the charges were dropped, and his run-in with the police did nothing to dampen his enthusiasm for his cause. Now, instead of abstractions which he didn't fully understand, like 'the patriarchy', he had a single, identifiable enemy, and that in turn gave him a stronger sense of who he was.

The Nazis are pure evil, so by them being so evil, it implies that we are good, he reasoned.

Shayne did wonder sometimes about the motives of some of his comrades. There were a few who seemed to relish the violence of the confrontations more than the cause itself. He always felt slightly sick when fights broke out. But he had to admit that there was something about the power he felt when he donned his black mask. It was not just the far right that he felt he had power over, but everyone – the police, journalists, anybody who was not as committed to the cause as he was. Dressed in a black hoodie and rumpled clothing, his sandy hair matted and his face unshaven, Shayne didn't look much like a warrior – but he felt like one. Which was how Shayne Hunter ended up on Cronulla Beach on 12 December 2015, heading in the direction of a group of white supremacists, including a deeply hungover seventeen-year-old called Toby Cook.

Toby had been at a friend's eighteenth birthday the night before, and it had been a predictably debauched affair, with huge quantities of alcohol and Ecstasy tablets doing the rounds. He only managed a few hours' sleep before he roused himself to get to the Cronulla barbecue, where he was now skulking on the outskirts, knocking back bottles of water. It was a bit of an anticlimax. His group had spent months preparing for the event, only for the courts to ban the march, so here they all were with a pig on a spit and a few dozen activists. But they had made the news, and Toby heard that Antifa were not too far away, creating a spectacle on the seafront. He was a bit disappointed that they were too far away for a scuffle, given how much he relished laying into his political foes. But their protest was amplifying the media coverage, so between the rows of police and the angry lefties, Toby reasoned that the reaction outweighed the actual action, so it was a job well done. Not for a second did Toby question what it actually was that he was marking with the barbecue. To many in Australia, it was offensive to commemorate such a shameful moment in the country's history. But at the time he stood on Cronulla Beach, Toby was fully committed to what he saw as a revolutionary cause to protect Australia. It was a cause that had grabbed hold of him at the lowest point in his life.

Born in Gosford on the New South Wales coast in 1998, Toby had spent most of his early years moving around. His parents split up when he was nine months old and he didn't see his dad, who had struggles in his own life. His mother was a teacher, and they always seemed to be packing up and moving again, often to tiny rural settlements where Toby didn't know anyone. When Toby was thirteen, they settled in Sydney, but he had lost count of the number of schools he had already attended and started to question the point of going to school at all.

How is this going to prepare me for adult life? he wondered.

An adolescent anger was also stirring in Toby. When he was little, he knew he had a loving mother who was doing her best for him and he hadn't questioned their transient lifestyle, but as he started to make friends in his Sydney neighbourhood, he could sense a difference between his friends' stable two-parent homes and his own chaotic upbringing.

I missed out on all this, he thought. *What did I do to deserve this?*

When he was fifteen, this anger and malaise coalesced into a full depressive episode. Toby felt completely overwhelmed by school and was gripped with fear about his future. He had an uncanny feeling of being utterly alone, even when he was surrounded by friends. Increasingly, Toby would refuse to leave his bed. If his phone rang, he would ignore it. One day, Toby found himself on the roof of a car park. He wasn't sure how he got there, but there were some railings in front of him. He started to climb over them. The next thing he knew, he was being tackled from behind. A security guard had prevented him from jumping, and Toby was committed to a psychiatric hospital for ten days. On anti-psychotic and anti-depressive drugs, Toby sat in a ward with a colouring book on his lap, just staring at the wall. When he was released, he was referred to counselling, which helped him to start to make sense of the feelings racing around his head. But there was still an anger deep inside that he couldn't put into words.

He started to externalize those feelings of rage, and his inner turmoil began to fuse with events happening around him. In December 2014, a few months after his release from the psychiatric ward, an Iranian-born man claiming allegiance to the Islamic State attacked the Lindt Chocolate Café in Sydney, holding a number of customers and employees hostage. Three people were killed, and Toby was incensed. In April 2015, far-right groups organized a rally under the provocative banner 'Reclaim Australia', and seventeen-year-old Toby Cook was there, relieved at finally being able to unburden his frustrations with the world. At the rally, he struck up a conversation with some older men who told him about a new anti-Islam group they had started called the Party for Freedom. Toby was flattered that these men in their thirties and forties would be interested in a teenager like himself, and he eagerly accepted an invitation to attend their meetings. The alcohol flowed when they all got together to right the world's wrongs, and he revelled in the boozy sense of camaraderie and in their righteous indignation. His new friends were so good at explaining what had gone wrong in his life and at making him feel valued. They would point out the people from China and Sri Lanka who owned businesses and had nice homes. Toby had never had any of that, they would also point out, so it must be because the government was favouring ethnic minorities. Suddenly, everything seemed to click into place. Less than a year earlier he had been on a psych ward staring at a wall. Now he was at fundraisers for Pauline Hanson's One Nation Party, surrounded by well-dressed politicians espousing similar xenophobic views to those of his new friends.

It's on TV, it's acceptable in parliament, it's acceptable wherever, he thought. *So why can't I say it? Why can't I believe it?*

Toby spent increasing amounts of time at the side of Nick Folkes, leader of the Party for Freedom, who cultivated a lightly bearded, homely 'guy next door' veneer, prompting much of the Australian media to focus on the incongruity of his appearance rather than on the hateful message he was spreading. They even gave him a platform for his views, on a prime-time television show called 'Living with the Enemy', where he spent time with a Sudanese refugee. Alongside Folkes, Toby looked like the burly enforcer, a heavy-framed six foot three, with dark hair shaved at the sides and a florid round face. But Toby was no mindless bodyguard. When he wasn't wasted on alcohol and drugs, he could be loquacious, and soon the group was putting him on the podium and in front of the media. The more important he felt, the more deeply committed he became to his new cause. Even as Nick Folkes proclaimed that the Party for Freedom wasn't racist or anti-Semitic, Toby was hanging a Nazi flag over his bed. There were no shades of grey for him any more.

Although they were ensconced in groups promising very different utopias, Toby and Shayne were consumed by similar emotions: feelings of importance and superiority; a sense of belonging, purpose and community; relief at having a cause and an enemy on which to project their own anger and insecurities. They were on different sides of the reciprocal extremism which continues all over the world today. The far right feeds on economic instability, increasing inequality, and cultural and social anxiety, finding scapegoats in migrant communities and religious minorities. Its rhetoric plays straight into the narratives propagated by extreme Islamist groups, which feed off the idea that there is an inherent bias against Muslims in the West. Attacks by Islamist extremists then appear to confirm the rhetoric of the far right, further swelling its ranks. As the far right grows, a more militant far left emerges using increasingly violent tactics, and the cycles of hatred are perpetuated.

But Toby and Shayne would admit to no commonalities between them. They knew of each other, and hated each other. Toby had seen Shayne at a few protests and court appearances, and he knew exactly what he would do if he came across Shayne in a dark alley one night. He joked about it with his mates, how he would jump him and teach him a lesson. He certainly could never see a time when they would become friends.

Part Three

Reckoning

13

Cathrine Moestue

Eskilstuna, Sweden, Spring 1986 to Stockholm, Sweden, January 1988

In the spring of 1986, just a few months before she was due to graduate from the Charlie Rivel Entertainer Art School, Cathrine Moestue disappeared. Her first good friend there, Christina, had been concerned by the change she had seen in Cathrine and had been worried about the company she was keeping, but she had no inkling of the world of fantasy Catherine had been drawn into, and was shocked when she simply vanished.

It had not taken long for Cathrine to feel overwhelmed by her new role as secret disciple to the Marxist guerrilla leader that Cornel had claimed himself to be. She would alternate between feeling excited to be part of such an important movement and feeling fearful that her life was in danger. And while Cornel had taken on a God-like quality, he had also become more threatening, aggressive and critical, now also chiding Cathrine for her studies.

'Do you really want to be an actress in a world where children are starving?' he asked her.

Cathrine quit her course. With no work to distract her, she became increasingly anxious. She summoned the courage to ask her mentor if she could go home and study philosophy in Oslo. To her surprise, he said yes.

'Educating yourself is part of the revolution,' he told her.

Just before she was due to leave, Cathrine brought Cornel

flowers and said goodbye. She thought she could continue to fight for a better world by herself now and would never have to see him again. She signed up at the University of Oslo and drove back west to her family. She had stopped smoking and had lost weight from the running and from her new vegetarian diet. Her mother would be delighted, she thought. Cornel disagreed.

'Your parents will not be pleased,' he warned her.

He was right. Her parents were dismayed at the change in their daughter. They had said goodbye to a bubbly, excited teenager full of life and expectations. Returning to them was a sallow, withdrawn young woman with haunted eyes and an air of sadness. They were clearly worried about her, but Cathrine imagined they were still harbouring the same old grievances.

How right Cornel was, she thought.

Despite moving to another country to get away from him, Cathrine remained under Cornel's spell, having internalized all his criticisms of her. She loved being back home – but then was consumed by guilt at living a life of wealth and frivolity while there were people who were starving and suffering. She experimented with some of Cornel's ideas, trying out his moral conundrums on her old friends. While they had such a powerful impact when they came from Cornel, Cathrine's friends seemed bewildered by her air of moral superiority. She felt alienated and lonely once again, and her anger built up: anger at her friends for not caring about the world; anger at her parents for not seeing the cause of her pain; anger at herself for not being good enough.

Then Cornel's letters started to arrive. The first one came a few weeks after Cathrine had returned home, and she felt that familiar combination of excitement and apprehension. The tone was chatty, intimate, confessional and conspiratorial, just like in those early days when they would huddle in the little café under the hat shop, sharing their secrets.

'I hope I find you in the mood for a letter from "yours humbly",' he began. Cathrine didn't think too long before replying. She was flattered that he still thought her worthy of these intellectual debates, and with the geographical distance that now existed between them she felt able to challenge him, asking him why they couldn't just send more money to help alleviate the famines. He answered calmly and respectfully, with none of the mean-spirited criticisms he had heaped on her back in Eskilstuna. He engaged with her and was humble in his rejection of her suggestions, informing her about the hidden agendas of the 'big fat capitalists' and about the misappropriation of foreign aid.

'The most important thing to campaign for in the third world is for capitalism of all kinds to get the fuck out,' he wrote. 'It wants to keep the People ignorant and uneducated so that it can use them as slaves.'

As their correspondence picked up pace, Cornel's letters would follow a familiar pattern. He would share some trivial information with her before making opaque reference to his clandestine struggles ('I've been betrayed so many times'; 'please keep my intentions and my whereabouts a secret'; 'I've been a little careless in my movements and actions and I'm lucky I haven't been punished for it'.) Then he would engage her in questions about the meaning of life, the nature of existence and the quest for self-fulfilment. The words 'injustice' and 'truth' jumped out from the page as he urged Cathrine to reject a wasteful life and instead follow the noble path to redemption and fulfilment.

'A lot of powerful people (parents, friends) will do their best to keep you with them, offering all sorts of goodies,' he wrote. 'They will have everything, except maybe the truth.'

Cornel's message was that she was going through a test of her commitment during her time back home, with the temptation while she was there of returning to her old bourgeois life. Once she had chosen the correct path, he was ready to be her teacher again.

Then, a few weeks after Cathrine had started her course at the university, he appeared at a student party in her neighbourhood.

Cathrine did not understand what he was doing there, and she felt the same chill she had felt on the day she first saw him. It was one of the rare moments when Cathrine could sense what Cornel truly was, and she felt disgusted. But she would not trust her instincts. For hadn't he told her that her instincts had been forged by decades of brainwashing and indoctrination by the rich and powerful? So she walked over to him. It was as though their months apart had simply melted away. Soon he was filling her head with questions, flattering her, criticizing their mutual friends and making her feel like she was the only person in the world worthy of his time and attention. The good feelings flooded back.

Not long after Cornel returned to Sweden, he wrote to Cathrine with an offer: he would pay for her to travel to Stockholm and would make all the arrangements for her new life of spiritual and intellectual fulfilment. The contradictions in her head had become so overwhelming that it felt like a relief to acquiesce, as then she would no longer have to make her own decisions about what was right and what was wrong. Cornel claimed to have all the answers, and Cathrine was ready to accept them.

A few days later, in February 1987, twenty-one-year-old Cathrine Moestue said goodbye to her family. Cornel had told her exactly what to say and scripted her responses.

'I am leaving now, and even if I make the wrong decision, at least it is my decision,' Cathrine said coldly and calmly.

Her mother seemed to sense that this goodbye was somehow final and begged her eldest daughter to stay, crying 'Don't leave! Don't leave!'

Unmoved, Cathrine picked up her bags and made her way through the snow to an address in Oslo that Cornel had given her. It was the apartment of a woman called Sofia. Cathrine knew Sofia from her extended social circle and was surprised that Cornel had so readily entrusted his secrets to a woman he had only just met during his recent trip to Olso. Sofia had the same radiant Scandinavian beauty as Lise and was one of the smartest people Cathrine knew.

I can't feel jealous because that's not pure, that's not for the revolution, she told herself. *I cannot have these feelings when people are suffering.*

Together, Sofia and Cathrine travelled to Stockholm, where they were greeted by Cornel and Lise. Cathrine transferred her studies to the University of Stockholm, and Cornel told her to move into student accommodation. He would live with Sofia and Lise. Cornel's wife had disappeared, apparently moving back to England. Ready to assume her role in the revolution, Cathrine asked Cornel what would happen next.

'Aren't we going to South America?' she asked him.

'No, it's important that you keep me safe here,' Cornel replied. 'I am doing more good living under cover in Sweden.'

So began Cathrine's life of absolute devotion to a man she now considered to be not only her saviour, but the saviour of all the poor and humble of the earth. She listened as he taught her the secret codes of his group, a patchwork of far-fetched stories that she was now primed to absorb without question.

'You see when the neighbour has the curtain down?' he asked. 'That means they have saved some children.'

The conspiracies grew: there was an agent from Paraguay posing as a student at the university who had been sent to spy on Cornel.

'She is following me,' he said. 'We have to find out where she lives.'

So they followed the young woman to her car and trailed her all the way home, sitting outside her apartment and watching it until Cornel told her it was time to leave. No matter how incredible his claims or unpleasant his requests were, Cathrine obeyed. If she listened and learned, he assured her, one day she would be a teacher of the revolution too. And it wasn't just the secrets of saving mankind that Cornel tempted her with.

'One day you will marry one of the leaders of the revolution,' he said.

Cathrine would go to bed filled with romantic thoughts about the brave warrior into whose arms she would one day fall. Maybe he would look like Kunta Kinte, the handsome slave whose desperate quest for his own identity had so stirred her when she had watched television in her youth.

But in spite of such promises, a threat of violence now overshadowed everything. Shortly after Cathrine moved to Stockholm, Cornel sat her down and placed a gun and a knife before her.

'Call your parents and tell them they are Nazis,' he said.

Cathrine did not want to make the call, knowing it would add another layer of distance between her and her already estranged family. But she obeyed.

I have to prove that I am a good person, that I want to save those starving children and that I really care about other people's lives, she thought.

She picked up the phone and dialled. Her mother answered.

'You are a Nazi!' she shouted into the receiver, and then hung up before her mother had a chance to respond.

Cornel always managed to balance his cruelty to Cathrine with messages of hope, reminding her of the better world their revolution would usher in, a paradise where there was love and equality for all and no racism or sexism. But Cathrine's mental health was beginning to suffer. She believed enemies of the revolution were everywhere, that her life was under constant threat. She had become convinced that someone was following her. Wherever she went, a man seemed to be there, standing under streetlamps, watching her on the subway platforms, loitering outside her apartment building.

This time Cathrine's paranoia was justified. Someone was indeed following her. Her parents, sick with worry about their eldest daughter, had hired a private detective to find her. They had initially gone to the police, only to be told that Cathrine was an adult who had left of her own free will and that any attempt to force her back would be a crime. Such an illegal intervention was a step that many families in similar situations had been prepared to take. In the United States, an entire industry had sprung up to meet this demand during the high-profile cult cases in the 1970s. Individuals touting their services as 'cult deprogrammers' would forcibly remove people from groups, often holding them captive for days as part of an intense 'de-brainwashing' programme. These interventions had little grounding in psychology and there was scant evidence of their long-term success. In many cases they caused lifelong mental damage. The idea that you could exorcise one set of beliefs and replace it with another without considering the layers of experience and human trauma that had led to those beliefs in the first place would eventually be discredited, and some de-programmers went to jail for false imprisonment. A few decades later, there would be a similar scramble for a solution to another deeply complex problem. 'Deprogramming' became 'deradicalization', a headline-grabbing quest for a silver bullet that would prove as elusive as it had done when rogue cult 'experts' tied men and women up in dark rooms to drive out the bad thoughts.

For Cathrine, the constant presence of this unknown man confirmed Cornel's stories about spies watching their every move. Instead of being sympathetic about her stalker, however, Cornel didn't seem to take her seriously.

Cathrine's paranoia intensified, and she felt herself begin to crumble. One day she retreated into her apartment and began crying. The tears and the howling would not stop, and other students began knocking on her door, asking if they could help. She turned them away, as Cornel had said they could never accept help from outsiders. He had already made her move from one apartment after he saw her talking to a man outside her building. Then one morning, Cathrine awoke and noticed two squirrels climbing the white wall of the house opposite. She immediately saw that they were Martians invading the world. She was petrified, frozen to the spot with fear.

What is happening to me? she wondered.

When she was able to physically move again, she called Cornel in a distressed state. Lise came round. She sat on the end of Cathrine's bed and comforted her. It was the first compassion Cathrine had experienced in months, as Cornel had told Lise and Sofia to withhold any affection from her. This was the only way for Cathrine to overcome her indoctrination, he told them. He was expert at playing the three women off against one another, provoking jealousy between the two he was sleeping with and referring to Cathrine humiliatingly as 'the monk'. So to have Lise offer her this rare affection felt monumental.

The day after Cathrine's breakdown, Cornel came for her. She was mentally wrecked and still confused from the visions of the previous day. He insisted that they had to leave. They needed to return to the apartment of the young female student they had followed home a few weeks earlier – the woman he referred to as 'the agent'. It was 31 August, the kind of crisp evening that tells you autumn is on its way, and they drove over to the apartment in Cornel's car as dusk was falling. Cathrine was to knock on the door, say she was a fellow student, and ask for a cup of sugar.

This is crazy, Cathrine thought as she climbed the stairs to the apartment. But she had long since lost the power to refuse Cornel.

To her relief, the woman was friendly, gave her the sugar and then closed the door. Cathrine returned to the car, hoping that this horrible test was over and she could go home.

But that was not how the evening was going to unfold.

'I have to talk to her,' Cornel said. 'I'm going up there too.'

They climbed the stairs together, and Cornel hid behind the door. Cathrine knocked, and as soon as the other woman opened it, he forced his way past her and into her home. Cathrine followed him in, and Cornel then closed the door behind them. He ordered Cathrine to close the curtains. She obeyed. The woman was terrified and tried to step backwards, begging them to leave.

'I have to talk to you, we have to stay a little bit longer, we are very important,' Cornel told his hostage.

He turned to Cathrine.

'Go and get the guns.'

It was a code he had given Cathrine earlier: it meant she must leave and wait in the car. Cathrine obeyed. Not for a second did she think that Cornel might hurt the woman. She was convinced the two of them knew each other and were somehow connected in this parallel revolutionary world that was now her only reality.

A numbness descended on Cathrine as she walked down the stairs and back to the car. It was an utter exhaustion of body and mind, coupled with a strange sense of detached relief that she would have a little time alone.

Thank God I don't have him next to me, she thought. *I can relax and close my eyes.*

As she eased into the driver's seat, the drowsiness became overwhelming and she could no longer resist the instinctive pull to drift off and relieve herself from her mental tumult. Time seemed to elongate, and she felt her eyelids close. Sleep came like a balm.

She awoke to a violent rapping on the window. Cornel. It was pitch black – the dead of night. And he wasn't alone. The young woman was with him. He pushed her into the back of the car.

'Give me the guns,' Cornel said.

It was the code again, and this time it meant she had to pass him the gym bag on the seat beside her. There were no guns. Just sweaty clothing.

She passed him the bag and glanced behind her at the girl. She seemed normal. Quiet.

'We have been talking together and we have decided to go and continue working,' Cornel told Cathrine. 'Drive us to your apartment.'

When they arrived there, he and the girl left the car.

'Wait for my call,' he said.

Cathrine then drove to the apartment Cornel shared with Lise and Sofia and waited there, still in a state of numb disbelief at the evening's events. She told them only that she had been out on a mission with Cornel. After a few hours, his call came. She drove back to her apartment, where once again Cornel put the girl in the back of the car.

Cathrine drove her home as if she had been on an evening out with friends.

It took a few days for the police to show up. During that time, Cathrine stayed at Cornel's apartment while he formulated his plan. He decided that he would take Lise and Sofia to Norway, and that Cathrine would be left behind to explain the situation to the police. She must tell them that the agent had been following them. Tell them the truth, he said.

It was a beautiful day when Cathrine finally returned to her own apartment. The sky was clear and the bright white northern sun lit up the leaves that were just starting to turn. When Cathrine arrived home, she discovered police tape across her door, along with an instruction to call the station immediately. She went to the pay phone in the building and made the call, and soon two plain-clothes officers arrived in a white unmarked Saab. She was surprised at their kindness to her. One officer told her that usually they would handcuff a suspect, but she looked compliant.

At the police station, the officers showed Cathrine the young student's statement. Cornel had raped her, once in her own apartment, and once more in Cathrine's apartment. He had told her that soldiers were outside, that a revolution was under way, and that he was a guerrilla leader. He had told her she had to do what he said because soldiers were threatening her parents' lives.

As she read the woman's detailed account, Cathrine knew that every word of it was true. In that bright interrogation room under the eyes of sympathetic investigators, her loyalty to her guru cracked. She was able to relate to the victim's story, and for the first time, she allowed herself the grace of considering that she may be a victim too. That brought a strange feeling of resentment: this young woman he raped bore physical wounds of Cornel's true nature. What did Cathrine have? The damage done to her was all within. She told the police everything she could – the truth as she understood it to be.

The months she spent in prison waiting for her trial felt almost like a respite. She slept constantly. She no longer had to fear Cornel because the police had caught him just over the border in Norway and he was now behind bars too.

I'm in prison, I am in safe hands, among people who want me well, she thought.

She was offered no counselling or other psychological support, nor did any police officer or social worker come to her cell to talk to her about the lies Cornel had spun. Nevertheless, a strange sort of peace overcame her. With it came an internal reckoning as she tried to piece together the real truth.

How could I have done so much bad when I wanted to do so much good? Cathrine wondered. *I have deceived my friends. I have deceived my family. I've been deceiving myself.*

While Cathrine was spending her days in confinement in quiet contemplation, a more frenzied mood had gripped the Swedish and Norwegian press. Cornel had stuck to his outlandish story of persecution at the hands of shadowy forces, and the newspapers relished publishing stories about this wild-haired, dark-skinned predator and the young blonde victims of his revolutionary

Marxist sex cult. Cathrine's father had spoken to reporters, telling anyone who would listen that his daughter had been brainwashed. 'She is like Patty Hearst,' he told them.

The case made it to court in January 1988. Cathrine testified, and was astonished at Cornel's behaviour. She knew how smart and polished he could be – the dashing professor able to hold a room in rapt attention – but this Cornel was acting like a madman. It was as if he were playing into all of society's prejudices and into the covertly racist slant of the media coverage. Throughout the trial he appeared distracted, tapping at his chair, leaning back and forth, looking under his seat and causing an irritated judge to repeatedly call for his attention. Cornel actually seemed to be enjoying himself, and suddenly Cathrine felt like she was watching an actor in a play – but one in which she was the only audience member.

My God, they don't see it, she thought, casting a horrified glace at the journalists, the judge and the lawyers. *He is fooling everyone.*

His performance worked. The judging panel postponed Cornel's trial pending a detailed psychiatric report.

Cathrine sat staring at the floor as the lawyers debated her case. She vaguely heard them talk about her delicate mental state, her dependence on a manipulative individual. Her trial ended with a caution for having been an accomplice to breaking and entering. She was free to go – but she had no idea where to go. Throughout her confinement, the only person she had seen was her lawyer. Her parents had conveyed a message to the lawyer that they wanted to take her out to dinner as soon as she was released, and Cathrine had agreed to this. She missed them and was desperate for a reconciliation. They had watched the court proceedings from the gallery, and Cathrine had seen them leave when the trial finished, her father's arm wrapped protectively around her mother's shoulders. But where had they gone? How was she meant to get to them? Her lawyer was nowhere to be seen either. It turned out there had been a misunderstanding: Cathrine's mum and dad were expecting her to come to their hotel.

Some other people were outside the court waiting to meet her, however – Lise and Sofia. Cathrine could have told them to go away, but in her delicate mental state, with no one else there to help her, she was grateful to see the smiling faces of people she knew. Besides, maybe she could enlighten them about all the lies Cornel had entrapped them with and help them break free of his spell too. So instead of going to her parents' hotel, she went with the two women back to the student apartment they had shared with Cornel. It was a decision that would cost her the next four years of her life.

14

Peter Cytanovic

Reno, Nevada, USA, 2017–18

When Peter Cytanovic appeared on KRNV, a Nevada television station, on Sunday, 13 August 2017, he cut an unapologetic figure. Hair gelled to one side, preppy blue shirt, Peter came across as amused rather than anguished, defensive but not reflective. He had just landed at Reno-Tahoe International Airport, arriving back from his trip to Charlottesville. His time in Virginia had lasted less than three days, but it doesn't take long for a life to spin off its axis. From his rage during the night-time protest through to his horror at the murder of Heather Heyer and his shock at seeing his face appearing in media all over the world, the twenty-one-year-old student had experienced a kaleidoscope of emotions. There had even been a clumsy attempt at redemption. On the morning of his flight, Peter had headed to a church in Charlottesville to try and explain his actions to a confused and suspicious congregation. As he made the return journey homeward, however, his position was crystalizing. Hateful messages were pouring in and his feelings of contrition faded, to be replaced by a much more familiar emotion: overwhelming animosity towards those he believed to be his political enemies.

Fuck it, Peter thought, *I have no choice. Everything I believe in I have to believe now without any hesitation or second thought.*

So when the KRNV reporter put series of perfunctory questions to him about his views and his role in the protest,

Peter said it clear as day: 'I am a white nationalist.' There was no sign of the anger that had contorted his face in the infamous picture. He remained composed and articulate, although at times his carefully considered words sounded more like he was parsing material for a politics essay rather than examining his culpability in a rally that had led to murder.

'I'm not a fascist,' he told the reporter, 'I don't believe in the ideology of Benito Mussolini.'

Peter had become so convinced by the sugar-coated version of white supremacy offered by Identity Evropa that he had become their ideal spokesperson, delivering half an hour of coherent defences of their ideology. Being a white nationalist wasn't hateful, he insisted, it was about taking pride in your own culture and heritage at a time when they were threatened by globalization. For all his polish, however, there were flashes of immaturity, and he came across as a young man with a deep lack of understanding of the consequences of his actions. For most of the interview he wore a smirk that veered quickly from charming to glib, and he seemed more consumed by his own travails over the last few days than by the violent death of a young woman at the hands of one of his fellow protesters. He lamented that no one was listening to him or letting him explain himself, despite the fact he was being given thirty minutes of airtime to do just that. But while he got off lightly in his interviews with the mainstream media outlets he derided, he was at the centre of a firestorm on social media.

The messages started flooding his phone soon after his photograph went viral. His name had been made public in a process known as doxxing, whereby a person's private details are revealed across social media with the aim of shaming or embarrassing them. While the scant policing of the Internet laid it open for extremist groups to exploit, it also offered opportunities for regular people to act as the police themselves, meting out 'justice' in the form of orchestrated and relentless online bullying. Anti-abortion campaigners had pioneered this form of group vigilantism, publishing the names of doctors and nurses who worked in clinics in the hope that supporters would hound them into quitting. Online, the Gamergate trollers became the forerunners in Internet doxxing, publishing the personal information of the female developers and journalists they were waging their misogynistic battles against. Now it had become a favoured tactic of some far-left activists, and after the Charlottesville protests a crowd-sourced campaign outed many of the marchers. The fact that more than one person was incorrectly identified didn't seem to deter its proponents, nor did warnings that heaping shame on people vulnerable to extreme ideologies merely reinforced the feelings of alienation that had led them to those views in the first place. Everyone appeared to be fair game: friends, relatives, people who had the misfortune to share a surname with a doxxed individual. Once again, it was a way for people disconnected from the structures of power to feel like they were reclaiming their right to be heard.

For Peter it started with a single message on Facebook Messenger: 'You'll be remembered forever, Nazi.' Within minutes the deluge started. Peter's phone wouldn't stop vibrating with all the messages flooding his social media accounts. Some were generic: 'Die Nazi scum.' Others were specific and frightening: 'I'm going to come to Reno and kill you.' Then there were some which were downright bizarre, like the one from the man who sent Peter a photograph of his feet along with the message: 'Does the Nazi want to suck on them?' There were also messages to his father and grandfather – who were both also called Peter Cytanovic – and his mother and sister. That made his blood boil. They had done nothing, but people were telling his mother – a slight woman still plagued by headaches from the brain cancer – that she deserved to die. The barrage of hatred served to reinforce the feelings that had fuelled his extremism in the first place. He had always thought people on the left wanted him dead, and now they were literally threatening to kill him. Peter resigned his membership of Identity Evropa, but he did that mostly to protect the group from the publicity he was generating. His beliefs remained firm as ever, and his outing even gave him a sense of relief at no longer having to hide his views.

I will stand for what I believe in, he thought. *The best thing I can do is dig in my heels. I am alt-right, I am a white nationalist.*

It was in this frame of mind that Peter returned to the University of Nevada: Reno a few weeks later. It wasn't how he imaged his senior year would be. Tampons were thrown at him in the university halls. One day, a bowl of urine was launched from the back of a motorcycle and missed him by a metre. 'Fuck you – kill yourself, Nazi,' the driver yelled.

More than 36,000 people signed a petition to expel Peter from UNR. The university declined to do so, reasoning that Peter had broken no laws and that his freedom of speech was protected by the US Constitution. Someone who had been angered by the university's response called the administrators and threatened to burn the place down, and from then on Peter was accompanied to and from his classes by campus police. The FBI turned up at his house asking questions, and the family suffered from all these intrusions into their lives. Money became even more of a problem. Peter quit his job as a campus ride-share driver, aware that no one would want to get in a car with him, and he was unable to find any other employment now that he was the face of American hatred. His family, however, stuck by him.

'You are not a Nazi,' his dad told him, 'you are a dumbass.'

Peter's older brother, who lived in a different city, offered him a place to stay if life got too hard in Reno. But Peter stuck it out at UNR, each day bracing for the vitriol from all sides. The online abuse continued to be relentless and vicious, and strangely incongruous with the liberal beliefs Peter believed people on the left claimed to have. The Facebook video of his KRNV interview attracted many homophobic comments and much speculation about his sexuality, as well as comments from people who genuinely seemed to believe that he deserved to be killed for his ideology. Peter didn't ignore these messages. He read them all, forwarding the most frightening ones to the police. He responded to anyone who seemed genuinely interested in what he had to say for himself, but those messages were rare. Then a few weeks into his senior year, a message caught his eye. It was from a woman called Hawah Ahmad. She had recently graduated from UNR and wondered if he would like to meet her for a coffee. She just wanted to chat, she said. But what on earth could she want to chat to him about?

Hawah was born in the United States a few years before Peter, into a family that had emigrated from Pakistan and India, and she had experienced the racism and xenophobia that many Muslims suffered in post-9/11 America. Those experiences had instilled in her a desire to make a positive difference in the world, and she had been working with homeless and transient kids, trying to help them get their lives on track. Being political came naturally to Hawah, and she joined the Nevada Young Democrats, becoming their state president. She was passionate about getting other kids involved in politics, and in the run-up to elections she and her counterpart in the Young Republicans would go to high schools and help seniors to register to vote, chatting to them about politics and their role in American democracy. When the picture of Peter went viral, she followed his story, curious about this young man from her former university. Then she discovered which high school he had attended. It was one of the schools Hawah had visited.

Oh my God, did I miss this? she thought. *Someone needs to reach out.*

When she contacted Peter she was surprised by his quick and gracious reply: the fact that he was willing to meet her signalled that he was open to discussion.

But Peter was wary of her intentions – so many people seemed to think they could bully his opinions out of him, as if being constantly under attack would somehow magically transform him into a completely different person – but he was intrigued enough to meet her.

You are one in a million trying to talk to me, he thought.

The campus Starbucks was quiet the morning they met in early autumn 2017, and the coffee shop manager cast him a wary glance. Hawah thought Peter seemed nervous and defensive, like an animal coiled and ready for a counter-attack, so she launched into a relaxed monologue about herself and her experiences at college. Hawah was not a specialist in deradicalization, but it seemed natural to her to try and find shared ground. They had similar views on student loans and the lack of financial help for poorer students. But as they talked, it felt like they had a lot more in common than that. They were both political, they were both smart and they both enjoyed a debate. And unlike most of Peter's college peers, Hawah also understood the world Peter had grown up in. Then she asked him about the rally.

'Why did you go?' she asked. 'What did the statue mean to you?'

Peter let everything out. It was like a valve had been released, and he talked Hawah through his fears and insecurities, and how they translated into the ideology that set him on the path to Charlottesville. At times he was intentionally antagonistic, but she listened without judgement, and while she often disagreed with him, she took him seriously. This was the sort of conversation Peter had longed to have in his early days at college, and their discussion flowed easily from politics and culture to identity and injustice. Still, there were some fierce disagreements. Hawah talked about how everyone had the same blood flowing through their veins, regardless of their race or religion. Peter seemed receptive, but when she started using an analogy involving Islamist extremists and drawing parallels between his recruitment to the far right and Islamic State recruiting young Muslims as foreign

fighters, Peter grew agitated. At times Hawah was taken aback
by the fervour with which Peter embraced his white nationalist
label – it was like he was ready to die for this movement. Their
voices became raised, their gestures more expansive. That was
more than enough for the coffee shop manager. Peter was widely
known as the campus Nazi, and here he was screaming at a young
woman of colour. The manager called the campus police, and
soon an armed officer was at their table.

'What are you doing?' the officer asked Hawah.

He seemed genuinely shocked that she was talking to Peter.
Even when she reassured him that they were fine and just having
a debate, he insisted on staying. For the rest of their conversation,
the officer sat between them, a silent and armed mediator, a
perfect metaphor for their polarized times. When they wrapped
up their two-hour long conversation, the pair parted on good
terms.

Peter did not come away from that coffee with Hawah a
changed man. But something had shifted in his mind. There
were questions that hadn't been there before. There had been
a connection with someone that he hadn't expected. Hawah
messaged him a few days later. How was he doing? Would he
like to chat again? And so began an unlikely friendship that
offered him the first genuine opportunity to begin to analyse
his beliefs. Hawah was now studying in a different state, so they
kept in touch on WhatsApp or the phone. Sometimes they
chatted about politics, but often it was about day-to-day life.
Hawah, a law graduate, read Peter's dissertation and offered
feedback. When they did talk about politics, she was patient,
allowing Peter the time to lower his ideological defences. With
so many other people, as soon as they made the connection
between him and the Charlottesville protest, he seemed to
transform into a monster.

I am not even human any more, he would then think, *I'm just
a thing.*

That always made him feel jittery and paranoid. But when he spoke to Hawah, he felt human again. In turn, she made him recognize the humanity of others. He began to see how the words he had been chanting in Charlottesville while holding a torch aloft against the pitch-black night would have triggered fear in others. Hawah helped him understand what being a white nationalist really meant, how racist it was, slowly breaking down all the narratives that Identity Evropa had carefully constructed. He started to recognize that he was not a blameless victim of some far-left conspiracy, and he began to experience some regret and remorse.

I didn't consciously cause harm, but I still caused harm and I have to make amends for it, he thought.

Quite how he would do that remained unclear in those early months of self-reflection, and while his understanding of the true nature of the rally was developing, much of his ideology was still entrenched. All Peter knew was that he needed to find a better path in life, and now he had some guidance on that path.

While the ugliness of the Charlottesville protest had over-shadowed his last few months at university, he wasn't going to let it obliterate all his dreams. Studying for a master's degree in the United Kingdom was still in his sights. Oxford and Cambridge turned him down, but this time he didn't make the same mistake he'd made as a teenager: he applied to all the top British universities, and the London School of Economics accepted him for its master's in political theory. The university even offered him a partial financial scholarship. Here was a chance to start again. Peter had a plan. He was going to read everything he could get his hands on – feminist theory, socialism, Marxism, social justice. He was going to retrain his mind, starting with a blank slate, and try and work out where it all went wrong.

15

Ibrahim Kamara

Brighton, England, January 2014 to Aleppo Province, Syria, September 2014

When Khadijah closed up her shop for the evening after Ibrahim's surprise visit and returned home, she was looking forward to cooking dinner for a family reunited. But Ibrahim wasn't there.

'Where is he? Where did he go?' she asked her younger sons.

They passed on his message about going off to study somewhere.

'He's lying,' Khadijah said.

The possibility that he was travelling to Syria to join a hard-line jihadist group fighting to overthrow President Bashar al-Assad didn't even occur to her. She had made sure his passport hadn't been renewed, so there was no way for him to leave the country.

But that was exactly what he was doing. On the afternoon of 28 January 2014, using his younger brother's passport, nineteen-year-old Ibrahim headed through security at Luton Airport flanked by sixteen-year-old Jaffar Deghayes and seventeen-year-old Abdullah Deghayes, the younger brothers of his best friend Amer Deghayes. Amer had left for Syria the previous October, joining an aid convoy then slipping into territory controlled by the al-Nusra Front rebel faction, which had that year become the official Syrian affiliate of al-Qaeda. The Brighton authorities, however, had appeared unconcerned by the fact that Amer had gone to Syria. It had taken a month for them to even realize where he was, and no action was taken to assess whether his young brothers might be at risk of joining him. Amer had always been considered the sensible one of the Deghayes family, so social workers took at face value assurances by his family that he was just there delivering humanitarian aid.

It should have been no surprise that British Muslims were heading in increasing numbers to actively participate in the Syrian war. Muslims across Europe were doing the same thing. By the end of 2013, around 1,900 Europeans were believed to have travelled to the war zone. But the British government appeared to have been blindsided by the hundreds of citizens who felt that their future lay on the battlefields of Syria and Iraq, and there was little framework in place for monitoring their activities or preventing their flight. Across Europe, there was general bewilderment about how to tackle the problem. Many governments were providing financial and logistical support to some of the Syrian rebel groups, so to criminalize the broad act of associating with Syrian armed factions would effectively criminalize their own policies. A patchwork of solutions was considered, from confiscating passports to stripping people of their residency if they left for Syria, but there was little information-sharing between nations or deeper analysis about what was drawing their citizens to a war zone. The mess of the Syrian conflict meant it was also difficult to know which groups the volunteers were joining. Such monitoring would require deep coordination between EU member states and security services, but the European Union was still grappling with the fallout from the financial crisis, and individual nations were focused on domestic issues, including the fight against growing populism as austerity measures took their toll. In Britain in 2013, Prime Minister David Cameron had promised a referendum on the country's EU membership, and the caustic debate over Britain's future in Europe would consume government and media attention in the coming years.

And in theory, Britain did already have a strategy in place for combatting extremism. It was called Prevent, and it had been launched in 2003 as part of a general counterterrorism push after 9/11. When fifty-two people were killed in London in 2005 by four al-Qaeda-linked suicide bombers, the focus of Prevent was narrowed to home-grown terrorism, and in 2011 it was amended again by the Conservative government to remove community integration work from its remit. But Prevent was controversial. It claimed to be tackling all forms of extremism, but Muslims were disproportionately targeted while being largely excluded from its design and implementation. Critics said the requirement for teachers, doctors and other public servants to report suspicious behaviour created a climate of distrust and fuelled the feeling that Muslims were under constant surveillance. Prevent was seen by some in the Muslim community as further alienating the communities from which extremist recruiters were filling their ranks.

Khadijah certainly never considered telling the authorities when Ibrahim started talking about Syria. By that point, she had given up on the police, having spent years trying to get someone to help protect her family from the relentless racist abuse. Not once had the police taken any action. So why would they help her now? She had taken the steps she thought she needed to to keep Ibrahim safe, not only withholding his new passport but also speaking to the imams at the local mosques. So when a call came one morning a few days after Ibrahim disappeared, it was a shock.

'Wa-Alaikum-Salaam,' came the voice of her first-born son. 'I am in Syria.'

Overcome with anger, Khadijah hung up. The phone rang again.

'Mum, did you hang up on me?' came Ibrahim's affronted voice from afar.

'Don't ever call me again,' Khadijah blurted out, hanging up once again.

How could Ibrahim have done this after all we have been through? she thought. *How could he turn his back on his family?*

Now Khadijah did go to the police. While she was telling them that her son didn't have a passport, she suddenly realized that he could have taken one of his brothers'. At first it seemed extraordinary that that ploy would have worked, as her three other boys looked nothing like Ibrahim. Besides, they were all under sixteen, so would not have been allowed to travel without a relative. The police told her to go home and check, and sure enough, a passport was missing. She was incredulous. Why had the border agents allow him to leave the country?

The fact that he was travelling with the stolen passport of an underage child was not the only reason Ibrahim should never have been allowed to leave the country. The two boys travelling with him were both under eighteen. Abdullah Deghayes was also the subject of a court order as he awaited trial for a criminal offence. And crucially, Jaffar Deghayes had been assessed under the government's Prevent strategy after a youth worker raised concerns about an anti-American tirade that he had launched into during one of their sessions. Jaffar had been referred to Channel, the process in Prevent under which a panel meets to assess an individual and decide the course of action. Throughout their lives, the Deghayes children had been brought to the attention of at least twelve local authority services and dozens of individuals, as they lurched between child protection and welfare agencies and police and youth offending services. The siblings were assessed to have suffered childhood trauma as a result of domestic abuse and the racist and Islamophobic campaign against them. But communication and cooperation between the different agencies was chaotic and mismanaged, and no one seemed able to connect with the teenagers or devise a coherent approach to their various problems. This miscommunication was apparent in the Channel meeting that convened in November 2013. Jaffar's anti-American outburst was discussed in isolation, and other significant connections were ignored or dismissed. Earlier that year a teacher at Jaffar's school had raised concerns about the vulnerability to radicalization of a number of young people in his peer group. That information was passed to Prevent, but it did not end up in their intelligence files, nor was it passed on to other agencies. Individuals at the Channel meeting who were aware of the information did not bring it up, considering the matter closed and unconnected. Similarly, when attendees at the meeting learned that Jaffar's older brother Amer was already overseas, that information was also deemed irrelevant. They discussed the possibility that Amer might be in Turkey helping Syrian refugees, but no connection was made to Jaffar's case. There were plenty of stories in the media at the time about young Muslims joining the war in Syria and about foreign fighters heading to the conflict from all over Europe. The British government was also aware of the threat. Foreign Secretary William Hague sent a letter to MPs in April 2013 in which he raised concerns that returning fighters could pose a risk to the UK. But these concerns had not yet coalesced into new policies, nor had they trickled down to the local authorities dealing with individual cases. Many of the people involved in Jaffar's case had been trained in the general principles of Prevent but not in any specifics, and certainly no connection had been made to a war on another continent. The possibility that a sixteen-year-old boy from Brighton would consider travelling to Syria was not even entertained. Those attending the Channel meeting concluded that there was no evidence that Jaffar was at risk of radicalization. The multiple red flags waving in their direction were ignored, and Jaffar had no problem flying out with Ibrahim and Abdullah to Istanbul, all of them with one-way tickets.

The authorities seemed to have been so careless that Khadijah wondered if it had been deliberate. Did they want young Muslims to leave the country? That seemed to be the only logical explanation. The authorities certainly did not seem interested in how Ibrahim had found his way to Syria. They told her that he was nineteen now – an adult – so they couldn't do much. Despite the fact that she reported Ibrahim's whereabouts to the police the day she received his call, the authorities only worked out that Jaffar and Abdullah were there as well a few weeks later. No police officer or community representative ever spoke to Khadijah's other three sons. Instead, Khadijah was again left alone to try and hold the family together. For months she managed to stick to her resolve, and ignored Ibrahim's calls. She did not want to hear the word 'Syria', and avoided any news about the country that had stolen her child.

Even if she wouldn't speak to him, Ibrahim never stopped thinking about his mother. Once inside Syria, he recorded a message for her on his phone in case anything happened to him, telling her that he loved her. He had crossed the border from Turkey into Syria with ease on 2 February, and had then travelled to an al-Nusra Front training camp in northern Aleppo province, where he was reunited with his best friend Amer. He underwent basic training, and a few weeks later the four young men from Brighton were deployed to the Turkish border to take part in an offensive against regime troops in Latakia province, a stronghold of President Assad. It was a success, and having now had their first taste of battle, the young men were eager for more. Next was an assault on Chalma, a mountain further south. This was a tougher proposition – an assault on a heavily guarded summit in difficult terrain. During a push forward in early April, regime gunfire rained down on them. The bullets hit Amer and his little brother Abdullah. Amer was injured; Abdullah was killed. The news reached Brighton.

The next time Ibrahim called, Khadijah answered. It was wonderful to hear his voice again. They started communicating via Facebook Messenger video calls, and after a few chats they resumed their easy, jocular way with each other. Sometimes she would tease Ibrahim about a hat he had taken to wearing, and she could almost forget where he was. Then reality would hit home again, and an immense weight would press upon her whole being.

'Oh Mum, I need to go for training now,' he said once as he rushed off a call.

Khadijah felt the fear creep back. Each conversation was a relief and a torment for her – her boy was safe, but would it be the last time she spoke to him? She had three other boys to raise, and worrying about Ibrahim every waking moment was exhausting. One day in July, she challenged him over whether he had stolen his brother's passport. He admitted he took it.

'The people brainwashed you,' she replied, incensed. 'They are not just cowards, they are criminals. They told you to steal someone's passport.'

Ibrahim started to defend himself.

'It was out of necessity,' he told his mother.

It was too much for Khadijah. She could not stand to listen to her son justify theft, after all the years she had spent trying to teach him to be respectful and to do the right thing. She felt herself getting breathless, her heart pounding in her chest. It was too much.

'No, I can't deal with this any more,' she said. 'You did something wrong and you are trying to justify it. That's it. You know what? That's it.'

Khadijah hung up. She never spoke to her son again.

Ibrahim was now fully embedded in life as an Islamist rebel. On Facebook, he was posting messages encouraging other Muslims to join the fight. He was popular among the other fighters and was known by the nom de guerre Khalil Al-Britani – the friendly Briton. Ibrahim appeared to have no regrets about his decision to leave Brighton, telling other fighters that he would never return to the UK and that he felt his destiny was to die a martyr. He had come a long way since first seeing those images of children suffering in Syria, and waiting with so much hope for the western powers to intervene. He had been desperate for them to end the bloodshed before it was too late. They didn't, and by the time Ibrahim found himself on the front line, at least 18,000 Syrian civilians had died. The war was becoming increasingly factional and brutal, spilling outside Syria's borders and threatening the security not just of the region, but of the world. Western journalists and aid workers had been kidnapped and murdered. Russia and Iran were starting to engage in action on Assad's side. Then in June 2014, Abu Bakr al-Baghdadi stood outside the mosque in Mosul, Iraq and declared an Islamic State stretching from Iraq across swathes of Syria. Now there was more than just an idea to entice people with – there was a physical entity to sell to the disillusioned young men and women seeking their own personal utopia. While many casual followers of the war in Syria believed that all the Britons who had gone to Syria were heading there to join ISIS, Ibrahim and his friends were actually battling against the Islamic State fighters. The al-Nusra Front had refused to join with the Islamic State, and they were now fighting not just Assad's forces but ISIS as well. And by mid-2014, there was another threat to their existence. The USA had finally decided to take military action in Syria, not to protect the civilians, but to protect itself.

In late September 2014, President Barack Obama received intelligence that an al-Qaeda-linked faction called the Khorasan group was embedded with the al-Nusra Front and was plotting attacks on US targets. He authorized a bombing campaign in Syria, targeting an al-Nusra Front training camp in Aleppo province. The first bomb fell on 22 September 2014. It landed on a young man called Ibrahim Kamara, born into a war and destined to die in one too.

16

Tom Olsen

Tom Olsen boarded his flight from Oslo to Johannesburg in late summer 1997 as a fully committed racist and neo-Nazi. At twenty-three, he had a history of violence and an utter conviction that he was fulfilling his destiny as a revolutionary in a righteous race war. He felt no need to hide his hateful views. He relished the effect he had on other people and sauntered on to the plane in his usual uniform: high boots and black clothes covered with swastikas. Shortly before landing, another passenger – a smartly dressed Black man – leaned across to him.

'Hey son,' the man said, 'are you sure you are on the right plane? This plane is going to Africa.'

Tom gave a snort of laughter and looked out the window again.

Yes, he thought, *I am on the right plane.*

Tom believed he was heading to South Africa to serve a just cause, in an odyssey which would find parallels decades later in the journeys made by thousands of men and women enticed to a brutal war in Syria and Iraq. The violent tactics of the Afrikaner Resistance Movement (AWB) in its fight to promote white Boer nationalism were no secret. In 1993, its members set up a fake roadblock and murdered four Black people, cutting the ear off one of the victims. In 1994, they killed twenty-one people in a bombing campaign aimed at disrupting the first post-apartheid election – an election which brought Nelson Mandela to power. The AWB claimed to be fighting to create a white-only state for the descendants of the original Boers who had first colonized the Africans' land hundreds of years ago. It was the same old promise of an exclusive utopia built on the blood of others that the Islamic State would rehash many years later as it waged its battle for a caliphate. Islamic State recruiters would even use the promise of marriage to a noble fighter to entice female recruits, and it was a hint of romance that had helped Tom make up his mind to come to this distant land too.

Christine, the woman who had beguiled him with the long letters she had written to him when he had been in prison, was waiting to greet him at the airport, flanked by her family, and carrying a big sign reading: 'WELCOME TOM!' The family lived in a modest house in a mining town just northwest of Johannesburg, and Tom quickly settled into the pace of life there. He and Christine fell into an easy relationship, going for long walks and losing themselves in conversation. There was no doubt about the family's politics: they spoke of South Africa's Black population with a venom which matched Tom's own, and while Christine was a few years younger than Tom and had a delicate air about her, he was surprised by the ferocity of her views. The family's evangelical approach to politics extended to their social mores, and while Tom and Christine would share a kiss now and then, it was a chaste relationship. Within a few days of Tom's arrival, the family were even talking about marriage, and Tom was a little taken aback. He couldn't help but wonder if perhaps they were after an insurance policy for their daughter, a safe European passport in case life in South Africa became too hard.

But Tom was also impatient to join the fight. He had come there, after all, to make war, not love. A few weeks after his arrival, Christine's father invited him to a large AWB meeting. It was an impressive gathering. Hundreds of people milled around a huge farmstead as a brass band played and a whole ox turned on a spit. Eugène Terre'Blanche, the firebrand leader of the AWB, was holding court with the assembled journalists, white nationalists, European skinheads and members of his black-clad Iron Guard protection unit. With his white hair, flowing beard, intense blue eyes and fanatical way of speaking, Terre'Blanche came across as messianic at times and as demonic at others, a cult-like figure revelling in the adoration of his followers. Tom was filled with nervous excitement when his turn came for an audience with the man.

'We are grateful you have come to South Africa to serve our cause,' Terre'Blanche told him.

It was then that Tom learned what his role would be in the glorious fight for a pure white state. He had dreamed of being on the front line, trained in horse riding, firearms and cross-country terrain. No, said Terre'Blanche: they needed him to work as a security guard on a farm. Tom's disappointment was intense. He had heard stories from other skinheads about the fate of these farm guards. They were posted to the middle of nowhere, barely given enough food and only a little pocket money, then expected to risk their lives guarding private property. Some had been violently attacked by criminals. Others, with no work visas or permits allowing them to carry the weapons they were armed with, ended up in jail. These gullible Europeans were treated as free labour for the high-ranking AWB members as they plotted an uprising which, by that point, was already in its dying days. Nelson Mandela had been South Africa's president for three years and had been welcomed on to the world stage. The Truth and Reconciliation Commission was helping put the country's divided history well and truly in the past, and many AWB members had requested and received amnesty. There was no revolution any more: just a bunch of angry and disenfranchised white people whose voices were increasingly drowned out by the emergence of tolerance, forgiveness and hope in the new South Africa.

Tom returned dejected to Christine and her family. They had another suggestion for him: why not stay with them instead? He could get all his paperwork and serve as foreman in the little factory they ran producing wooden desk ornaments. Tom reluctantly filled in the forms requesting a work visa. Overseeing the production of carved rulers and ornamental paperweights while settling into a life of domesticity was not exactly what he'd had in mind when he boarded his flight a few weeks ago with the ambition to change the world. But what choice did he have? He could hardly go home now, especially given the drama with which he had told his parents he was leaving.

Tom sought solace in alcohol, spending increasing amounts of time in a bar favoured by AWB members and European skinheads, with whom he quickly struck up a rapport. One evening he took some CDs of English neo-Nazi music with him to the bar and cajoled everyone into a drunken singalong of racist chants. The bartender even put up a swastika flag in his honour. The Nazi symbol was not too different from the AWB emblem, which clearly referenced it in shape and colour, but some of the older AWB members were irked by this interloper and his open support for Nazism. When Tom started playing an anti-Semitic song, he felt a shift in the mood. He spotted someone barging across the bar towards him – it was a man known as the Preacher, whom he recognized as a friend of Christine's family. Before Tom understood what was going on, a revolver was in his face, pressed right up to his nose, causing him to topple backwards off his bar stool and hit the floor. The Preacher kept coming at him, shouting, and accentuating every word with a wave of the gun.

'You are not allowed to insult the chosen people of God!' he screamed.

Tom lay on the floor, petrified. Eventually the man stopped

screaming. The bartender turned off the CD and took the swastika flag down. The party was over.

Tom was nursing his dented pride the next day when the Preacher came to Christine's house. He invited Tom out for a drive, and Tom was made aware that it wasn't the kind of invite he could turn down. After a while, the Preacher's white Mercedes pulled into a churchyard.

What's next? Tom wondered. *Is there a grave for me?*

It was time for a lesson on the exact strains of hatred acceptable in this sect of white supremacy. The Preacher sought out some graves with the Star of David on them.

'All these are Jews who died fighting for South Africa in the wars,' he said. 'The Jews are our friends.'

Tom was incredulous. He had wholeheartedly bought into the idea that the Jews controlled immigration, and that they were ultimately responsible for racial mixing in societies.

You have really lost it, Tom thought as he looked at the Preacher. *You have got sunstroke from being here too long.*

His disillusionment deepened. Tom wanted desperately to join the great fight for a better world, but so far all his attempts had been ridiculed and rejected. Over the next few days, he pondered his future. He needed some time to clear his head. He lied to Christine, telling her he had a meeting with a Ku Klux Klan member, then packed a bag and headed off to Johannesburg.

In the late 1990s, Johannesburg was abuzz with the creative energy of a city in transition. The counterculture was thriving, the energy spilling out of the clubs, bars and makeshift galleries on to the streets, a celebration of the many identities of South Africa coming together to form one future. The district of Yeoville encapsulated this spirit, as a multi-racial neighbourhood which showed the best and worst of the new South Africa. There was petty crime, as well as drugs and biker gangs, but they existed cheek by jowl with the bohemians, small business owners and music lovers drawn to the anarchic and inclusive energy of the area. On Yeoville's main thoroughfare, Rockey Street, every night was party night, with people thronging the streets and the noise of booming sound systems and excited shouts all but drowning out the occasional gunshot. Kosher food was available for the many Jewish families, alongside Indian supermarkets, shops selling African carvings, unofficial gay bars. Everybody was catered for here – even a white supremacist with swastikas on his clothes.

Tom had ended up at a backpackers' hostel just off Rockey Street by chance. He had picked up a leaflet for the hostel at the bus station and handed it to a taxi driver. Aware of his environment, Tom tried to tone down his appearance, but it was difficult given that most of his clothing had white supremacist symbolism on it and his head was closely shaved. Many of the foreign backpackers at the hostel were frosty, but the South Africans in the bars just seemed to take him for what he was at that moment: a paying customer keeping himself to himself. In a strange way, Tom felt like he fitted in there, among all the other outsiders trying to figure out how to navigate this strange new territory.

His days followed the same pattern: he would wake up, have some breakfast and go for a meandering walk around the area, before ending up in the late afternoon at his favourite bar, where he would stay until dark, watching rugby and chatting to the bartender. One evening Tom befriended an Englishman, and they decided to head downtown. Two drunk white men staggering through the dark streets of a city still wracked by poverty was not the best idea, and the pair had not got far when Tom realized they were lost. Searching out a street sign, Tom noticed a gang of Black men coming towards them. He sensed trouble, and soon the men were closing in, forming a horseshoe around them. One of the men pulled a pistol from his trousers and turned it on Tom, demanding money. Tom turned out his pockets. There wasn't much there – maybe twenty or thirty rand – but the Englishman handed over his ATM card and told the men the PIN code. Tom felt the adrenaline pumping, acutely aware of how provocative his AWB T-shirt must be. Then he was seized by an unexpected calm. His life was under threat, but instinctively he knew what to do. He had to make some sort of connection to the man with the gun, to show him he was human too.

He looked him in the eye, holding the contact.

'I hope you don't shoot me, because I would love to see the rest of your beautiful country,' Tom said slowly and deliberately.

The man held his gaze for a second, then snapped the gun down and walked away.

Tom stood there, the adrenaline draining from his body. He felt unmoored. All his indoctrination had taught him that Black people were not humans like he was, but barbarous animals. So what the hell had just happened?

Why didn't he shoot me? Tom thought. *If I was in his shoes, I would have shot me. And if I'd had a gun and I had the possibility to, I would have shot him.*

Tom and the Englishman made their way back to the hostel and called the police, who mocked them for their drunken foray on to the city's dangerous streets.

'Stupid tourists,' the officer said, and hung up.

Tom's adventure in South Africa now seemed like a series of humiliations. But fate hadn't finished with him yet. One morning, he woke up and looked for his wallet. It had disappeared – stolen or lost, he didn't know. Now he was penniless too. A call to the Norwegian embassy proved as successful as his call to the police. They told him that if he had living relatives back home, there was nothing they could do. Dejected, Tom called his parents and asked them to send him a cheque. It would take a few weeks to arrive, but the owner of the hostel – a white woman from Zimbabwe who was sympathetic to his politics – said he could stay there until his money arrived. She also gave him breakfast on credit, so each morning Tom ate as much food as he could, and then spent the day wandering the streets getting increasingly hungry until he showed up in the early evening at his favourite bar. The staff knew him and didn't mind if he just sat at the bar drinking water. Sometimes they would even give him a free beer.

One evening, Tom was watching the rugby when the man next to him ordered two lagers. The man casually slid one of the beers over to Tom and raised his glass.

'Cheers!' said a friendly voice.

Tom glanced over and was surprised to find himself looking at one of the blackest faces he had seen in South Africa. This stranger – well dressed and clean shaven, unlike a lot of the other regulars on Rockey Street – was smiling at him. He seemed to emanate an aura of kindness and good cheer. Tom on the other hand was a skinhead. He was wearing clothes bearing the signs of the Afrikaner Resistance Movement.

Are you completely insane? Who are you? Tom thought.

Just in case there was any confusion about his allegiance, Tom turned to face the man to make sure he could see the racist symbol emblazoned across the front of his shirt. Then he realized what must be going on, and anger swept over him.

He is from the South African intelligence and this beer is poisoned and he is planning to kill me, he thought.

There could be no other explanation. Tom stiffened. The bartender noticed the tension spreading across his face. He reached over the bar and placed his hand on Tom's shoulder.

'Tom, relax, the guy just wants to buy you a beer,' he said. 'Say thank you.'

It took a few seconds for these words to permeate into Tom's consciousness. Then he tried to rearrange his face into something other than fear and anger and managed to stutter out a half-hearted 'Thank you.'

The stranger laughed. Tom found himself laughing too.

It was an icebreaker, but Tom still was on guard, keen to return to his pint and the rugby. But his new companion kept talking. The rapid-fire questions came at Tom so quickly that he didn't have time to compose his face back into a wary glare between each answer.

'Where are you from? Have you been here long? Have you seen the Big Five?'

Tom tried to answer politely, knocking back his beer as quickly as possible to try and get out of there as soon as he could. But when it was finished another beer appeared, and the questions kept coming. Tom learned about his gregarious drinking companion too: he was a businessman from Zambia with a wife and young children, and he worked in telecoms and travelled a lot. He was around the same age as Tom and liked to meet interesting people, so always stayed in backpacker areas rather than in business hotels. In fact, he was staying at the same hostel as Tom. He didn't once mention Tom's appearance. When they finished the next round of beers, a couple of Springbok shots arrived – the electric green of crème de menthe topping the soothing tan of Amarula Cream. Tom knocked a couple back, and remembered little of the rest of the evening.

The next morning, Tom woke with a crushing hangover. At first he was only able to focus on the pounding in his head, and on his tongue that felt like sandpaper. Then he remembered what had happened the night before, and a sense of shame spread over him. He had been out drinking – and enjoying himself – with a Black man. He was embarrassed that other backpackers from the hostel might have seen him. It was a strange reaction given that most of the other backpackers barely disguised their dislike for him. There was one American woman – young and petite and on her honeymoon – who would look at him with utter venom every time she passed him. He knew the look well: it was the same look he would give to mixed-race couples back home, a look that said: *I would kill you if I could*. Tom never imagined he would be on the receiving end of such a look. It felt different to the looks of fear he inspired in Norway, and it made him feel deeply uncomfortable. What if these people had seen him getting drunk with a Black man? They'd think him a fraud. At the same time, Tom remembered the warmth and good humour of the man and couldn't deny that it had been an enjoyable evening.

Tom spent much of the day brooding, nursing both his hangover and his existential crisis. He went for his usual walk. By late afternoon, he was back at the hostel and his stomach was growling. He was sitting in the lounge when the Zambian man walked in, carrying two bags of groceries.

'Hey Tom!' he shouted across the room, his free hand waving enthusiastically.

Before he was able to stop himself from returning the wave, Tom's arm shot up.

'Are you hungry?' the man asked.

'Yeah,' Tom replied.

'Well come on over and help me make some food,' the man said.

Tom joined the man in the kitchen and was put to work chopping onions. He loved cooking. During the periods he had spent in jail for committing acts of white supremacist violence, he had spent a lot of time in the kitchens, learning different techniques and honing his skills. But he decided to keep this to himself as he busied himself with the preparation, letting himself enjoy the simple pleasure of a shared experience. Soon the pair were sitting side by side, eating a delicious Zambian dish. During their dinner, the young American woman walked in. Tom would never forget the look of astonishment on her face when she saw the pair eating together.

Soon it was a daily ritual, Tom and the man he was beginning to consider a friend cooking side by side and then sharing the meal and a few beers. It became the best part of Tom's day. The pair would make small talk as they cooked, chatting about South Africa, their families, the different cuisines of Zambia and Norway. The conversation flowed easily between topics. Tom's new friend never brought up his openly racist appearance. It should have been the elephant in the room, but somehow it wasn't strange. Both men looked beyond the other's appearance, choosing instead to focus on the small pleasures they had in common.

One morning, a few days into this new routine, Tom woke up and looked in the mirror. He ran a hand over his bald head, ready to grab the razor with which he had rigorously shaved it bare for five years. He felt the fuzz of a night's growth. He paused, put the razor down, and went for breakfast.

It only took a couple of days to grow about five millimetres of hair, a strange sensation after so many years as a skinhead. But it was also comforting not to be constrained by the physical symbols of his identity. It was somehow freeing. His new fuzz raised no comment from his Zambian friend, but Tom felt a bit better standing alongside him chopping onions now. A few mornings later, Tom carefully cut the labels from all his T-shirts, as he was going to wear his clothes inside out now. It wasn't a conscious repudiation of his ideology. Far from it. He still considered himself a neo-Nazi. But it just didn't feel right, standing in the kitchen next to his friend while wearing his Nazi and AWB gear.

Ten days after Tom lost his wallet, a cheque arrived from Norway. He settled his bill with the hostel owner, and then calculated how much he owed the Zambian man. Every day when the man bought food, Tom had assured him he would pay him back. His friend had brushed him off, telling him not to worry about it. Now Tom sat down and worked out exactly how much to give him, factoring in a bit extra as a token of appreciation. But when he tried to hand over the money, the man was affronted.

'I chose to help you, and I didn't do it to get paid,' he said. 'It was my choice alone and I'm happy to see that you got your money. Now spend it wisely, and not on me.'

Tom brooded over this, but acquiesced. He knew what he had to spend the money on. He was going home.

Today, Tom cannot remember the name of the man from Zambia who showed him such generosity, nor does he know why this man chose to strike up a friendship with someone who clearly marked himself out as a racist. Tom feels bad that his name has faded over time, and that he didn't even ask the man where in Zambia he was from. He would like to see him now, to thank him again. But at the time, the friendship in Johannesburg didn't feel like a turning point. It felt more like a glitch, another strange thing in an already strange odyssey to South Africa. It was a journey that challenged the narratives Tom had cemented in his head throughout his youth, not through any forced intervention, but through the mundane fact of having stepped outside his bubble and exposed himself to other people. It wasn't just the initial disenchantment with his reception in South Africa, followed by the mugger who didn't shoot him and the Zambian man who offered the hand of friendship, that provided this challenge. There was also the date arranged after a flirty phone call, in which Tom unexpectedly found himself having a romantic dinner with an Indian woman. Then there was the Black taxi driver who had experienced a run of misfortune and was working twenty hours a day to try and provide for his family; when Tom suggested he find less honest ways to pay off his debt, the indignant man looked like he was about to throw Tom out of his taxi.

'I can't feed my family on money that has been acquired illegally!' he shouted. 'How would I look my son in the eye and tell him that the bread he is eating is stolen?'

This man's moral code was far superior to Tom's, and that shocked him.

Tom had gone to South Africa with the aim of fighting anyone of colour and installing white-only rule. Instead, he found himself immersed in a multiracial society seized by energy and optimism after decades of oppression. He spent only a few weeks in Johannesburg, but each day he spent away from Christine and her white nationalist family and surrounded by people from all backgrounds, his perspective inched ever closer towards a lasting change. But while Tom's reckoning in South Africa opened the door to such a transformation, it would take a few more years before he was able to walk through it.

When Tom returned home in December 1997, his old neo-Nazi friends were there waiting for him, and he slipped easily back into their company, even if he wasn't quite convinced by their ideology any more. Within months he was behind bars again, this time for an assault on a young man while working as a bouncer. In jail, he reconnected with a prison guard he knew from his previous stretches inside. This guard had always spoken to him like a human being, and while he enjoyed his company, their discussions had not in the past had any impact on his beliefs. Now, though, Tom already had some questions in his head, some sense of nuance about the world that wasn't there before. His conversations with the prison guard became deeper, more profound in his questioning of his life choices. There was also a priest in the jail who took the time to listen to what Tom said and offer support without judgement. All these experiences built up, layer upon layer, reinforcing what had come before, and steering Tom towards a different future.

When Tom came out of prison in late 1998, he had made up his mind: he was going to leave his neo-Nazi past behind. It would take many years for Tom to get his life back on track. He worked for some time on a remote salmon farming island, where he met his future wife. Then he began studying social work, but it was such a hard task to get people to believe that he had turned his life around and wanted to help others do the same too. He understood the scepticism. Sometimes he couldn't even be sure if he had really changed.

You can't just take a urine test and see if the swastikas are gone, he thought. *You never know if the ghost is still there.*

Then in 2004, his niece had a baby. The father was Nigerian. When Tom looked at the photos of the beautiful mixed-race baby, he felt nothing but joy. Finally, the ghost was gone.

17

Hadiya Masieh

London, England, 2003–15

When twenty-five-year-old Hadiya Masieh turned on the television on 15 February 2003, she was struck by a powerful feeling of dissonance. In front of her, millions of people around the world were marching against the upcoming war in Iraq. Hadiya pressed up to the screen with the same intensity as when she was a child watching Live Aid, mesmerized by this new spectacle of shared humanity. Years later, many people would look back at those protests and pinpoint them as the moment they lost faith in their power to effect change. But gestures we think are futile can have an impact in ways we may never understand.

At the time she watched the protests, Hadiya was a fully indoctrinated member of Hizb ut-Tahrir, immersed in the extreme ideology of a sect that campaigned to abolish democracy and create an Islamic caliphate. Her existence was every bit as insular as the group itself. The only time she interacted with people outside the circle of Hizb ut-Tahrir was when she was recruiting, and then it was with the purpose of winning them over to her cause. She knew the truth – the unbelievers had no respect for Muslims and were all out to destroy their religion.

So why are millions of people – most of them non-Muslims – marching to save lives in a Muslim country? Hadiya wondered as she watched the screen.

It was a mass of individuals coming from all corners of society to voice disapproval over something unjust. Suddenly these non-believers no longer felt like her enemies – they felt like human beings with a shared purpose. This disconnect between what she'd been taught and what she saw planted the first seed of doubt in Hadiya's mind, and over the next year, it grew. One of the central tenets of her indoctrination – the idea that there was only us and them, with no in-between – had started to crack. That opened her mind to other questions about what she believed.

If the movement is meant to create a utopia full of perfect people, why is there so much petty squabbling among group members? she wondered. *And why do my fellow believers refuse to engage in any debate about their beliefs?*

For more than a year, these questions swirled around inside Hadiya's head. She began to share her doubts with her husband, and while he listened and took her worries seriously, they were both so busy. There was endless organizing and proselytizing for Hizb ut-Tahrir, and another baby was on the way too. The questions never went away, however, and they all came together in the most unexpected of places: on a hospital bed during the early stages of labour. It was 21 July 2005, and Hadiya's third child seemed reluctant to come out. Hadiya understood why. On the television in her room, news was breaking about the failed effort by four Islamist extremists to detonate bombs across London. It came just a few weeks after four al-Qaeda-linked suicide bombers killed fifty-two people on trains and buses in London. One of the bombs had struck King's Cross station, not far from the hospital where Hadiya was about to bring a new life into the world.

Am I just like them? Hadiya wondered.

Hizb ut-Tahrir did not advocate violence, but the organization's grievances and aspirations were the same as those suicide bombers': seeking justice for the victims of western foreign policy in Muslim lands, and waging a campaign for the establishment of an Islamic state.

What I believe is not that different to what they say, thought Hadiya. *But is this mercy? Is this peace?*

Suddenly, she felt the baby coming. Hadiya believed that in the purity of labour, God was listening, and there was a higher chance of him answering your prayers. In the weeks running up to her due date, she had wondered what to ask for. Now, as the pain of the contractions convulsed her body, she screamed one phrase over and over.

'Show me! Show me! Show me!'

To the midwives, it was just another woman dealing with the pains of childbirth. To Hadiya, it was a specific request for God to tell her which path she should travel, how she could change, what to do with her life. It felt like her body was rising to the ceiling, while the voices of the medical staff faded away. The emotions came quick and fast: fear, regret, sorrow, anger and confusion. Hadiya let out one more almighty scream and pushed.

When her baby was placed in her arms, the pain was forgotten, but her questions seemed to have been answered. It was time to leave Hizb ut-Tahrir.

The first few months were difficult and alienating. Hadiya had believed the people she had spent the past seven years with were her friends. She had shared with them her formative years in her new faith, her marriage, the birth of her three children. But when she returned home from the hospital, she discovered just how tenuous those friendships were. The epiphany she had at the birth spurred her to ask questions about the Hizb ut-Tahrir teachings, to explore whether there was still a way to salvage her faith in the organization and reconcile the internal disputes. But dissent was not to be tolerated. The group now saw her as the enemy and closed ranks.

Together with her husband, Hadiya began to rebuild her life. They were lucky that Hadiya's husband had a profession outside the group, so financially they were secure. Hadiya had also managed to maintain a relationship with her parents after the initial upset caused by her conversion to Islam. She had been under pressure from Hizb ut-Tahrir to sever all ties with the world outside the organization, but she had not been willing to give up her family. To have them supporting her now, as she struggled to acclimatize to life outside the group, was a blessing. Now she returned to the same question that had consumed her when she left the family home for university nearly a decade ago.

What am I going to do with my life?

Caring for her three young children gave her such pleasure, but she was never going to be happy with a domestic life and nothing else. She wanted to salvage something positive from her experiences, and spied an opportunity when three other Hizb ut-Tahrir members, all men, left the organization too. They would all gather around Hadiya's kitchen table and talk into the night about how to use their collective experience to counter extreme narratives. Hadiya had been one of Hizb ut-Tahrir's best recruiters and had a unique window into the mind of female extremists, so she felt she had a lot to offer. But when the men eventually established the Quilliam Foundation, which would become a key partner of a British government looking for a very precise archetype of a 'moderate' Muslim, Hadiya did not find a role in it and felt sidelined. So she kept searching, and after all those years in a group which tore people apart, Hadiya found herself drawn to work which brought people together. She joined a Muslim–Jewish theatre group after being deeply affected by the stories she heard at the Bereaved Families Forum, which brought together Israelis and Palestinians who had lost loved ones in the ongoing conflict. It was an exercise in relearning everything, this time from a completely different perspective, one which focused on the commonalities people have rather than on what divides them. With her gregarious, enthusiastic nature, Hadiya quickly made connections in this new world. She worked with the Faith & Belief Forum and the Austrian NGO, Women without Borders, and enjoyed the feeling of being on a new crusade, this time on the side of right. But there was always a nagging feeling that this utopia could be as flimsy as her last one. Although she met lots of inspiring people and believed in the goals of many organizations, there was an awful lot of self-promotion too. People seemed to want to use Hadiya's experience and inside knowledge, but then take all the credit for it. It was a price she was willing to pay, however, if she thought she could make a difference.

I'll keep in the background because it's a bit of a dog-eat-dog world, she thought.

Hadiya soon came to the attention of the British Home Office, and in 2009 started doing occasional work as a counterterrorism advisor. In 2013, she was invited to be part of the Prevent counter-extremism strategy and was listed as a potential mentor for individuals in the Channel deradicalization programme. She knew many members of the Muslim community had their concerns about Prevent but figured if she could stop even one young woman from going down the same route as her, then it would be worth it. It was still early days for the newest incarnation of Prevent, with the Channel intervention scheme only rolling out across the UK in 2012, and Hadiya's training was basic. There were some role-playing sessions, but she was mostly expected to draw on personal experience. In her role as mentor, Hadiya would visit women suspected of harbouring extreme beliefs and try to get them to talk about their ideology. She would then report back to the police. If the security services decided to take the case further, a tailored intervention plan would be devised, with social workers, psychologists, police and mental health professionals all working together to attempt to deradicalize the individual. At first, Hadiya kept being given cases which conformed to the stereotype of the programme: white women who had converted to Islam. The assumption seemed to be that if a white woman wanted to be a Muslim, there must be a problem. Hadiya would supress her annoyance, have a chat with the women, and then reassure her superiors that there was nothing to worry about. Other than those cases, she rarely heard from Prevent. Even when there was growing concern in the communities she worked with that radicalization was on the rise, her phone didn't ring.

In late 2013, a twenty-year-old from Glasgow became one of the first British women to travel to Syria to join ISIS. More would soon follow. As far as she knew, Hadiya was the only female mentor on the Prevent database. Yet still they didn't call her. By early 2014, Ibrahim Kamara had travelled to Syria as had four other youngsters from Brighton. The police identified at least half a dozen other Brighton youths, including a young woman, who they believed were considering joining them. But still Hadiya didn't hear anything.

In October 2014, Prevent finally contacted Hadiya with a case. A sixteen-year-old girl from London had disappeared to Turkey. The authorities had done nothing, so her parents had gone to Turkey and brought her back themselves. Could Hadiya go round and speak to her? It was Hadiya's first meeting with a young person who had been in contact with ISIS recruiters, and when she met the teenager, she was shocked. The venom with which she spoke about Britain was alarming, as was the speed with which she had been transformed from a diligent schoolgirl into a single-minded zealot.

This is weird, Hadiya thought. *What is going on?*

She didn't have a chance to find out. Days later, the girl was on her way back to the airport. Her mum called Hadiya, begging her to stop her daughter from leaving. Hadiya got on the phone to her police liaison officer.

'Tell the airline not to let her board the plane,' Hadiya said. 'Or have her arrested at passport control. Or take her off the plane.'

'I'm sorry,' the police officer replied. 'We simply can't do that. We don't have the power.'

The girl left for Syria and would never return. Hadiya was distraught. Something was happening to Britain's young people, and no one seemed to be taking it seriously.

That was all about to change. In February 2015, three teenagers from the Bethnal Green Academy in East London – Amira Abase, Shamima Begum and Kadiza Sultana – calmly walked through security at Gatwick Airport dressed in hoodies and trainers and looking like any other British schoolgirls heading off on summer camp. In fact they were about to board a plane to Istanbul, from where they would travel into Islamic State territory in Syria. Their pictures were splashed over the front pages of British newspapers, the sensational stories that accompanied them about 'jihadi brides' sparking equal measures of soul-searching and Islamophobia.

Suddenly Hadiya's phone didn't stop ringing.

The hysteria surrounding the Bethnal Green girls finally seemed to spur the British government into action, and throughout Europe security services were scrambling to understand this exodus to the battlefields of Iraq and Syria. From 2013 until the fall of the Islamic State, an estimated 10,000 European men, women and children would head to Syria and Iraq, and slowly governments realized that they might one day come back and threaten the safety and security of others.

In May 2014, a Frenchman opened fire in the Jewish Museum of Belgium in Brussels, killing four people. He had spent a year in Syria fighting for Islamic State. It was the first attack by a returned foreign fighter, and more would follow. Of the nine men who attacked Paris nightspots in November 2015, most had spent time with Islamist fighters in Syria. So had at least two of the men who bombed Brussels Airport and Metro in early 2016. Suddenly deradicalization 'experts' were in as much demand as the controversial cult deprogrammers had been a few decades earlier. An easy solution would prove equally elusive.

Lessons could have been learned from experiences with cult members in the 1970s and '80s, when the approach moved from the deeply flawed deprogramming method to a more nuanced approach. Psychologists found that people's brains cannot switch from one ideology to another in a short space of time, and that a whole host of past experiences must be considered as an individual embarks on the long and difficult process of recognizing and accepting the different identities that define them. But these lessons were largely overlooked. Vast amounts of money were spent across Europe on deradicalization programmes with little evidence of their success. Thousands of academic papers were penned; new think tanks and non-governmental organizations (NGOs) emerged; people touted solutions ranging from cage fighting to cultural re-education, desperate for a share in this new and rapidly expanding business.

France invested millions of euros in its counter-extremism programme, repurposing an eighteenth-century countryside château as a 'Centre for Prevention, Integration and Citizenship' – an Orwellian name for the first of twelve deradicalization centres it planned to roll out across the country. The 'guests' at these centres were taken away from their families and communities and subjected to a rigid routine, coupled with lessons in French history, literature and philosophy, in the hope that these messages would somehow supplant any extremist narratives. No evaluation was made of the effectiveness of a strategy dreamed up by people with no experience working in counter-extremism, and in 2017 the centre closed.

In the Netherlands, a newspaper investigation found that the city of Amsterdam had hired a man who still had connections to extremist groups to work with youths at risk of radicalization. They alleged that he was actively recruiting vulnerable people to head to Syria, and as a result, the authorities in Amsterdam stopped deploying former extremists. Yet with the proper checks and balances, the use of former extremists like Hadiya to work with people at risk of radicalization could be crucial. They understood the nuanced process by which a person fell for extreme narratives and were able to respond with genuine empathy. Once again, however, it was not the silver bullet that some thought it was. Hadiya even came across people who exaggerated their extremist background, or even made one up, in the hope of getting work in this booming sector.

There were some countries that made progress in understanding the many factors that drive people towards extreme beliefs. Denmark's Aarhus model was an early success story and was praised for not only focusing on changing people's minds but also working on their underlying problems. It looked at every aspect of a person's life – their family, education, health, housing, jobs, relationship, religion – then came up with a plan tailored to the individual that involved cooperation between all the relevant agencies. It had impressive results, and these results could have been replicated elsewhere. But in the mid-2010s, Europe wasn't in a collaborative mood. The economic crisis had already frayed relations between nations, and the subsequent refugee crisis was driving them even further apart. Borders hardened again, and countries retreated into a wary us-and-them nationalism.

Even within individual countries, there could be a staggering lack of coordination. Belgium had Europe's highest per capita number of foreign fighters in Syria and Iraq, but not a single one of them had come from the town of Mechelen, which had a significant Muslim population. The progressive mayor of Mechelen had long worked to bring all the different communities together and level inequality, and his holistic approach over many years meant that there were fewer grievances to exploit. Less than ten miles away in the city of Vilvoorde, at least thirty people in a population of around 30,000 left for Syria and Iraq. If two towns fifteen minutes apart could not effectively share their knowledge, there seemed to be little hope for the rest of Europe.

In London, Hadiya just kept her head down and focused on

the girls she was trying to help. She mentored dozens of young Muslim women who had tried to travel to Iraq and Syria to join Islamic State or who showed signs of drifting towards Islamist extremism. She met the families and school friends of the three Bethnal Green girls and worked on some of the most high-profile cases in the UK.

It was a steep learning curve. Hadiya saw so much of herself in the young women she met – that desire for knowledge and purpose, that struggle for an identity, that rage against injustice. She could understand how many of the early recruits were driven by a sense of outrage at the brutality of the regime of President Bashar al-Assad. But even when the horrific actions of the Islamic State became clear – the reports of gay people being thrown from buildings, the hostages being beheaded on camera – the converts kept on coming. When Hadiya asked why, their answers echoed those of the far-right extremists: the negative coverage was fake news. The alleged atrocities by Islamic State were lies invented by a media that hated Muslim people, they told her, and Hadiya once again saw parallels with her own experience. There was, however, one major difference. In the late 1990s, Hadiya's quest for an identity required a concerted effort to read books and newspapers, trawl different social groups, and finally venture into university prayer rooms. For the girls she was working with, their automatic response to feelings of isolation and alienation was to go online.

If you were passionate about something in the 1990s, you had to be bloody passionate about it because you had to make that extra effort, Hadiya thought. *Now everything is on Twitter – that is the world at your fingertips.*

The sophistication of the IS propaganda astonished Hadiya. It tapped into those wistful dreams of a better world and lured recruits with slick and polished media campaigns, as well as enticing young women with the promise of romance with heroic fighters. Of course, the promises were as shallow as those in recruitment materials used by the far-right AWB to draw young men to South Africa in the 1990s. The reality for many of the female IS recruits was daily hardship and loneliness as they lived under constant bombardment, at the same time being treated poorly by their 'heroic' IS husbands and reduced to domestic drudgery with ever-dwindling resources.

Trying to get the world to feel any empathy with these youngsters proved difficult. In the weeks following the departure of the Bethnal Green girls, the media coverage and public debate was largely sympathetic, portraying the three teenagers as children who had been manipulated by IS and failed by the authorities. But the emerging panic over foreign fighters coincided with the height of the refugee crisis and the wave of terror attacks on European soil, and these issues converged in people's minds. The majority of the million refugees entering Europe in 2015 came from Syria and Iraq and were fleeing the same Islamist extremism that the West feared so much. The far-right and populist parties, however, portrayed these refugees not as the victims of terror, but as potential perpetrators of it. Many governments began to put even more emphasis on security and exclusionary ideas, despite all the evidence showing that such policies accentuated the alienation that drove people towards extremism in the first place. Parents who sent a few hundred euros to children who had travelled to Islamic State territory in Iraq or Syria were prosecuted for financing terrorism. Young people who had gone there were stripped of their citizenship. Teachers were asked to spy on the children in their classrooms and report any suspicious behaviour. The climate of mistrust grew. And with governments so focused on the Muslim communities, a resurgent far right went almost unnoticed. Until more blood began to spill.

18

Mak Kapetanovic

Jacksonville, Florida, USA, 2015–20

By the time he was eighteen, it was like there were two Maks. There was Mak in class, withdrawn and quiet but still playing drums and spending time with people at his school from different ethnic backgrounds. Then there was Mak online, a young man convinced that people with a skin colour other than white were genetically and intellectually inferior and that the Jewish people were conspiring to suppress the white race and replace it with a nation of immigrants. That a Bosnian-American child of Muslim refugees believed he was a victim of this replacement conspiracy was astonishing, for it was the same 'demographic jihad' theory that the ultra-nationalist Serb regime in the former Yugoslavia had claimed was being perpetrated by the Bosnian Muslims, laying the groundwork for the ethnic cleansing that had sent Mak's parents fleeing to America in the 1990s. But Mak was in too deep to see any parallels.

Mak kept his two worlds wholly separate, only once venturing to share his views with a few friends. 'Isn't it weird that there are all these Jewish people in charge of all these companies?' he asked. His friends looked at him as if he were mad, and Mak realized that these theories weren't ones he could share outside 4chan. In fact, though, he wasn't sharing them there much either. He remained one of millions of anonymous lurkers on 4chan. It wasn't like Facebook or Twitter, where you posted something for public consumption and then basked in your 'likes'. No one ever knew who you were, and you could just immerse yourself in the content without worrying about any consequences. No one ever overtly attempted to recruit Mak to a far-right cause. That wasn't the way extremists on 4chan worked. It was a place for testing and spreading ideas, theories, lies and conspiracies, poisoning the soil in which hundreds of young minds would grow.

Mak was a bright kid, however, and he went to a diverse school, which meant his daily experience acted as a counterweight to the ideologies he encountered online. About half of his fellow students were Black, and for a while Mak became hyperaware of these other kids, actively seeking out any behaviour that would fit into his racist narratives. But it just didn't work, because Mak liked many of them. Some were clearly smarter than he was; others were better at playing drums. When they worked together, he learned a lot from them. It became impossible to equate these students whom he respected and admired with the racist caricatures he saw online. In the end, the simple fact of being in daily contact with the people he felt he ought to hate was enough to uproot the ideas that had been planted in his head the year after his mother had died, when he was vulnerable and unable to separate his emotions from the anger of others. As he moved beyond the initial shock of grief, the fog began to clear and questions emerged.

If these ideas and arguments are as good as I think they are, let me go and seek out the other side and see what they have to say, he thought.

He applied his quiet curiosity to a new quest: unpicking each of the theories he had accepted as fact. Mak would check the sources used on the 4chan posts, then cross-check them elsewhere on the Internet. In doing so, he came across websites which debunked far-right conspiracy theories, and then he cross-checked those as well. As he did more fact checking, more cracks started to emerge. The biggest crack of all was in relation to a book by Richard Lynn which argued that race and intelligence were intrinsically linked. When Mak read criticisms of this book, it blew his mind. As he unpicked the methodology and saw how flawed and biased the research was, he was struck by that familiar feeling of privileged knowledge he had harboured before, only now he had followed the path to the genuine truth. When he raised these discrepancies on 4chan, people there insulted him. Now that he was on the outside, Mak could finally see the conspiratorial narratives for what they truly were: a house of cards built with lies, which collapsed the moment one card was removed.

Mak gradually withdrew from the world of white supremacy through the same confused fog by which he had entered it. To onlookers, he was still a brooding and unreachable teen glued to his phone. Yet inside, he was struggling with this process of enlightenment and grappling with doubts and questions as he tried to separate himself from an entire belief system.

In the summer of 2015, Mak graduated from high school. Despite having skipped so many classes, he got decent passing grades, and was once again weighed down by the expectation that he should be mapping out his future when he had no idea what he wanted to do. His anxiety returned and he found himself falling back into his old habit of looking at 4chan, which had been his emotional support at the most testing times. He did not believe the racist and anti-Semitic conspiracies espoused on there any more, but the escapism they provided was addictive.

Maybe I just like feeling angry, he thought.

Mak decided to start an electrical engineering course at community college, hoping to use those skills in the music industry. As he embarked on this new phase in his life, 4chan remained a constant companion, only now the relief it once brought was supplanted by feelings of guilt that he wasn't able to shed that part of his past. When he finally stopped looking at 4chan in 2016, he felt an enormous void in his life. He had never fully addressed his depression or processed the grief over his mother's death, and the dark clouds returned. He transferred his studies to a new university in 2017 but started skipping classes again. Mak would tell his family and friends that he was in school, but then just sit in his car doing nothing all day. He felt overwhelmed, and now he had nowhere to escape to, no avatars of hate to project his own fears and anxieties on to. But he still had his father. Throughout everything, his dad had been there for him. The traumas his father had experienced in Bosnia had left their mark, and he could be undemonstrative and emotionally distant. He was also old-fashioned in his views about mental health, and so Mak had resisted telling him about his struggles and about the extremist beliefs he had held. Mak knew he was loved, however, and eventually he decided to confide in his father. Together, they agreed that Mak would see a therapist. As the therapy progressed, Mak realized that he had been suffering from depression for much of his adolescence, and slowly he began to feel okay about his place in the world and a little bit more positive about what lay ahead. However, his real reckoning was yet to come.

Although Mak's extremism had been intellectually and emotionally all-consuming, it had been confined to the online talk boards where he read and indoctrinated himself in white supremacist narratives. He had never considered acting on the feelings they evoked in him. But others in the same environment would internalize the far-right rhetoric – and then unleash that hatred in the real world, with tragic results.

Throughout the early and mid-2010s, governments were consumed with panic over Islamist extremism. While they directed huge amounts of money into various schemes to try and counter the threat, they overlooked the potential for violent far-right extremism. When the Norwegian far-right terrorist Anders Breivik killed seventy-seven people in Oslo and on Utøya island in 2011, the attack was treated as an anomaly. Newspapers breathlessly reported on every aspect of the attacker, republishing swathes of Breivik's racist manifesto along with photos of him posing in military-style outfits. They had so little experience of covering far-right violence that they did exactly what Breivik wanted them to do: they amplified his message to a broader public.

The horror over the attacks gradually subsided, and people returned to worrying about Islamist violence. But anger was brewing across all sections of society, particularly in Europe and North America. As the economic crisis turned into the refugee crisis and populist and nationalist politicians found easy votes from stoking division, hate crimes against minority groups rose. It was obvious to people working in extremism that more far-right violence was coming, but it was difficult to get that message across to governments that were in thrall to the politically expedient idea that terrorism only came from one demographic. When Donald Trump became the US president in 2017, he instructed the Department of Homeland Security to channel its funding into countering Islamist extremism. More than eighty-five per cent of such grants went to groups focused on Muslim and migrant communities, despite a clear rise in violence from the far right, not just in the USA but around the world. In 2015, in the USA, a white supremacist killed five Black churchgoers in Charleston, South Carolina. The following year in Britain, the Labour member of Parliament Jo Cox – a passionate supporter of refugee rights – was shot dead just before the 2016 vote on Britain leaving the European Union by a man with links to a neo-Nazi group. A few days after Trump's inauguration, a man killed nine people at a mosque in Quebec City, Canada. A wave of anti-Semitism was affecting Jewish communities in Europe, and officials in Belgium, France and Germany advised Jews to stop wearing skullcaps. In the USA, in 2018, a man with anti-Semitic and neo-Nazi views shot dead eleven people at a synagogue in Pittsburgh. Deaths at the hands of far-right extremists had long surpassed deaths caused by Islamist extremists in America, where, in the nine years up until 2017, right-wing extremists carried out nearly twice as many attacks as Islamist extremists. But you wouldn't have known it from listening to the rhetoric from the country's leadership.

Then, on the afternoon of 15 March 2019, a man walked into a mosque in Christchurch, New Zealand. He turned on a video camera, started livestreaming on Facebook, and then opened fire as the worshippers began Friday prayers. He then left, walked to another mosque and opened fire again. In total, fifty-one men and women were killed, in a tragic manifestation of what experts had been warning about for years. The New Zealand security services had been so focused on the potential for Islamist extremism that they had ignored reports from the Muslim community of rising hate crime against their people.

It was late evening in Jacksonville when Mak heard about the Christchurch attacks. He was lying in bed watching television and scrolling through Twitter when he saw the shocking news. Soon his sense of horror had deepened to a more harrowing feeling of intense guilt: the killer had been immersed in the same narratives that had ensnared Mak himself just a few years earlier. The shooter's grievances had been forged on 8chan, a chat board similar in format to 4chan. Mak tracked down the killer's manifesto and found it littered with everything he used to read and believe. Its central concept of the white replacement genocide theory was sickeningly familiar, but what horrified Mak the most was the tone and structure of the manifesto. It was imbued with that same sardonic humour, irony and sarcasm that had so enthralled him in his early days on 4chan. Many of the memes and jokes that Mak had laughed over were now being regurgitated by a mass murderer. He even recognized the list of songs the man had played as he carried out his massacre: one was a Serbian nationalist anthem that had made Mak uncomfortable even when he was fully immersed in his far-right beliefs. By the time Mak finished reading the manifesto, it was close to three in the morning. Tears were streaming down his face.

I believed the same thing as this person who killed fifty-one people, he thought. *Maybe this man was also in the same thread I was in, maybe I said something in this thread that helped incite him, maybe I read the same material that helped incite him.*

The sense of guilt was overwhelming. Mak did not know where to turn. Then he saw a tweet from a young woman Mak knew from school, a Muslim-American girl of Pakistani heritage. Her tweet read: 'Hey, I'm not going to be able to sleep because of the attack that happened. If anyone wants to talk to me, you can send me a message, I'll be up.'

On an impulse, Mak sent her a message. She responded quickly, and the pair chatted well into the morning. Mak had not seen the woman in years but found himself telling her about the white supremacist beliefs he'd held and the guilt he now felt. She responded with empathy and reassured Mak that he was not the same person now.

A few days later, the young woman got back in touch. She was doing an internship at NPR, the US national public radio station. Would he do an interview about his experiences? Mak had never thought about speaking publicly before. His family had always been private about their traumatic personal experiences, and he had inherited that sense of reserve. But now he could feel his ideas shifting and a sense of duty emerging.

Maybe I can do something about this, maybe I can use these experiences that were bad in some sort of good way, he thought. *If not me, then who? If I speak up, maybe I could stop one of these attacks from happening.*

After mulling it over for a few days, Mak felt ready to tell his story. He could see now that he had an important message to share. If a Muslim-American son of migrants could become a white supremacist, it could happen to anyone. In the end, the NPR interview didn't come to pass, but Mak contacted Christian Picciolini, a former neo-Nazi from Chicago who ran a counter-extremism organization called the Free Radicals Project. Mak volunteered to help in any way he could, and soon Christian arranged interviews with a local newspaper and NBC. Taciturn yet analytical, Mak was not suited to quick TV soundbites. But there was an authenticity about him that stood out at a time when many people were proclaiming their credentials as former extremists in the interests of self-promotion and absolution. The public dawning of understanding about the far-right threat heralded the same rush for easy solutions and media-friendly 'experts' that had accompanied the panic over foreign fighters a few years earlier. Suddenly people who months earlier had been at the forefront of the new far-right movements conveniently transformed themselves into deradicalization experts. Two organizers of the Charlottesville rally claimed to have reformed and joined a counter-extremism group, raising questions about the timing, given they were facing lawsuits over the violence. Many other people found that being publicly linked to far-right extremism had similar consequences for their lives and careers, and quickly shifting sides could be an easy fix.

Mak was not one of those people. He had never been doxxed, he had never attended a protest, his face had not appeared on social media and his name had never been linked to any far-right cause. He could have quietly forgotten that period in his life and moved on without consequence. Instead he chose to put himself forward, and with that reckoning came some relief – that he now had a new path to follow and clarity about what to do with his life. Mak transferred to an anthropology course, hoping to gain a deeper understanding of the human motives for a drift towards extremism. Eventually, he wanted to work in the field of counter-extremism and reach other vulnerable people before they fell into the same trap he had.

But the world now was dramatically different to how it had been when he'd fallen into far-right extremism just five years earlier. In that time, the presidency of Donald Trump had emboldened far-right groups and driven a wedge through

American society. Similar divides had cleaved communities in Britain and elsewhere in Europe. Misinformation was swaying elections, and the truth had become an even more ethereal quality, constantly slipping away from the grip of reality. Boards like 4chan where Mak had found solace and humour were no longer just testing grounds for extreme ideas and juvenile pranks – they were places where real groups would organically form, leaderless entities rooted in extreme ideas and tantalizing conspiracy theories. Groups like the Boogaloo Bois, which originated as a meme on 4chan only to morph into an extreme anti-government group whose armed adherents turned up at protests in Hawaiian shirts and black face masks. Then there was QAnon, a shadowy and impenetrable concept first posited on 4chan suggesting that Satan-worshipping Democrats, Hollywood stars and billionaires ran the world while engaging in paedophilia, human trafficking and harvesting of the blood of abused children. Its origins were possibly a joke or a hoax, but within a few years its many-tentacled belief system had infected millions of people in all corners of the world.

Sometimes, Mak would watch the news and feel hopeless. His anxiety would return, and thoughts about the future would overwhelm him. He would dream about running away to a small farm in the countryside and living a simple life where he could pretend everything was fine. And in fact by mid-2019, Mak and his dad had already started living more in tune with the world around them. They built their own house on an acre of land, and planted vines and pomegranate trees. Mak was delighted when they discovered wild onions growing on their plot. This connection to the land gave Mak a sense of peace, a rare feeling in a world that seemed to be getting angrier by the day. His knew now how quickly a person could succumb to dangerous ideas, and he worried about the scale of the lies and disinformation he saw all around him. But in a way Mak himself had been lucky: he had escaped from extremism relatively quickly and with his most significant relationships intact. He had emerged with a clear understanding of what had made him vulnerable to the lure of division and conspiracy, and with a strong desire to speak out. For others – especially those who made the leap from theory to practice – it would be an altogether murkier journey back from the extreme.

Part Four

Redemption

19

Cathrine Moestue

Stockholm, Sweden, 1988 to Oslo, Norway, 2021

When Cathrine Moestue left the courtroom following her exoneration in January 1988, she was a deeply vulnerable and traumatized twenty-two-year-old woman who had been reduced to a child-like dependency on a man who was by then recognized as dangerous and unstable. A psychiatric evaluation carried out soon after her arrest found that Cathrine had been contaminated by another person's paranoia and recommended close care and follow-up. This did not happen. No legal order was put in place to prevent Cornel from contacting Cathrine, nor was she offered any assistance or counselling, or a safe location where she could go after the trial.

In America, in the wake of the disastrous cult deprogramming schemes of the 1970s, a new approach was being pioneered in the late 1980s in which people were guided away from their belief systems in a collaborative and non-confrontational environment. This expertise had yet to make its way to Europe. During Cornel's trial, newspapers in Sweden and Norway had thrown around terms like 'brainwashing' and 'cult', but no one seemed to understand what those words truly meant: not the police, not the lawyers, not the probation service, not Cathrine's parents, and certainly not Cathrine herself. There was only one person who understood the exact nature of Cathrine's mental state at that moment, and that person was the man who had created it: Cornel.

It was Cornel who had told Lise and Sofia to meet Cathrine outside the courtroom. As she followed her friends home, Cathrine remained convinced that she was now the one in possession of knowledge. Soon she would reveal the truth to them and expose Cornel's lies. When they arrived back at the apartment, however, a sense of camaraderie enveloped her, and Cathrine didn't feel it was the right time to bring up Cornel's deceit. She was enjoying the familiarity of being back among people she knew after having been in prison for months. But it did not take long for that good feeling to shatter. That same evening, the phone rang. It was Cornel calling from the mental institution.

'So many children have died because of what you said.'

In an instant, Cathrine disappeared down the rabbit hole again, her mind reclaimed by the man who had abused and manipulated her for the past three years of her life. The police, the lawyers, the prison psychologists and her family had all expected Cathrine to behave rationally following Cornel's arrest: they had expected her to believe the facts they presented to her, as if the simple act of telling her the truth would override anything that had gone before. But that isn't how indoctrination works. The power to be believed is held by the person who can convey their truth with the most conviction and the strongest emotional connection, and that spell cannot simply be broken in a matter of weeks. Cathrine thought she was free when she had read the woman's account of her rape by Cornel and had believed every word. That had indeed created a crack in the reality Cornel had created, presenting an opportunity to guide Cathrine away from her oppressor. But nobody had seized that opportunity, and as soon as Cathrine was back in Cornel's world, his reality was just as powerful as it had been before. It was like a switch had flicked in her head and she reverted to everything she had been previously. But having made it to a place where she was beyond his power and failed to break free, the veil of indoctrination would now prove even more difficult to penetrate.

Cornel served just six months for the rape of the young woman. His psychiatric evaluation concluded that he was mentally unfit for trial and he was sent to a prison for the criminally insane, with no minimum or maximum amount of time to serve specified: it depended on his response to treatment. Apparently, the skills with which he had been able to manipulate three young women also worked on experienced psychiatrists, with a doctor at the institute concluding that Cornel was experiencing a realistic paranoia brought on by society's prejudices. If he were able to reconcile with his wife, the doctor said, he would pose no danger and could be released. Cornel walked free and flew to England. Within days he told his wife he wanted a divorce, and made plans to reunite with Cathrine, Lise and Sofia.

During his six months' confinement, Cornel had also been allowed to make a phone call every day with no one checking who he was calling or what he was saying. So he would call the three women and give them detailed instructions on how to live their lives until his release. He told Cathrine she could stop seeing her probation officer. He had already been coaching her on what to say in those sessions, but the inexperienced young officer didn't seem to notice or be particularly interested in Cathrine's welfare or well-being. When she failed to attend, no one followed up. Another condition for Cornel's release was that he could not return to Sweden, so he ordered Cathrine, Lise and Sofia to pack their bags and leave the only country where the authorities were aware of Cornel's crime and Cathrine's vulnerable situation. Instead of being monitored to make sure she was safe from this predatory man, she was allowed to disappear with him.

And so the three young women began a nomadic life following Cornel across Europe, moving between countries and cities at his command. Lise and Sofia remained in a sexual relationship with Cornel, while Cathrine would take a separate room, continuing her demeaning existence as 'the monk'. They would alternate between spells in Norway, Finland, Germany, Denmark and the Netherlands. The quartet at first survived on the women's student loans and money from their estranged parents, but when that ran out Cathrine took care jobs in hospitals, while Lise and Sofia made money acting and modelling. Cornel never worked, but he came up with a scam in which they would stop attractive women on the streets, then claim to work for a modelling agency and offer to take photographs of them for a fee. It was a long way from Catherine's dream of fighting injustice and changing the world.

'What happened to the starving children?' Cathrine once asked.

'We have each other now,' Cornel replied.

From time to time, he would throw out the old promises of finding her a revolutionary husband and of ensuring her bright future as a teacher and mentor. But it was no longer those promises that kept Cathrine from leaving. It was fear. Cornel had always fuelled Cathrine's paranoia by warning her about the imagined enemies of their revolution, but now he himself was the main source of her fear. He had started directing violence at her, always subtle and humiliating. Out of the blue, he would kick her hard in the shins. Even in the face of this physical abuse, she would remain silent. Sometimes she felt like she was outside her own body, watching perplexed as this young woman took the punishment without a word. She couldn't even cry properly. If she did, Cornel would become enraged.

'Fucking pack that in,' he would shout.

Cathrine was afraid of Cornel's temper; afraid of his increasing violence towards her; afraid of the constant humiliation; afraid of the gulf she now felt between her and her family. Somehow this fear made her cling harder to him. Cornel had convinced her that she was deserving of this constant torment, and no part of her doubted it any more.

Then, the year after Cornel went on trial, Lise gave birth to his son. They were living in Finland at the time, in a nice house on one of the Swedish-speaking islands of Åland. Cornel had been dismissive of hospital births, spinning his conspiracy theories about how people in power wanted to control women through medical interventions during childbirth. So the child was to be delivered at home, he decreed. They would lie to the authorities and say the baby arrived before they had a chance to get to the hospital. Cathrine took her new role as midwife seriously, reading books about natural childbirth by the author Sheila Kitzinger. As the due date approached, they prepared the house sauna for the delivery. When Lise finally went into labour, Cornel sat in the living room and ignored her. It was up to the three young women to bring this new life into the world. Lise was in labour for eight hours. To Cathrine, it was a beautiful eight hours. She was awed by her friend's radiance and strength as she helped her through her contractions. When the baby finally emerged, Lise was standing up. Cathrine thought the child was going to fall on its head, but instinct made Lise swoop down and scoop her son straight into her arms. Cathrine had never experienced such wonder as that moment. She cut the cord, and the three women shared a rush of euphoria at the perfect little boy who had entered the world so peacefully.

After the high of the birth subsided, the household began to adjust to this new life at its centre. Lise called him Jacob and loved him dearly. But Cornel started to use the baby against her, telling her she was a bad mother and taking the child away from her while she was breastfeeding him. He lied to Cathrine, telling her Lise was suffering from post-natal depression, so she would have to comfort and care for Jacob instead. It was another way for Cornel to try and turn the women against one another, but Cathrine was delighted with her new role as Jacob's nanny. She spent increasing amounts of time with this tiny human, developing a bond unlike any other she had known. He may have been born into their claustrophobic circle, but he existed as his own person, a new and pure life. Nurturing this life and protecting its purity gave Cathrine a purpose beyond pleasing Cornel. Now her priority was Jacob, not Cornel. But while the immediate effect of her growing relationship with the baby was to bind Cathrine closer to the group, it also gave her the courage to think about a future in which she might be free. Deep down, she knew that one day she would have to leave in order to keep Jacob safe. And the love she felt for Jacob also made her see that she was capable of having relationships outside the small world Cornel had created. Although it would take a while for these feelings to blossom into actions, the cracks had been created into which light and kindness would one day be able to penetrate.

In the summer of 1992, a few years after the birth of Jacob, Cathrine and Cornel visited the town of Aarhus in Denmark while Lise and Sofia were away with Jacob in Sweden. One afternoon, Cathrine went to a fruit and vegetable shop. Behind the counter was a young man named Haissam, who had arrived in the country from Lebanon in 1982 when he was ten years old. Haissam's family were Palestinian refugees who had been living in the Shatila camp in West Beirut. The Red Cross evacuated them three days before a Lebanese Christian militia laid waste to the Sabra and Shatila refugee camps in a massacre that claimed at least 800 lives. Haissam and his family were resettled in Denmark and set about building a life in Aarhus. Haissam learned Danish and ended up at university, where he studied engineering, while also helping out in the fruit and vegetable shop of a family friend when he could. Haissam felt immediately drawn to Cathrine. She looked thin and her blonde hair hung limply around her face, but there was something about her – a kindness in her eyes

– that caught his attention and they exchanged smiles. The next time she came in, he summoned up his courage.

'I would like to have coffee with you,' he said.

The girl looked shocked and a little scared.

Why is she so worried? Haissam wondered.

'Yes, I'd love to have a coffee, but I can't,' she replied.

'Why?' asked Haissam.

The young woman didn't answer, and quickly left the shop.

The next day, she returned. She seemed to have a new confidence as she walked up to the counter.

'I would like to have coffee, but we have to do it here in the shop,' she declared.

Haissam told her to come back at five.

For Cathrine, it was the most significant independent action she had taken in four years. There was something about Haissam that just made her trust him. In the hours before she returned to the shop, her whole body felt alive with adrenaline and fear, as she hoped that the huge mobile phone Cornel had given her did not ring. At 5 p.m., Cathrine went to the shop and Haissam took her to a room behind the counter. She didn't know what to expect, but within a few minutes they were kissing. It didn't feel like a betrayal. It felt like a liberation. Then Haissam noticed some blue marks around her shoulders – bruises made by Cornel.

'Has somebody hit you?' he asked.

'Yes,' Cathrine said quietly.

Haissam looked at her with genuine concern.

'Why don't you marry me?'

It was an impulsive suggestion given that the pair had only just met, and it was more of a romantic gesture than a genuine proposal. But Cathrine had so little experience of the world outside the reality Cornel had created that she had lost her ability to judge the nuances. She took Haissam at his word and was moved by the unexpected kindness of his gesture, something she didn't know she was craving so fiercely until it was offered.

He made her feel safe. At twenty-seven, she was seven years older than Haissam, but emotionally she was like a child. Haissam gave her his telephone number and made her promise to call him if she needed any help. Cathrine only stayed for about half an hour, but in that short time her world had shifted.

Cornel will know what I've been doing, she thought. *He sees everything. I am dead.*

But when she returned to their apartment, he was oblivious.

I can do things he doesn't see, she thought with relief.

The next day, Cathrine and Cornel went back to Copenhagen to reunite with Lise, Sofia and Jacob, but Cathrine's exhilaration at her small rebellion lingered. The morning after their return, she decided she would carry out another independent act. It was nothing dramatic: their mobile telephone had become too expensive to keep using, so Cornel said they were going to return it to the shop.

I can do that by myself, Cathrine thought, and she set out with the phone while Cornel was still asleep. But she had forgotten that it was Sunday, and when she got there the mobile phone shop was closed, so she returned to the apartment. When she opened the door, Cornel was standing there, a look of fury on his face.

'Where have you been?' he demanded.

Cathrine tried to explain, but he seemed not to hear her. Instead he started shouting and waving his arms around. Then she noticed that he had a knife.

I am going to die, she thought.

Before she knew what had happened, she was lying on the floor, her legs kicked out from underneath her. Cornel was sitting on top of her and pinning her down with the weight of his body. The large hunting knife was pressed right up against Cathrine's eyeball. Cornel was screaming and ranting about how she was about to die, and how nobody would miss her. His furious speech seemed to last forever, as it wove into familiar territory about her evil parents, her insignificance, her egotism.

'Before you die, I'm going to cut your eyes out,' he screamed.

He pressed the knife harder against Cathrine's face, breaking the skin.

'Open your fucking eyes!'

So this is what dying feels like, she thought.

It wasn't how she had imagined it would feel. As she lay under the weight of this man who had moulded her and tormented her for eight years, she felt like she was playing the lead role in an American horror film. She was terrified beyond anything she had ever experienced, yet she also felt detached from what was happening around her. She tried to keep her eyes closed as Cornel's voice pounded in her ear. Her mind raced through her life with him. She could see herself in the car while he raped a woman nearby; she could see herself at her trial; she could see the evil that Cornel had done to her and others. It was like a red thread weaving through her life over the past eight years, connecting all the moments when she had been lied to, manipulated, terrorized. As all these memories came rushing in, they brought with them an amazing feeling of clarity. Finally, Cathrine had the truth she had been seeking for so long. In this moment when she was so close to death, her own mind finally unravelled all the lies, and she felt free. This was her liberation.

Then Cornel got up.

'You have to stop scaring me in this way,' he said matter-of-factly, and walked off.

Cathrine lay on the floor. She was alive. But everything had changed. She now saw Cornel for what he truly was. That act of extreme violence had broken the psychological spell he had cast, and for the rest of the day her brain was functioning on another level, planning all the tiny details by which she would escape. When they went out later that day, Cathrine snuck into a telephone box and called Haissam.

'I'm coming tomorrow,' she said.

That night, Cathrine could not sleep. She stared at the ceiling, replaying her plan in her head. She was in survival mode, finally letting instinct take over her mind and body. The face of Jacob floated before her too.

One day, he will come looking for me, and I need to be ready to protect him, she thought.

When the sun rose, Cathrine started putting her plan into action. She could not risk waking Cornel, so she moved slowly and with painstaking care. She had to get the bag with all their cash. Each footstep felt laborious, like walking through syrup, and she winced with each creak of the old Danish floorboards. To focus her mind, she kept looking at the big wooden front door, until finally, her heart beating in her ears, she touched the handle. When it opened, it seemed unreal: freedom. Cathrine closed the door behind her and walked down the stairs. When she reached the street, she started running. Suddenly she remembered: the soldiers of the revolution!

Are they here? she thought. *Will they see me?*

Although she had unpicked many of the lies Cornel had told her, others remained and would do for many years to come. Paranoia was her constant companion as she made her way to Copenhagen Central Station and bought her ticket to Aarhus. When she got off the train, she was confused. No one was there to meet her. But then she remembered that she hadn't told Haissam when she was coming or where she would arrive, so of course he was not there. Then fear took over again: people were coming up the escalators.

Are they here to kill me? Cathrine wondered.

She managed to hold herself together sufficiently to find a telephone. She called the number Haissam had given her for his student lodgings. Someone answered. Haissam was at the shop, the person said, but she was welcome to come to the dorms and wait for him there. Cathrine noted down the address and paid for a taxi with the money she had taken. When she got to the dorms, she sat and waited for Haissam, paralyzed by a mixture of fear, bewilderment, excitement and relief. He arrived about an hour later. He had bought some food, cigarettes and beer. He took Cathrine into the communal garden. The weather was beautiful. It was a perfect summer day – 5 July 1992. They sat on a bench drinking Tuborg Green beers and smoking cigarettes. Cathrine had hardly drunk any alcohol or smoked a cigarette in years. Both tasted of freedom. The Guns N' Roses song 'November Rain' played on the stereo. She had never felt as safe as she did sitting in that garden with Haissam.

Cornel will not find me here, she thought. *I have made it.*

Cathrine's future would hold many more challenges. There would be a wedding to Haissam; a divorce; a lifetime trying to make sense of her past. But for now, there were just the cans of Tuborg Green, the cigarettes, the hot July sun and the sound of 'November Rain'.

Cathrine lived quietly with her story for twenty years, trying to process everything that had happened. It was a tough journey. No matter how many years passed, she could never fully shake the feeling that Cornel's spies could be lurking in the bushes, and that any happiness was transient and could be taken away from her. Cornel's lies were ingrained in her, but at least she knew now what they were, and she could live with that. There were joys too: a few years after leaving Cornel, she spotted Lise at a swimming pool in Oslo. She had escaped from Cornel as well, and Cathrine would be reunited with Jacob. Once again they became like family, and together helped each other heal.

Cathrine embarked on a career in psychology, determined to help others while also trying to unravel the process by which she lost herself all those years ago. She had never denied her past – friends and family knew parts of her story – but she had never wanted to put the whole jigsaw together. There was too much pain; there was too much shame. For years feelings of guilt consumed her, and she longed to be able to put right all the hurt she had caused, but she was torn between understanding that she had been a victim herself, and feeling the urge to take responsibility for her actions and forge something positive and lasting from her experiences – to obtain some sort of absolution.

Then, in 2013, she read about two Norwegian sisters who had travelled to Syria to live in the Islamic State. Suddenly, she could once again see the red thread that all those years ago had revealed the truth of her life with Cornel. Now this red thread was weaving her story in with the story of these two girls. When Cathrine read the letter they had written to their parents explaining their decision, it took her breath away: exactly the same words could have come out of her own mouth nearly three decades earlier when she told her mother she was leaving the family home. The recruitment process, the appeal to teenage vulnerabilities, the promise of a role in a revolution to bring about a better world: the parallels were striking. But everything she read about the girls focused on their religion. There was nothing about the emotional connection or the commonalities that transcended the ideology. Cathrine realized then that to make people understand, she had to tell her whole story. Because now it was not just the story of one young woman and one manipulative individual: it was the story of so many other people in the world today too.

20

Shayne Hunter and Toby Cook

Sydney, Australia, 2015 to Ontario, Canada, 2020

By the time Toby Cook was nineteen, he'd been active in the Australian far-right movement for two years, drifting ever further to its most extreme fringes. He slept under a swastika flag, wore T-shirts emblazoned with Nazi slogans, and would happily do Heil Hitler salutes for the camera while knocking back bottles of Little Fat Lamb eight-per-cent-proof cider. He read neo-Nazi propaganda all day, as he and his friends would ping racist memes and videos to one another on Facebook.

As his views became more extreme, Toby drifted away from his old friend Nick Folkes and found himself hanging out with people more obviously on the outskirts of Sydney society. His friends on the extreme fringes of the far right were drug addicts and alcoholics; people who struggled to find regular work; lonely souls – an assortment of people who had a hard time with everyday life and sought refuge in the false promises of divisive ideologies. In the waning years of his own adolescence, Toby spent much of his time drunk or on drugs. He had spells in mental institutions, where he was detained against his will and treated for bipolar disorder and depression. Then there were the court dates for crimes ranging from criminal damage to firearms possession and assault. Much of that brawling was gang related, but his real vitriol was reserved for left-wing activists. Sometimes he would lie in bed for hours and wish they were all dead, the anger seething through his body. When the chance came to let out that rage, he would launch violent attacks on his political foes with no thought for the consequences for himself or his victims, and then he would be back under arrest. There were so many court dates that standing trial became like any other chore. He never went to prison, getting off with cautions, suspended sentences or transfers to mental health facilities. But nothing tempered his extreme views. He would leave court or check out of the hospital with more pills, and head straight back to his gang of white supremacist friends. The only disillusionment Toby felt was with the authenticity of some of his comrades. There was a lot of drinking, partying and casual violence, but he was aware that little actual work was ever done on overthrowing democracy and establishing neo-Nazi rule, and he was beginning to feel jaded and burned out. Rather than making him question the ideology, however, these feelings merely pushed him in even deeper, convincing him that he was the only one capable of changing the world.

In early 2018, Toby became entranced by videos coming out of Ukraine showing highly disciplined soldiers fighting for a cause. They were members of a Ukrainian paramilitary unit called the Azov Battalion, a nationalist militia with openly neo-Nazi ideology which had been luring recruits from overseas with the same promise of adventure and purpose made by groups as disparate as the South African AWB and the Islamic State. The Azov Battalion was notionally battling against Russian incursions into Ukraine, but had become legendary in far-right circles as the only well-armed and well-organized white nationalist group training foreign fighters. The first overseas recruits started showing up in around 2014, and extremism monitors claimed that eventually as many as 2,000 fighters would join from all over the world. That figure would prove difficult to verify, being clouded by the same confusing swirl of conspiracies, disinformation and government cluelessness that had formed around the flight of Islamist radicals to Syria. But as a propaganda tool, the Azov Battalion had acquired a mythical reputation. The New Zealand mosque shooter had worn a symbol used by the Azov Battalion on his clothing. A former US soldier jailed for planning a terrorist attack in the USA had also aspired to join its ranks. Then Toby began talking to people online who claimed to have travelled to Ukraine, and he became excited by the idea of leaving his increasingly chaotic life in Australia behind and finally fighting for a tangible cause.

I want to commit to this permanently, Toby decided. *I want to fight and die for my beliefs.*

But Toby was not going anywhere. In mid-2018, Australian intelligence officers confiscated his passport. Toby figured they had been monitoring his communications and had got wind of his plan to go to Ukraine. Instead of heading out to the wilds of central Europe, Toby was enrolled in the Australian government's deradicalization scheme. This was a surprisingly late intervention in the life of a young man who had already been involved in extreme movements for three years and who had been on the radar of the authorities and mental health services for some time.

The aim of the programme was to find Toby some friends outside the movement and help him get a job, but it all seemed rather casual to Toby. Over six months in 2018, two social workers came to his house every few weeks and asked him how he was doing. That was it. He didn't give the process much credence, but the intervention coincided with the questions that kept recurring in his own head about what exactly he and his group of misfit friends were achieving. Whenever his motley gang of drunk or hungover white nationalists tried to accomplish the simplest political goals – like printing some signs for an anti-Islam protest – their plans always seemed to descend into farce.

You talk about a revolution, you talk about all this shit, you can't even get a banner printed, he thought.

So Toby decided to start exploring life beyond the fringes.

He had not suddenly seen the error of his hateful and violent ways – the anger was still there. It was more that he now sensed the futile nature of the far-right movement, and he wanted something more. He enrolled in a psychology course, hoping it would help with his ennui. He found it hard going, but simply being around normal people was a revelation. For three years, Toby had been cocooned in the far-right world, the only community he had ever felt part of, and he had lost a sense that there was life outside that narrow world. Now, he saw other people his own age – often from similar socio-economic backgrounds – who were not consumed by rage and who were optimistic about the future. Many of them were also from different ethnic backgrounds. The more time he spent with people from outside the movement, the more he started to feel he had things in common with them. He began to see the person, the individual, rather than a racist caricature. He became friendly with a young Muslim woman on his course who had had some problems with Australian intelligence herself when she veered too closely towards Islamist extremism. They shared a camaraderie about their brushes with the law. He didn't give up all his friends in the neo-Nazi movement, but he did start spending less time with them. As the months passed, he began to realize that normalcy was an option for him.

I can have a decent life outside the movement, Toby thought.

It was such a freeing thought that for a few months, Toby was overwhelmed by elation at all the opportunities opening up for him. His partying continued, but now it was in the form of raves with childhood friends. But this drug-fuelled euphoria at rediscovering the Toby he once was couldn't last. With the highs came the inevitable lows, as his mind tried to come to grips with everything he was leaving behind. The far-right movement had been like a family to him, his saviour at the very darkest moment when he had tried to end his own life. In some ways, throwing in his lot with the far right had been an easy option: he didn't have to think about his past or future; he didn't have to weigh up what was right and what was wrong, what was true and what was not. But what was he without those beliefs? Toby had been a neo-Nazi since he was seventeen years old. He had no idea how else to live.

This has been my life's mission, this has been my life's work, this was my sole purpose for existing, he thought. *What do I do? What do I have to fill that?*

The answer at first was more drinking, more drugs, more partying. Then he remembered his nemesis Shayne Hunter on the far left. Perhaps he could help. Toby sat down and composed a message:

'How the fuck do I adapt to regular life?'

Shayne Hunter had always had a unique approach to his political foes. Unlike Toby, he didn't want to inflict violence upon those who did not share his beliefs. He was more inclined to view them as idiots. Sometimes, he would even grudgingly admit to some common ground between himself and his adversaries on the far right, like the time he was disrupting one of their demos and realized they were both shouting similar anti-globalization slogans at each other. Once, after showing up outside the court to picket the trial of some white nationalists, Shayne invited them to have a beer with him. They declined, but the seed of the idea that discourse may be better than shouting 'Nazi!' and 'Fascist!' at each other had been planted in Shayne's mind.

While Shayne's approach was non-violent, other Antifa activists around the world seemed much more comfortable with the idea of causing harm. The election of Donald Trump as US president had galvanized many on the far left, and his inauguration in January 2017 brought groups of black-masked protesters to Washington DC, where they smashed windows and set cars ablaze. The Antifa position was hardening, and in the coming years clashes between the far left and far right would become increasingly heated. Throughout the Trump presidency, the amount of serious violence by far-left activists in America would remain small compared with the amount of blood shed in the name of far-right ideologies. There were no mass shootings by activists linked to Antifa. But their actions had far-reaching political ramifications. President Trump amplified them and fuelled the illusion that the disruptive actions of a few were somehow reflective of all people who held more left-leaning or socially progressive beliefs. Far-right media outlets also gave their conservative audience the misleading impression that a huge, violent and extreme left movement was threatening the safety and security of America. Meanwhile, the more established and liberal media fell into a different trap. Whereas once many mainstream media outlets had been so focused on Islamist terror that they overlooked a growing far-right threat, in the waning years of the Trump presidency there would be a downplaying of violence by the far left, even as it became clear that many people in that sphere now felt violence was justified to achieve their political goals.

By the time Antifa had become Donald Trump's favourite catch-all bogeyman, Shayne had already begun his retreat from the movement. There had been no eureka moment – more a series of incongruities that exposed flaws in the beliefs he had previously held so fervently. Like Toby with the neo-Nazis, he had become exasperated at the disorder of the movement. He had been lured over to the anarchist fringes by the promise of a role in building a rule-free utopia in which humans threw off the chains of structure that shackled them and entered a new era of universal freedom and equality. Many of his comrades, however, seemed incapable of carrying out basic admin tasks, let alone of changing the world. And so much time was consumed by petty internal battles. There was always one member ganging up on another and – given that they didn't believe in due process or hierarchy – disagreements would descend into cantankerous arguments in which accusations of racism, sexism, transphobia or some other transgression would fly. Eventually the mood would settle, and an individual would be booted out on the collective will of the group rather than on the basis of any verifiable evidence. Shayne had always been interested in fighting injustice, but that didn't feel very just.

It's either self-flagellation or scapegoating, Shayne thought. *There is nothing in this ideology that has anything to do with forgiveness.*

The casual attitude of some group members towards violence also shocked him, as did the reaction whenever he questioned decisions or plans. There seemed to be no space for any dissent.

In 2016, Shayne had also moved, leaving Sydney and heading home to Brisbane to live with his parents to try to save some money. Now that he was no longer completely cocooned in the Antifa and anarchist community, he gradually found himself drifting away.

Early in 2017, Shayne decided to cut all ties with the far left. It was a big leap. He was twenty-nine years old and had been unemployed for three years and living in squats. Luckily for him, stand-up comedy was not the sort of job where a three-year gap in your resumé caused problems, and soon he was on the circuit again and looking at ways to incorporate his years with the far left into his routine. But he didn't give himself much time to truly reflect on those experiences; instead, he launched a full-throttle attack on his old friends, incensed at what he saw as four wasted years.

It's like I was in a zombie movie, he thought. *I threw away the important years of my youth championing this ideology.*

A few months after leaving the far left, Shayne collaborated with a journalist on an opinion piece for an Australian news website in which he claimed that Antifa was more dangerous than ISIS. Shayne wanted revenge, and a naivety permeated the piece, which was picked up and ridiculed by other media outlets. Shayne was furious with himself – he had spoken to the journalist for just half an hour, and then had not bothered to read the piece before its publication. He could see that the article did not get his views across in the best way, but he was still upset by the negative reaction. Seasoned commentators seemed unable to grasp the fact that violence on the left was increasing and that it did indeed pose a danger to society. The blinkers were on again, and Shayne was worried about the increasing polarization he saw all around him.

For the next few years, Shayne focused on re-establishing himself on the comedy circuit, but the feeling of guilt and shame about his past haunted him, and he wondered how he could make amends. He enrolled on a psychology course, hoping to gain a deeper understanding of his experiences. He learned about concepts like cognitive dissonance, cognitive biases, tribalism, confirmation bias – all psychological theories that helped explain why human brains are susceptible to extreme narratives. He was particularly fascinated by the backfire effect, which showed how the mind worked when its most intrinsic belief systems were aggressively challenged. A psychological defence mechanism made the challenged individual become more entrenched in their views, and more actively seek out information which confirmed those views. Shayne's psychology studies cemented his concern about the limitations and dangers of Antifa, as what he was learning suggested that screaming at or demonizing people with different political views only prompted them to become more entrenched in those views.

You are creating the very monster that you are trying to destroy, he thought.

Shayne wondered if he could apply what he was learning and try to approach people from the far right in a more compassionate way, using his humour and sociability to forge a connection. He made a video speaking about his experiences and was encouraged when some far-right figures got in touch. But after a few Skype chats with them, he concluded that they were more interested in using his experiences to further their own cause. Then, in mid-2018, the message from Toby arrived.

Shayne was not entirely surprised to hear from Toby. After he left Antifa, he had a few communications from his old foe, who just seemed to want to vent his hatred about the far left. Shayne had been careful to engage with Toby on the fallacy of all extreme ideologies, whether left or right, and hoped his non-judgemental approach would have some impact. When Toby contacted him to tell him he had left the far-right movement, Shayne was delighted and replied immediately, sympathizing with Toby's struggle to cope outside the group and sharing stories about his own difficult experience acclimatizing to normal life. But it quickly became clear that a challenging transition was not all they had in common. Both had left their respective groups in part because of the ineptitude of their fellow revolutionaries, and both were now studying psychology. The more they chatted, the more parallels emerged, linked not just to their exit from extremism but also to what had lured them into those narratives in the first place: their mistrust of mainstream media; the feeling of power and superiority they had from being in the group; the sense of shared purpose. Now, Shayne hoped, this connection between them could help others escape from their darkest places too. Shayne set up some podcasts with Toby, reasoning that having them both on the same platform would inspire others on opposite sides of the political spectrum to focus on their own commonalities rather than on their differences. And in 2018, there were still political differences between Toby and Shayne. It was still early days out of the movement for Toby, and certain far-right beliefs lingered, along with a general sense of disorder about his life. He was hungover for most of the podcasts and did not seem reflective about the hurt he had caused others with his virulent Islamophobic and anti-migrant speeches and protests. He still used some derogatory terminology for people from ethnic minorities and spoke with nostalgia about his old friends in the far right. When he condemned the movement, it was on the grounds of its uselessness rather than because of any intrinsic errors in its aims or on account of its hateful and divisive rhetoric. Shayne didn't judge, however. He just tried to listen to Toby and let him speak. He worried about the quantity of drugs his friend was taking and the state of his mental health but figured the best thing he could do was just be there for him. Toby was still only twenty-one. He had a lot more work to do in coming to terms with his past, but he had taken the most important step: he had left the movement.

You can't believe in your own redemption if you don't believe in redemption for someone like Toby, Shayne told himself.

Besides, Shayne knew life had a way of throwing you curveballs, and he had a feeling that Toby was in the right frame of mind to seize any opportunities that came his way.

In late 2018, Toby was scrolling through Facebook. It was 9 a.m. and he was still high on amphetamines from a binge the night before. A woman popped up in his friend suggestions. He couldn't figure out who they had in common, but she looked pretty, so Toby pinged over a friend request. She replied, and soon they were chatting on Messenger. They felt an immediate connection, but it could not have been a more unlikely one. While Toby was enjoying the heat of the Australian summer, this girl was nearly 15,000 kilometres away in a snowy Canadian winter. She was also from one of Canada's indigenous groups. A year earlier, Toby would never have instigated a conversation with somebody from a different ethnic group. Now, however, the fact that she had a darker complexion had not even entered his mind. As the months passed, their interactions became the highlight of his days. He had not clicked like this with any girl before, and he knew he had to find a way to create something tangible from this long-distance online relationship. A few months into their correspondence, Toby made an impulsive decision. He booked a ticket to go and visit her. He felt nervous as he took the circuitous route from Sydney to the small town in Ontario where she lived, and jet-lagged when he arrived in Canada, but the girl was waiting for him at the airport, and they quickly settled into the same easy relationship they had online. When Toby returned home to Sydney, he knew he would be going back to Canada soon, and in June 2019, Toby moved permanently to Ontario. It was a fresh start, but he still came with baggage. Toby had always been open about his neo-Nazi past with his new girlfriend and had been struck by her willingness to see the best in him. Some of her friends were less accepting, however. He had already experienced a culture clash: the first time he went to meet his girlfriend's friends, he crunched up some Ritalin ahead of time and snorted it, thinking it was going to be that sort of party. When he arrived, however, everyone was sitting around drinking wine and playing Monopoly. Then they uncovered some of his hateful speeches on YouTube and became confrontational. Toby understood that they wanted to protect their friend, but he was infuriated not to be given a chance to explain himself. They claimed to be liberal, but Toby saw a hypocrisy in their actions and wondered if they would have been quite so unforgiving with someone from a different strain of extremism.

If I had been to Syria and come back, they would have been falling over backwards to make me feel included, he thought.

In the face of such hostility, the old, combative Toby resurfaced. Whenever he was challenged and not given a chance to explain himself, he would get aggressive, drinking more and provoking arguments. In the end it seemed better not to see them at all, and Toby felt bad that his girlfriend was alienated from her friends because of him. Within a few months of arriving in Canada, however, there was some unexpected news: Toby was going to be a father. He was still so young, and the news made him reflect on his own childhood and how his absent and troubled father had had such a negative effect on him. He saw his own past in a new light and desperately wanted his child to have a good male role model. This was one of those curveball opportunities to make a definitive change.

Many people emerging from divisive ideologies are driven to seek redemption through work which serves the greater good of society or to use their experience to help others leave extreme groups. Some former extremists become vocal opponents of the ideologies that entrapped them. But Toby, scarred by a difficult childhood and coping with serious mental health problems, struggled to process his feelings of remorse or channel them into any social project. He thought his best chance lay with the people most dear to him.

The best thing I can do to make amends is to make sure there is someone who does not turn out like me, to make sure my child does not turn out like me, he thought.

He clung to the positives in his life and tried to build on them. He reached out to a deradicalization expert in Canada, seeking guidance on moving forward. He found a job working in a cannabis dispensary and took his new role as provider and protector very seriously. At times Toby still felt overwhelmed by everything he had been through and everything that lay ahead of him, but at least there were people willing to give him another chance: people like his girlfriend and her family, and his friend Shayne Hunter, who he remained in regular contact with.

In the spring of 2020, Toby became a father to a baby boy. He looked down at the tiny new life and knew that change was possible. There in his arms, he held the possibility of his own redemption.

21

Peter Cytanovic

London, England, 2018–19

England was predictably grey and damp the day Peter Cytanovic landed at Gatwick Airport in late September 2018. He didn't care about the dismal weather. If anything, it added to the frisson.

Yup, this is England, he thought as he made his way into London, watching the rain make its diagonal progress across the train windows, and feeling pleased at how closely reality so far matched his expectations gleaned from magazines and movies.

He had never been to Britain before, and now here he was, a graduate student about to embark on a master's course at the London School of Economics. It was a clean slate. Back home, he was the face of white supremacy. But here in London, he was just another foreign student among many looking to learn and grow. There would be none of the loaded preconceptions about working-class rural American kids that had bedevilled his early days at college in Reno.

I'm going to put everything behind me, he thought.

At first, London was all Peter hoped it would be. He was housed in student accommodation with two young women and quickly settled into the rigorous academic pace of his postgraduate course in political theory. Sure, it was costing him a lot. He had a partial scholarship and some savings from weekend jobs, but most of his year in London was being paid for with student loans. Peter knew it was worth it. It was intellectually exhilarating, and he was delighted by the diversity of debate and political thought among the student body, which seemed much more expansive than in the USA. He quickly made himself at home in the university library, where he intended to interrogate his own ideologies and expand his thinking. Feminist theory, socialism, Marxism, social justice: he read it all. He remained in frequent contact with Hawah, who was spending a semester in Iceland, so was roughly on the same time zone.

Peter still felt constantly on guard, however, as a steady stream of hate mail from back in America continued to clog his inboxes. The photograph of his enraged face at the Charlottesville protests seemed to be everywhere, a handy way to illustrate any article or tweet about the far right. Peter figured it was only a matter of time before his fellow students saw it, so he decided to pre-empt any surprises. He sat down with his two roommates and explained the events leading up to Charlottesville. He spoke for two hours, trying to convey the complexities of the feelings that had led him to attend the protest, and to emphasize how he wanted to start afresh in London. He was as honest as he could be, explaining that he still wanted to be able to talk about immigration and white culture in America, but he regretted taking part in the rally and was looking to make things right. The women seemed to take it well. There were a few questions about what he believed now, and then they slipped back into regular conversation.

Awesome, I've nipped it in the bud, Peter thought.

The next few days however, Peter sensed that something was amiss. His dorm seemed unusually quiet. He was so distracted with his studies that it took him a few days to realize that his roommates had moved out. The LSE authorities confirmed his suspicions. One woman had packed her things and left the next day. The other woman had taken a few more days to find alternative lodgings, and then she had disappeared too. Peter was left alone and upset in a small flat with two empty beds. Why had they seemed so understanding if they were in fact so horrified at his past? Why didn't they talk to him about their feelings and ask him more questions? Peter felt suddenly unmoored from his new London life, and that feeling of dislocation was about to be amplified. Within a few days of the women moving out, stories about the face of the neo-Nazi rally attending LSE started to appear, first in the student newspaper and then in the national press. A petition to expel Peter circulated. Just like his senior year in Reno, Peter was now the most infamous person on campus. Students staged a protest on campus with signs reading 'No hate at LSE' and 'LSE protects racists'. Once again someone flung tampons at him in one of the halls.

While he was attending university in Reno, Peter had been somewhat hardened to the abuse, still hiding behind the armour of a cause. Now, at this moment when he was trying to change, it felt devastating. He put out a statement saying he regretted attending the Charlottesville protest, but it made no difference, and he retreated into himself once again.

Most people want me dead at the LSE, so I don't want to talk, he thought.

This time he wasn't alone, however. There was Hawah, who was there for him at the other end of the phone day or night. And there was the college, which stood up for Peter's right to be there. LSE issued a statement defending its position, although it was not clear if it had been aware of Peter's background when it had accepted his application. Peter once again also found solace in religion, spending increasing amounts of time at a beautiful church in Kensington. With these pillars propping him up, he tried to stay positive and continue with his internal reckoning.

Within months, another opportunity arose. The LSE Faith Centre ran an annual trip to Israel and the Palestinian territories for a handful of students from different religious backgrounds. The trip aimed to help students understand the complexities of conflict and the importance of inclusivity in peace building. Peter decided to apply, even though he knew that, with his reputation, it was a long shot.

The application landed on the desk of Dr James Walters, the founding director of the Faith Centre. He knew exactly who Peter was but nevertheless read the letter with interest. Peter made a strong case to join the trip, and Walters invited him for an interview. While Peter had avoided mentioning his white nationalist past on his application, it came up immediately at the interview. Peter told Walters exactly what he had told his roommates: he was deeply sorry for going to the protest and was trying to figure out how to move forward in a more positive way in his life while remaining true to his religious faith.

'I believe you,' Walters told Peter.

Peter was going to the Holy Land. His presence on a trip to Israel was always going to be controversial. Peter strenuously claimed not to be anti-Semitic himself, but his willingness to stand shoulder to shoulder with anti-Semites and neo-Nazis that day at the protest was incontestable. Still, Walters was willing to give him a chance. One of the points of the trip was to bring students from different faith groups into contact with one another and challenge any preconceptions they held. Walters believed that universities should make people question their world view, rather than reinforcing it. During their time in Israel and Palestine, the students would learn that conflict was not a simple story of the good guys versus the bad guys. It was about conflicting visions of what is good. In his many years working in inter-faith relations, Walters had found that the most effective way to get people to recognize their shared humanity was to get them in the same physical space with each other. Online, people were reduced to a one-dimensional caricature of their worst moments, and any depth of experience was lost. Walters also believed that people should be given the chance to say they were sorry. He would look at the world around him and wonder where the idea of redemption had gone. He saw a lot of righteous anger, but the space for someone to apologize and repent seemed to be shrinking by the day.

Peter left for Israel just before Christmas 2018. At the start of the trip, he felt like he was walking on eggshells. He knew that some of the other students had lobbied to have him removed from the trip, and he felt like every word he uttered would be analyzed for signs of lingering white nationalist views. Peter would oscillate between sympathy and understanding of their wariness and resentment that he was being prejudged. As the days went by, he began cautiously interacting with the other students. He chatted to the Muslim students, who seemed most open to giving him a chance. The Jewish students were understandably wary. When they visited a Holocaust memorial, he felt their eyes upon him, expecting some sort of epiphany. He nervously shuffled around, struggling to take anything in given the immense pressure he was feeling. After the visit, one young man kept asking him question after question about his views, trying to see what effect the memorial had had on him. Peter did his best to be patient and answer the questions, and as the days went by, relations began to thaw. On the last night of the trip, a young Jewish woman who had been deeply sceptical about his presence on it asked to speak to him. They talked for three hours. Peter told her as much as he could about how his beliefs had changed from the day he had attended the Charlottesville protest, and about his efforts to find a better path. He felt like his words reached her.

Peter returned home to Reno for Christmas, and then headed back to London for the 2019 term, feeling invigorated by the trip to Israel. As the months passed, he fell into an easier relationship at the university. Sure, there were still those who looked at him in the hallways as if he were little more than an animal. But slowly he started to make friends with people from his church and with students on his course. Many of these new friends were from different ethnic backgrounds, and from across the religious and political spectrum. Peter got caught up in the energy and creativity of the diverse multicultural city he was living in, and at times he felt like any other foreign student, far away from the increasingly noisy and divisive US politics. He vowed to avoid personal politics and did not vote in the 2018 US midterm elections. If anyone asked him about Donald Trump's presidency, he would tell them he was too far away to worry about it.

Peter was also beginning to realize that merely being sorry for attending the Charlottesville rally was not enough: he needed to find a practical way to make amends. He thought that his first-hand understanding of the frustrations that could lead people down the path of far-right extremism could be helpful to any debate on that subject, but he wasn't sure how to make such a debate happen. He sent out CVs and letters to all sorts of organizations in a quest for internships or voluntary work that could help him make sense of his past. Hardly anyone replied. A brief Google search of Peter's name was probably all it took for any prospective employer to make a decision.

And Peter did not always help himself. While he had gained more empathy and insight into other people's experiences and understood why white nationalism was racist, he still could be insensitive to people's feelings. He was born and grew up in a socially conservative and religious community and was deeply wedded to his Catholic beliefs. More than two decades of lived experience forged Peter's world view and personality. But Peter sensed that many people in college didn't want him just to condemn neo-Nazi ideas – which he was ready to do – they also seemed to demand that he undergo a complete reversal of who he was and embrace a liberal and left-leaning world view. He could not do that. His conservative beliefs were particularly stringent: he did not believe in sex before marriage, pornography, abortion or same-sex marriage. He also still worried that white working-class Americans were being demonized and sidelined, and his views on migration and demographic change could still veer towards the alt-right. He had a live-and-let-live attitude, but he had no intention of staying silent on the issues that mattered to him.

I want to help without losing what I think is right still, and what makes me me, he thought.

Peter was not always adept at explaining the intricacies of his beliefs. In the spring of 2019, he agreed to give an interview to the *Beaver*, the LSE student newspaper. The interview started well, as Peter talked about his desire to use his experiences to help others understand how the frustrations of the white working class can lead some to embrace extreme viewpoints. He was then challenged on his reasons for going to the Charlottesville protests, and his defences went up. He spoke about the Confederate statues and his continued belief that they should stay, leading the interviewer down a path that focused on the Confederate legacy, rather than on the shifts in Peter's white supremacist world view. Peter felt like the journalist was equating his strong sense of American nationalism and his social conservatism with far-right extremism, and he became agitated. His answers veered off from the topic, and he ended the interview by making some derogatory comments about transgender people when trying to explain how his belief system was rooted in his Catholic faith. It was a disaster. The piece came out with a trigger warning about transphobic remarks, and showed Peter twisting himself in knots trying to justify his presence at the rally. It described Peter as someone who 'leans back on the same right-wing talking points that drove him to the fatal rally'. And it was right in part: Peter was still not far into his deradicalization, a journey which takes many years, if not an entire lifetime. Peter was crushed. Once again, his attempt at doing the right thing had backfired. He desperately needed more guidance – and it would come soon, from an unexpected source.

At around the same time as the *Beaver* interview was published, one of the many letters Peter sent out looking for work made its way on to a desk of someone who was willing to see his potential for change in the future, rather than condemn him for a past he was trying to atone for. That person was a rabbi who worked for an inter-faith organization. Something about Peter's application caught his attention, and he asked him to come in for an interview. In the end, Peter didn't get the internship because it involved graphic design, in which Peter had no experience. But the rabbi did see enough potential to call up a friend and talk to her about Peter. That friend was Hadiya Masieh.

22

Ibrahim Kamara

Brighton, England, January 2014–21

The day after Ibrahim Kamara was killed by a US missile strike in Syria's Aleppo province, his mother Khadijah was working at her small charity shop in Brighton. She was not feeling well and had been trying to contact one of her younger sons to ask him to come and help her out. When she finally got through, he assumed she must be calling about Ibrahim. Not long before, he had received a message on Facebook Messenger:

'Congratulations, your brother Ibrahim has died a martyr.'

That devastating sentence was accompanied by a photograph: Ibrahim in an unzipped body bag, his young face covered in blood and sand.

'Yeah Mum, I know, Ibrahim has passed away,' the teenager said to Khadijah before she'd had a chance to say anything to him. 'They sent a message to me.'

And that was how Khadijah Kamara found out that her first-born son – the little boy she had tried to save from war – had been killed in a conflict far away from home. Her mind only permitted one thought at that moment.

From God we came and to God we return.

Her younger son came to the shop and helped her home. Khadijah could not remain alone and silent with her grief, however. She needed to redeem her eldest son in the eyes of the world, and try and make people understand how this funny, kind boy could have come to feel that the battlefields of Syria offered him a better future than the streets of Brighton.

You either cry, Khadijah, or you tell your story, she thought.

Just hours after hearing about the death of her child, Khadijah embarked on a marathon of interviews with whichever journalists called her or turned up at her home or shop. The death of a British resident in a US bombing raid in Syria was big news, and Ibrahim's photo was soon splashed across websites and on the pages of national newspapers. The picture most media outlets used was not the Ibrahim his friends and family remembered. The Ibrahim in their memories was always smiling, goofing around, making people laugh. The Ibrahim in the picture looked angry, his lazy eye half-closed behind thick glasses and his mouth open in mid-sentence, casting his face into a glowering sneer. He wore a black shirt, his index finger raised to the sky, a gesture that referred to the oneness of God and that had been adopted by Islamic State fighters. Given that Ibrahim had gone to Syria to fight with the al-Nusra Front and was not linked to the Islamic State, he probably had the original religious meaning of the gesture in mind, but the overall impression was of an austere and hostile young man.

I have to speak out to make people understand, Khadijah thought. *These kids were not monsters. They just met the wrong people, who brainwashed them.*

The day Khadijah heard about Ibrahim's death, she spoke to nine different newspapers and TV channels. Over the next week, the journalists kept coming. Some of the newspapers ran derogatory articles despite her best efforts. The *Daily Mail* tracked down a neighbour from one of the streets where the Kamara family had suffered racist abuse. They printed her complaints about the Kamara boys playing football and about Khadijah taking deliveries for her charity shop, portraying the normal actions of a young family with a working mother as being somehow nefarious or ill-intentioned. Khadijah hardened herself to reading such distorted facts about her family and kept trying to get the truth out. Hearing the voice of the grieving mother did humanize a lot of the coverage of Ibrahim's death. When Khadijah spoke, she was authentic and emotional, powerfully conveying the anger she felt at the local authorities and the police for failing to provide a safe and stable environment for her boys.

Losing her son did not immediately change that situation. Neither police officers nor community support staff came to talk to Khadijah or her three surviving sons after the news broke about Ibrahim's death. The same pattern of inaction and indifference continued. A few days after Ibrahim was killed, one of Khadijah's neighbours came to the house at around 6 p.m. to complain about noise. The neighbour was aware of Ibrahim's death, but nevertheless she shouted and swore in front of the children. Khadijah had always tried to be patient and polite with her neighbours, even in the face of abuse. This time, however, still in a fog of grief, she was enraged. She began to shout back at the woman, hopping around, even swearing herself. She felt like she had a djinn inside her, and now it was coming out.

Other neighbours came out on to the street and the police turned up. Once again, Khadijah felt the blame for the disturbance fall on her.

'Maybe the neighbour had a child who was trying to sleep,' one of the police officers suggested to her.

When Khadijah tried to explain what had happened, another officer kept telling her to shush. It was humiliating and deeply upsetting, and compounded her grief. Khadijah spent the night crying and told her sons that she wanted to go home to Sierra Leone, but over the next few weeks, she collected her thoughts together and toughened her resolve.

She tried to piece together everything that had happened to her son and all the moments in his life that might have contributed to his eventual fate, buried in an unmarked grave on a mountainside in Syria. Khadijah could not absolve herself of all blame. She thought back to the withdrawn five-year-old who had joined her in the Netherlands and wished she had not been so overwhelmed with the other children and her unhappy marriage that she had failed to give him enough attention. Maybe if she had taken the time to listen to Ibrahim and had really tried to understand how traumatic his early years had been, he would have had a stronger emotional grounding on which to grow.

I have my own guilt, she thought. *I have my own part that I played. I will not hide that. I will never hide that.*

But most of her fury was reserved for the various British authorities that let her family down, time and time again. She wanted people to hear Ibrahim's story in the hope that they might start to understand the myriad experiences that mould a person's sense of themselves and their future. Maybe then his decision would make more sense. Maybe then she could prevent other young people from making the same mistakes. Maybe then the authorities would start to think about the systematic racism in an underfunded system that had constantly made her family feel they were criminals rather than victims.

Soon she would have her chance. There had been a lot of bad press around the Brighton case. It wasn't just Ibrahim who needed redeeming, but Sussex Police and the local authorities too.

A few weeks after Ibrahim was killed, the other teenager who had walked through Luton Airport passport control alongside him was also dead. Aged sixteen when he left the UK, Jaffar Deghayes had been one of the youngest British residents fighting in Syria, and he was killed at the age of seventeen in a gun battle with President Bashar al-Assad's forces in northern Syria. While Abdullah Deghayes and Ibrahim were technically adults when they were killed, Jaffar was still a minor, and pressure was mounting on the Brighton authorities to explain how so many of the city's young people had become radicalized right under their noses. As the scale of the city's radicalization problem because clear, so did the need for damage limitation. The Brighton & Hove Local Safeguarding Children Board commissioned a case review, while police and the council hastily put together a consultation with Muslim community groups to establish how relations could be improved. Khadijah proved to be a valuable commodity in this PR push. Many of the parents of foreign fighters were reluctant to speak publicly, fearful of a backlash in a country where suspicion of the Muslim community was regularly stoked by much of the media and by nationalist politicians. But in the years after Ibrahim's death, Khadijah remained determined to get her voice out there. When anyone came asking for her help on anything to do with the issues that had ultimately led to her son's death, she said yes. First she said yes to the council, which invited her to contribute to its report on the Deghayes brothers. Khadijah sat in Hove Town Hall and patiently answered their questions, going into detail about her family's experiences with social services and the police. She told them how she tried to raise her boys well, but said it was a struggle with so little support.

'Being a victim is a crime here,' she told them.

Next, she was asked to speak at a new community initiative launched by Sussex Police in response to the radicalization of at least four of its young citizens. The police chief attended the launch, and Khadijah told her story all over again, ending with a powerful plea to the police to help restore young people's faith in the justice system.

'I told my kids not to take the law into their own hands,' she said. 'But the law that is supposed to protect them did not protect them. For how long do I have to keep telling my children not to take the law into their own hands?'

She spoke with such conviction that the police chief apologized for everything she had been through and asked Khadijah to address a meeting of police officers. Once again, Khadijah accepted, giving a similar speech at the end of 2014 to a large audience at Sussex County cricket ground. By then, Khadijah was saying yes to so many requests, still buoyed by the sense that people were listening and that she had the power to effect change. She said yes to a counter-extremism organization that wanted her to speak at its government-funded training courses for Muslim mothers across Britain. She said yes to the journalists who kept turning up at her door with questions about her son. She said yes to the Muslim organizations that wanted to use her photograph on their websites. She kept saying yes, but as the years passed, she began to look around her. Had anyone listened to her or acted on what she had said?

Nothing had changed in her own life. When she gave her talks or travelled for media interviews, nobody paid her for her time. In fact, whenever she gave a talk she had to close the charity shop, so each time she actually lost money. One organization didn't even refund the cost of her train ticket to London. After Khadijah had given her emotional speeches to the council, they had promised to help the family find a permanent home after years of being shuttled between different houses along the south coast. But in 2015, the family were evicted from their council house and once again forced to go into emergency accommodation. The bed & breakfast they ended up in was in Eastbourne, more than an hour's travel from the boys' school and Khadijah's shop. It was not sustainable, so the large family slept on the floor of the charity shop for three months. When a council officer used racially offensive language in front of her, Khadijah brought the incident up at one of the community-building initiatives she had been asked to join. Once again, nothing happened. Khadijah became even more disillusioned. These organizations had exploited her grief and pain for their own ends and had given nothing back.

Once they have finished with you, they dump you like an empty basket, she thought.

In 2017, the serious case review into the Deghayes brothers

was published. It identified a catalogue of missed opportunities and mistakes in the care of the boys. It did not, however, hold anyone responsible for these errors, and maintained throughout – despite clear evidence showing otherwise within its own pages – that the people who came into contact with the boys could not have been expected to know that they were susceptible to radicalization.

When Khadijah saw the news about the report, she felt sick. She was done.

'Take my name off your list,' she told the various groups she had lent her backing to over the years. 'Don't send me any emails again.'

Not much had changed in Brighton either. For all the hand-wringing over how to improve relations between the different communities, links between the police and Muslim community leaders remained stagnant. The case of Ibrahim and the Deghayes brothers was treated as an unfortunate and embarrassing anomaly, rather than being seen as representing any systemic failure. The city was so blinkered by its own narrative as an inclusive and diverse liberal utopia that it failed to heed the voices in its own midst which questioned whether that narrative was actually true. It foisted a hymn of diversity upon its citizens from ethnic minority groups, without making any real effort to listen to or understand the needs of those different communities. The flagship One Voice community-building initiative launched by Sussex Police held a few meetings and released the odd statement every few years, but its website was soon out of date, with broken links and an email address that didn't work. Although youth workers who had known the Deghayes brothers were hopeful that the scandal over their care would lead to more positive intervention in the lives of those in Brighton's marginalized communities, instead, funding for new projects simply disappeared, falling victim to the sweeping austerity measures.

But if the lessons from Ibrahim's case seemed glaring, the

solutions remained opaque. Britain's chaotic social housing system was rooted in decades of dwindling funding and neglect by successive governments. The systematic prejudice and bias across public services around Britain was both well documented and deeply entrenched, and changing an entire mindset was a task of epic proportions. By 2020, however, new hope for change was emerging. The murder of the Black American man George Floyd by a Minnesota police officer in May 2020 sparked a global reckoning. The horror of the killing and a surge in support for the Black Lives Matter movement prompted people from all backgrounds to examine their own culpability in a system stacked against minority groups. But the swelling of outrage was exploited by extreme groups on all sides of the political spectrum. In the United States, some protesters – including far-left activists – used the protests as an opportunity to loot and riot, actions which far-right groups then magnified on social media. President Trump fanned the flames, associating the whole anti-racism movement with the actions of a few. The aims of this necessary reckoning about the sins of the past and the shape of the future became distorted and led to a greater sense of alienation and deeper divisions in society. Yet the fundamental goals of the Black Lives Matter movement remained critical: people from all backgrounds needed to truly listen to and then amplify the voices of historically marginalized communities, accepting the reality of their lived experience and then putting those voices at the centre of efforts to create a more equal society.

For a brief time, Khadijah was under the illusion that her voice would matter. When that illusion shattered, she retreated to her old life, a daily struggle to raise her beloved children against the odds the British system stacked against her.

The good people, they don't have the power, she thought.

Khadijah's health suffered, and she would have days when she could not get out of bed. She would languish on lengthy doctors' waiting lists, always feeling like she had to fight harder than everyone else to access the most basic services. When COVID-19 struck, she was forced to close her shop and apply for state assistance, a difficult and confusing process that again gave her the humiliating feeling that she was somehow being judged for suffering from hardship that was beyond her control. At times, she would revive her dream of returning home to live under the colourful skies of Sierra Leone. Her charity shop had raised enough money for various projects aimed at helping vulnerable children there, and Khadijah was proud of that work. But there was still much keeping her in Brighton. Ibrahim's three younger brothers were doing well in their education or were embarking on promising careers. She also felt she still had more to give back to her community. Her charity shop was on a run-down stretch of road in eastern Brighton, where the paint peeled off the pastel-coloured Regency buildings and a general air of neglect pervaded the shopfronts. The people living and working in the area, however, were warm and friendly, sharing a sense of camaraderie as they negotiated the hardships of life on the fringes of society. Her larger-than-life personality had always drawn customers into her charity shop, and it was there, surrounded by other people's unwanted things, that she began to feel a renewed sense of belonging and purpose. When she had the energy, Khadijah would organize events for those less fortunate than herself. Some weekends she would put a selection of her wares outside the shop for homeless people to take for free. Other days, she would open her doors to Brighton's refugee community to give them items they might need. Compassion came her way too. After Ibrahim was killed, Khadijah was deeply moved by the small kindnesses she experienced. People would come into the shop to offer their condolences, many bringing flowers or even home-cooked meals. When she spoke on television, some hate mail arrived accusing her of being a bad mother, but most of the letters praised her for her dignity. The schools her children attended made huge efforts to ensure the boys continued their education even through the periods of greatest turmoil. One of Ibrahim's former teachers even came to the shop to comfort Khadijah with warm words about her lost son. These small gestures went a long way in helping her feel a step closer to that elusive sense of acceptance in a country that never let you forget you were an outsider. Then, one day, a woman walked into the shop.

'Are you Khadijah Kamara?' she asked.

Khadijah nodded, then listened as the woman explained that she was a teacher. She had seen Khadijah's television interviews and had been deeply moved, so had started using those interviews in her class to teach her students about empathy and understanding the experiences of others. Khadijah felt her heart swell. She had been so disappointed when her words had failed to touch the people in power, but now at least there was hope that they might, in some small way, touch the next generation.

23

Hadiya Masieh and Peter Cytanovic

London, England, 2015 to Reno, Nevada, 2021

For a few frantic years, Hadiya Masieh was at the centre of Britain's fight against Islamist extremism. Working with the government's Prevent counter-extremism programme, she mentored dozens of young women who had tried to travel to Islamic State territory in Iraq and Syria, and she was astonished by the sophistication of the IS propaganda and the speed with which its mutating messages responded so precisely to people's changing insecurities and vulnerabilities. She had joined Prevent at its faltering start but felt it had gained confidence as the years had passed. It had grown closer in its approach to the Danish Aarhus model, tailoring each case to the needs of the individual and offering its mentors training and counselling.

The spell cast by Islamic State was powerful, but Hadiya also had her own tricks for countering it, and it was her personal experience that she drew on the most. She adopted the same empathetic persona she had used to recruit people back in her days with Hizb ut-Tahrir, beginning by establishing trust and then guiding people towards asking their own questions. Then she would gently introduce alternative interpretations of Islam. It took patience and perseverance, but Hadiya knew that lecturing them and aggressively challenging their beliefs would not work. Often the simple act of offering an alternative perspective without judgement was enough to spark that crucial process of self-reflection. With this approach, Hadiya was able to help people break down the ideology they had internalized while offering them hope that they had a future in the UK.

But it was emotionally draining work, and there were failures too. Some of Hadiya's clients ended up in jail, and each setback felt like a blow to her. Hadiya's role was to work on the ideology, but there was an army of other professionals involved too, and they did not always have the depth of understanding of radicalization or Islamist extremism that Hadiya possessed. While she was able to draw on nearly two decades of experience in extremism, many of the police officers and social workers seemed out of their depth in this field.

The wider political climate did not help either. Since 2016, when Britain had voted to leave the European Union, hate crime had risen across the country. The UK had also experienced a run of attacks by Islamist terrorists, some of whom had been through Prevent or other government deradicalization schemes, leading to difficult questions about how these programmes could have failed in such a devastating way. The British government responded with an even more severe, security-focused approach, increasing terror sentencing laws and surveillance, despite warnings that such an approach would backfire, especially if it was not coupled with deeper investment in tackling the root causes of extremism. Complacency about foreign fighters was also creeping in. By late 2018, the US-led military effort had eradicated the Islamic State's physical territory in Iraq and Syria. As an idea, however, IS remained powerful, and it was still active online, shifting its efforts towards planning attacks elsewhere in the world. But western governments breathed a collective sigh of relief at the fact that there was no longer an actual state to entice recruits to.

A new problem was brewing, however. After the Islamic State territory fell, thousands of European and American fighters and their families ended up either in the custody of Kurdish soldiers allied with the Americans, in refugee camps in Syria, or in the hands of Iraqi security forces. It wasn't just adults. Around 700 European children were also detained. These children had been taken to Islamic State territory by their parents or had been born there, and they were deeply traumatized by their experiences. They were European citizens, but many governments were reluctant to bring them home, and after the demonization of their parents, the public felt little sympathy for these children. Some governments did choose to repatriate their citizens, realizing the importance of intervening in these young lives as early as possible and aware of the potent symbolism of looking after their own nationals, regardless of race or religion. Britain, however, opted for the harshest policies – and there was a high-profile case with which to demonstrate this lack of mercy. In February 2019, one of the three girls from Bethnal Green, Shamima Begum, was discovered by a journalist in a camp in northern Syria. She was still only nineteen but had given birth to two children while in IS territory. Both had died, and now she was heavily pregnant with her third child. Shamima asked to return to Britain to have her child in safety. Her request was denied. Her baby boy, Jarrah, was born in a freezing and squalid refugee camp on 16 February. He died there of pneumonia less than three weeks later. Shamima's British citizenship was revoked on the grounds that her parents were originally from Bangladesh. Shamima herself had never been to Bangladesh.

Hadiya watched the saga of Shamima unfold, appalled at the lack of compassion for this young woman and others like her. Hadiya had made mistakes in her life, but she had been given a second chance and had used it to improve the lives of others. These young people would be given no such opportunity for redemption. Hadiya was growing disillusioned with her work with the Home Office, and the calls were less frequent now that Islamic State was no longer actively recruiting.

When she finally had time to catch her breath, Hadiya

looked inward at everything she had been through. She felt her layers of experience like a matryoshka doll: the indignant young Hadiya was still there at her core, surrounded by the shell of her years in Hizb ut-Tahrir, then the early community-building and interfaith work, followed by the tough outer layers forged in these gruelling recent years with Prevent. Few people in the country had the insight into the causes of radicalization that Hadiya now possessed. Time and again she heard the same story: people searched for meaning in a confused and uncertain world, and the extremists were the only ones who seemed to offer them answers. Alternative and moderate voices were often drowned out, but in among all this sound and fury, Hadiya could see the opportunity for change. It lay in the everyday interactions between people. When people from different communities came together, their commonalities outweighed their differences, and she could see the sparks of hope ignite. Those human connections were rare now, as polarization drove communities apart, so Hadiya decided to find a way to manufacture them. In late 2018, she launched her own organization. She called it Groundswell. At its heart was the quest to find new ways to promote unity, using technology and old-fashioned connections to bring people together. Hadiya found the best interactions were face to face, so she planned tree-planting afternoons, town hall meetings and other gatherings bringing communities together across religions and ethnic and political divides. She started gathering contacts, networking, fundraising, trying to spread her enthusiasm. It was tough going. While Hadiya had twenty years of experience in counter-extremism, she was not a public relations specialist, and she struggled at times to articulate Groundswell's goals. She also still harboured her own prejudices. She had an intuitive understanding of Islamist extremism, but little personal experience with the far right beyond the torment inflicted on her family by the National Front when she was a child. As a dark-skinned Muslim woman, she had experienced prejudice her whole life, and struggled to sympathize with white nationalists.

How on earth could someone with white skin feel like they were the ones at a disadvantage? she wondered.

Then, in early 2019, Hadiya received a call from a rabbi she knew.

'There is someone looking for an internship – would you be interested?' he asked. 'His name is Peter Cytanovic.'

Hadiya Googled the name, and there was Peter staring back at her in all his rage in the dark Charlottesville night. Instantly she thought she knew exactly who he was and everything he stood for. Then she realized she had heard his name mentioned before. A friend had a daughter attending the London School of Economics, and during the controversy over Peter's attendance the friend had asked Hadiya for her opinion of this young man. Hadiya had not given Peter much thought at the time, beyond feeling general rancour at the double standards in society.

He has been allowed to have a scholarship to the university, she thought bitterly. *If his face had been brown and Muslim, it would not have been the same story.*

But then she felt something stirring, a familiar feeling of fate playing her a hand she could not ignore.

Something is going on here, Hadiya thought. *Let's meet this Peter because he keeps coming up in my life. Maybe it's meant to be.*

Hadiya and Peter met in London in May 2019, at an upmarket hotel bar in St Pancras station. Under the ornate railway arches that recalled a cathedral, the pair sank into the lush chairs and fell into an intense four-hour conversation. They spoke about their backgrounds, politics, inequality, Hadiya's work, Peter's studies, the struggles of their respective communities, the inability of people to communicate outside the narrow worlds in which they cocooned themselves. Hadiya felt her preconceptions falling away. Listening to Peter describe his early days at college in Reno, she saw a mirror image of her nineteen-year-old self.

'We were both on a similar journey,' she told him, 'not feeling like we belonged, not feeling accepted, not feeling listened to.'

Hadiya could still see remnants of the angry young man in the photograph. She found Peter complex and intelligent, but also naïve and combative, and saw how easily he could fall back into far-right dogma when challenged. He was clearly still on a journey away from his extreme beliefs, but so was Hadiya. That journey did not have a definitive finish line that you crossed one day, becoming a perfect person acceptable to everyone in society. Such a person did not exist, and Hadiya felt immediate kinship with Peter's awkward and messy retreat from his past beliefs.

I am still changing my ideas and thoughts – fourteen years on and I'm still learning, she thought.

When the pair finished their conversation, Hadiya knew she was going to give Peter the internship. She wanted to help him stay on his new path.

During Peter's final term at LSE, he met Hadiya at least once a week. Together, they worked on the Groundswell newsletter, writing up reports on local community initiatives and trying to find new ways to get their message out. Peter scoured the Internet for groups fighting hate speech and helped put together the presentations for funding. Hadiya found him diligent and hard-working, fully committed to the project and its goals. In the few months they worked together, she could see him grow in confidence and allow himself to be challenged, his defensive edge blunting a little more each time they talked.

It was to be a short, productive burst of cooperation as Peter's time at LSE was coming to an end. He headed back to Nevada in early autumn, but the pair vowed to continue working together from afar. Hadiya last saw Peter in December 2019, when he returned to London for his graduation. They went to a busy fish and chip restaurant and huddled over their table to catch up. From there in the centre of crowded and buzzing London, neither could know that the world was about to change, throwing everything they had worked towards into jeopardy.

In March 2020, Hadiya wasn't feeling so good. She had all the symptoms of COVID-19 and struggled to get out of bed. It felt like there wasn't enough space in her lungs for any air, and just walking to the bathroom was like running a marathon. Still, she kept working, sometimes making calls from her bed, other times struggling down to the kitchen table to her laptop. As soon as coronavirus shut down normal life, Hadiya knew it had the potential to devastate not only people's health, but their societies too. All the feelings coronavirus sparked in the population – trauma, alienation, fear, uncertainty, distrust – matched the conditions in which extremism thrived. And it had struck at a time when trust in government was at a record low, creating the most fertile ground for conspiracies to thrive in. Hadiya knew how easily those negative feelings could be exploited by extremist groups looking for any cracks in society, and she saw that society was at a crossroads: COVID-19 could send people further down the path of bitterness and division, but if they harnessed the outpourings of community spirit, she believed they could emerge from the crisis more resilient to extremism and hate. So Hadiya threw herself into new campaigns, lobbying community leaders and counter-extremism experts to amplify the positive messages from the crisis. Every day there seemed to be someone else to talk to, a new task that required her energy. Even as her body was struggling to recover from COVID-19, she forged on. She often thought about Peter, so far away in Reno. They spoke on the phone now and then, and he would reassure her that everything was OK and that he was coping. Each time Hadiya put the phone down, she was never quite sure if he'd been telling the truth.

Peter had returned to his dad's house in Reno in autumn 2019, invigorated by his transformative year in London. He planned to get a job, save some money and start applying for PhD courses in politics or theology. His past, however, could not be erased, and it seemed ready to haunt him with a new ferocity. While Peter was in London, the hate mail had slowed to a trickle, but when he visited his old Reno university for references, word got around that he was back. The vitriolic messages resumed, and soon Peter felt a sad sense of déjà vu every time his phone buzzed.

'Die Nazi.' 'I can't wait to see you so I can kill you.' 'Hey racist kid, fuck you.'

Peter's return coincided with an uptick in far-right activity at his old college. Someone had painted swastikas on one of the halls of residence, and fliers for white nationalist groups began appearing. This reflected a rise in white nationalist sentiment across the USA, with the divisive rhetoric of President Donald Trump emboldening a new generation of right-wing extremists. Peter had had nothing to do with the swastikas and fliers at the University of Nevada, but he understood that his return had offered up an easy enemy to blame. It still hurt though, and even as he tried to respond with his new live-and-let-live attitude, a part of his resolve ebbed away, to be replaced by a sad sense of resignation.

I just don't care, if people want to hate me go ahead, he thought. *There is nothing I can do. It's just the way of the world.*

Peter's frequent contact with friends in London helped remind him of the positive connections he had been able to forge, but in November, that lifeline was cut off too. He was scrolling through his Facebook timeline one day when a message popped up: 'You have been logged out of this session.'

That's weird, Peter thought, and tried to log back in again.

Another message appeared: 'Your account has been deactivated.'

Peter appealed to Facebook, providing his ID. Within ten seconds, a message came back saying his appeal had been denied. Peter was mystified. He tried to think about what he had posted on his Facebook timeline. It was the usual mix of memes and jokes, nothing offensive that he could recall. He was offered no explanation. He was simply excommunicated from the world's biggest community and shut off from many of the people who had helped him shed his extremist views. Peter assumed an algorithm had associated his name with the Charlottesville protests, and that was enough for the social media giant to cut him off without appeal.

As the role of social media in the spread of extremist material and misinformation became clear following the 2016 US election, social networking sites came under increased pressure to act. But rather than enacting meaningful change to an architecture designed to grow and multiply advertising revenue regardless of the consequences, Facebook opted for token gestures. These included culls of fake accounts and accounts which they claimed had violated their terms of service. The exact criteria under which people could be removed was opaque, and no thought was given to the potential consequences of excommunicating a person from a platform that had made itself indispensable in modern life. For Peter, it accentuated the feelings of isolation and alienation that had been growing since his return to Reno – the same feelings that had led him to adopt extreme views in the first place. But he was more resilient now, and he welcomed the new year still feeling hopeful that there were people willing to give him a second chance. He had already managed to get a job. Most of his applications had been ignored, but his dad had helped him find some temporary work in warehouse logistics. It was not challenging work for a graduate in political theory, but it allowed him to save for college.

Despite his Facebook ban, Peter was able to speak to Hadiya regularly on WhatsApp, and the pair were always planning something: a podcast, some research, a virtual conference. Hadiya put Peter in touch with a researcher in Canada, and they started a collaboration on the links between religion and far-right extremism. These collaborations gave Peter a purpose and a connection to his self-exploration in London, and he approached them with childish enthusiasm.

But these connections were soon thrown into jeopardy by COVID-19. Hadiya was consumed with her work on her coronavirus projects in England. The pandemic led to funding cuts in academia and the research with the Canadian expert was put on hold. Then there was the bitter political atmosphere. By the summer of 2020, coronavirus was ravaging the USA with a ferocity unmatched anywhere else in the world. The elections were approaching, and the political climate had reached a rancour unprecedented in modern America. COVID-19 deepened the polarization, with Trump using xenophobic terms to describe the virus and alluding to far-right conspiracy theories. Peter had vowed to jettison personal politics until after his period of self-reflection, but that promise was proving difficult to keep. Politics was everywhere, and there was little else in Peter's life. Six months earlier, he had been living in London, engaged in challenging work with Hadiya and enjoying the company of friends from all over the world. Now the lockdown restrictions meant he was shuffling between a mundane job and his dad's house, where he would sit in front of his computer or on his phone, deprived of contact with much of the outside world. It didn't take long for the virus to take a financial toll on Peter's family too. His dad's hours were being continually cut back, and then Peter lost his job because the crisis was hitting demand for the products in the warehouse. He managed to find some more temporary work in logistics, which was a relief because his sister soon was out of work too. Her small business had become one of the many casualties of COVID-19, so Peter was not only saving for college, but also helping various family members pay their rent. His world became even more unsettled in May, when George Floyd was killed by a policeman in Minneapolis. Peter's initial reaction to the murder of an unarmed Black man and to the outpouring of anger at systematic racism in America was a shared sense of shock and horror. Then statues started to topple across the country, and Peter watched, horrified, as his heroes like Jefferson and Washington crumbled. At some rallies, protesters became violent and destructive. In Reno, demonstrators stormed an old police building and burned the American flag. Some of the Twitter accounts Peter followed blamed the violence on the entire Black Lives Matter movement, and his old feelings of hostility towards the people on the left stirred.

They don't just want to fix America, they want to burn it down, he thought.

This fear of the protests was fed by social media, with a morass of fake accounts and sophisticated information manipulation stoking the tensions. But Peter didn't think too long and hard about how or why different groups would manipulate the content he was consuming. He simply saw tweets from far-left accounts threatening the guillotine for conservatives if Joe Biden won the upcoming election, and many others with similar undertones of violence, and a familiar rage returned. He had not forgotten his pledge to be more understanding and more empathetic to those who did not share his views, but the internal battle for his soul was becoming increasingly fractious as America became more deeply mired in partisan hatred. The political environment was at boiling point, and this trickled down into every aspect of life.

In late 2020, Peter was enjoying a day off work when his phone rang. It was his employer. They were letting him go because of historical ties to a neo-Nazi movement. Peter searched for a new job, but it was fruitless. He had a few offers, but they were always rescinded after background checks. He applied to join the National Guard, a move which appealed to his sense of civic duty, but his application was put on indefinite hold after the recruiters found out about Charlottesville. He carried his past with him everywhere he went. One evening, while he was having a drink at an outdoor bar in Reno, a former schoolmate spotted him and encouraged others at his table to yell 'Nazi!' at him.

Peter descended into depression, and he became increasingly withdrawn from family and friends. He had spent the last few years committed to changing his ideologies and making amends for his past. But it had made no difference, so what was the point?

No one ever believes I have good intentions, he thought.

Peter was once again embedded in polarized America, cut adrift from everything that had pulled him out of that world. The chance of redemption that had been so tantalizingly close in London felt in danger of being snatched away. But while coronavirus had initially accentuated all the problems in Peter's life, as the end of 2020 neared, it started to bring some clarity. Whereas in the past he may have been receptive to the partisan conspiracy theories about the origins of the virus, the effectiveness of any countermeasures, and the safety and efficacy of the vaccines, he now saw the misinformation for what it was. When election day arrived, he did not cast his vote for Donald Trump. After Joe Biden won, Peter watched with horror as Trump's baseless conspiracies and lies about electoral fraud proliferated in his own community. It strengthened his resolve to try and help his country heal.

By early 2021, Hadiya and Peter had managed to re-establish their close connection. Despite a difficult year, they fell back into their easy rapport and started planning more work together. Hadiya knew that Peter had been through a lot, but she was struck by his renewed positivity about the future. There would be challenges ahead, but Hadiya was determined to help him through them. Peter decided to apply to study law at a Catholic university, using his faith as a framework to fight for the common good. Perhaps he would work in social justice and labour rights, he thought, helping the very migrant communities he had once denigrated. Peter was trying to be a more tolerant and open-minded person while staying true to himself, which he figured was the most authentic truth of all.

Epilogue

In February 2020, I travelled to the small town of Oulu in central Finland. It had been one of the mildest winters on record, and it had come after a year in which devastating forest fires in Australia and California and heatwaves across Europe had thrust the undeniable effects of climate change into our already unsettled lives. Frigid Oulu, however, was reliably blanketed in snow as my plane descended to the little airport. As ever, a feeling of mild disquiet accompanied me as I traversed the various airports, my own narrow escape from the Brussels bombings always teasing the edges of my memory. I never lingered long in departure halls, my consciousness shorn of that comforting belief: *it can never happen to me*. It is a necessary belief which allows us to get through each day without dwelling on the worst possible outcome, but it can also betray us, making us push away reality. Such a denial was apparent in the airports I passed through on my way to Oulu. Only a handful of people wore face masks. The World Health Organization had just declared coronavirus to be a global health emergency, but most people – myself included – carried on as if nothing were amiss, clinging to that human desire to preserve our reality against incomprehensible threats.

I was in Oulu to meet a man named Esa. In 2008, when he was a teenager, Esa had set up the Finnish branch of a pan-Nordic neo-Nazi movement. He had become a cause célèbre among the far right in the United States after he travelled there in 2009 and claimed political asylum on the basis that he was being persecuted in Finland for his neo-Nazi beliefs. While in America, he was thrown in jail for overstaying his visa, and he spent two months in solitary confinement. Upon his return to Finland, Esa continued to be an influential leader of the Nordic far right. But he had recently renounced the neo-Nazi movement, and I had travelled to Oulu to find out why.

I was quite far into my research for this book by then and felt I had a good grasp of the factors that led people into radical beliefs. I had interviewed many former extremists and had been struck by the commonalities. So often people had experienced early trauma: the loss of a parent; sickness of friends or relatives; troubled family backgrounds; racism and prejudice. Then there were feelings of depression, loneliness and alienation, coupled with a search for identity and a desire for meaning and purpose. So I came armed with my preconceptions as I sat down with Esa. Had there been any trauma? No, he had had a happy childhood with a loving family. Did he feel like he belonged? Yes, he was introverted at school, but he had friends with similar interests. Was he searching for an identity? He looked bemused. No, of course not – he was Finnish. So why did he become a neo-Nazi? The only reason he could muster was that he was interested in military history as a child.

When we follow the experiences of many people in this book, we can trace the moments in their radicalization when an early intervention might have made a difference. But then we meet someone like Esa, who shows us everything we cannot know, and it is bewildering. There are so many questions to which there are no easy answers. How can we prevent extremism when some people appear to have no reason for having followed hateful beliefs? Why do some people who experience trauma find solace in extreme views, while most do not? How does one person who consumes far-right rhetoric on chat boards simply drift away from it all one day, while another picks up a gun and kills? Then there are all the things over which we have so little control. The problems in our society related to wealth inequality and institutional racism have evaded solutions for decades, and continue to do so. How can we as individuals have any impact on these deep-rooted ills?

In the face of all that is unknown, it is tempting to retreat further into our own beliefs and find solace in the vilification of others. That is easy to do today when anyone with access to a phone or computer can broadcast their views, take others to task, and enjoy an immediate sense of power and moral superiority. This is especially true when world events conspire to cut us off from all that is familiar in daily life and plunge us into enforced isolation. COVID-19 has shown how many of us can cast around in a confused world and seek solace in conspiratorial narratives which claim to provide easy answers. Loneliness and depression are rising, and a whole generation of people who lived through the fear and uncertainty of the pandemic will feel an even more precarious grip on their futures, aware that everything they build could be taken away from them by factors entirely beyond their control. The after-effects will be with us for some time, and there are other global catastrophes on the horizon. The full impact of climate change remains unclear, but it too casts a shadow over any assumption of a safe and secure future. And the more uncertainty and fear there is in the world, the more we cling to those things which promise to bring meaning and control back to our lives. So if we are able to identify and understand the factors that might lead someone to extremism, how might we prevent this from happening?

Governments bear a great responsibility. They need to take measures which truly address economic inequality and start reinvesting in the social structures that protect people and better their prospects. There needs to be greater provision for mental health services, and an overhaul of education systems that can fail to connect with struggling students or to assist the most vulnerable. Classes must be introduced on critical analysis of the media we consume, so that the next generation will better be able to separate fact from fiction. The politics of fear dehumanizes vast swathes of the population and needs to be forcefully rejected. Western societies must undergo a calm and collaborative reckoning of how they prospered through the exploitation of others, and then systematic racism needs to be acknowledged and rooted out of every sector it permeates. Pressure should remain on social media companies to transform their business models, although the idea that some magical change to the technologies that dominate our lives will vanquish extremism is wishful thinking. Indeed, right now, many of these measures seem fancifully idealistic since their implementation requires sustained political and societal will. When nations emerge from the grip of COVID-19, all their energy and resources will be directed to trying to keep their economies afloat. As the long-term societal and psychological consequences become clear, policies relating to extremism will likely be reactive and punitive rather than preventative and constructive. The kinds of systematic failures that led Ibrahim to feel so unmoored from his life in Britain are likely to remain in place, nudging yet more people towards the false comforts of extremist ideologies.

With governments stretched, the actions of individuals take on an exaggerated importance. In every role we have – as friends, neighbours, parents, relatives, partners, teachers, employers and employees, community members – we all play a part in creating the conditions in which extremism either thrives or is vanquished. Because when we look at the stories in these pages, we see again and again that it is not massive political shifts or official interventions that have the most profound impact, but humane actions and everyday connections. In some of these stories, these connections are acts of extraordinary tolerance and kindness. Both Peter and Tom were helped on their path to redemption by people from communities they had previously demonized. This raises an uncomfortable issue that pervades many accounts of former far-right extremists – the suggestion that change only happens when the persecuted are nice to their persecutor. But these kinds of interventions should be viewed as evidence of the strength of character of those extraordinary individuals rather than as a specific blueprint to be promoted. Instead, we must draw out the lesson at the heart of these interactions: that the chance for change comes not when we close other people out, but when we let them in.

This is a difficult leap to make. Extreme views are frequently offensive, hurtful and dangerous, and when faced with hatred and division it is our natural inclination to try and shut it down or aggressively challenge it. Of course, we should stand up to hate speech, especially when it comes from people in positions of power. The mainstreaming of extreme thought galvanized many people in this book to head deeper into their ideologies, and so a general sense that hateful and divisive narratives are socially unacceptable must be maintained. The question is how we do this without further alienating the people we are hoping to reach. From the cult recruits of the 1970s up to the QAnon conspiracy theorists today, experience shows that you can't just argue someone out of an ideology or present a set of facts and expect them to be believed. Everyone thought Cathrine would shake off Cornel's lies the moment the rape he committed was exposed, but they failed to understand how deeply an ideology can take root. For Peter, every time he faced insults and threats from people on the other side of the political spectrum, it reinforced the far right's claim of an intractable and violent battle looming between left and right and sent him inching back to their ideology.

Treating people like human beings, even when we disagree with them, is a much more powerful tool. Hadiya discovered that listening without judgement was her most effective strategy when dealing with radicalized young women. Toby would have struggled to make sense of his future without the empathetic guidance of Shayne. Peter's world view underwent a huge shift because of his friendships with Hawah and Hadiya. In these cases, specific people stepped forward for that non-judgemental role, but everyday interactions are just as important. Throughout this book, we have seen that the more non-confrontational encounters an individual had with people from outside their narrow world, the more carefully they questioned their beliefs and the closer they moved towards lasting change. For Tom, staying in a multicultural Johannesburg neighbourhood exposed him to people and ideas he had spent years locking out. Attending a diverse high school helped Mak break down the racist material he was consuming online. And for all my confusion about Esa's entry into the world of white supremacy in Finland, his exit followed a more familiar path. Esa fell in love with a Chinese woman, throwing all his internal narratives into question.

Families are also crucial, as they help maintain a connection with the world outside. While there may be a temptation to cut off a friend or relative who chooses to adhere to a divisive belief system, doing so means there is nothing for them to come back to, making it less likely that they will feel able to return from their extreme views. What we can do is respectfully and calmly correct misinformation – either online or in person – and speak passionately about the values we hold and explain why we hold them.

But this book is not intended to be a step-by-step guide to deradicalizing extremists. Rather, it is about looking at what their stories tell us about the world we live in today, then drawing lessons that each of us can apply in our everyday lives in pursuit of a more tolerant and just society for all. Because this is how we prevent extremism. Through the experiences of the people in this book we can see how important it is that everyone feels that they have a voice in their family and community, and that their concerns and fears are taken seriously. How we foster that sense of value and inclusion depends on our individual situations. For people in possession of those rare commodities called time and energy, getting involved with the local community in any initiatives helping vulnerable people or bridging divides helps create a more resilient society. But it can be as simple as thinking about how we connect with the people around us. Being open to understanding the motives of others must guide the interactions we have with everyone in our lives, both in person and on social media, because even the simplest gestures can have the most profound effects.

If someone does end up on the path to extremism, we cannot expect a miraculous transformation. Decades after her escape, Cathrine still occasionally glances over her shoulder, on the lookout for Cornel's spies. Hadiya left Hizb ut-Tahrir more than fifteen years ago, but still considers herself to be going through a deradicalization process. There appears to be an expectation from some that former extremists – especially those from the far right – must immediately and publicly renounce their views and embrace a liberal, left-wing belief system. This risks further alienating people who are considering leaving extreme groups and represents a fundamental failure to understand how humans work.

Every one of us is moulded from our different identities, our layers of experience forming how we see the world and other people in it. These layers cannot be erased or replaced, and life cannot be bundled into neat transitions from one set of beliefs to another. If we believe in such a one-dimensional view of humanity, we fall into the same trap as the extremist recruiters who reduce life's complexities to good and bad; friends and enemies; us and them. At some point in their lives, everyone in this book sought solace in such easy answers. Eventually they saw the fallacy of these promises, and when they finally emerged from those ideologies, it was with an understanding that such simplicities do not exist – and that life is infinitely richer and more hopeful because of it.

Sources

The primary source for this book consists of interviews with the people featured in its pages, and more detail is given below on the interviews I conducted for each chapter. Additional sources and suggested further reading are also indicated below. Incidents that were widely reported by numerous media outlets are not sourced, but where I have relied on one specific article or book to describe an event, I have given full details. Quoted speech is reported as recalled by one or more of the protagonists. Italicized text denotes direct quotes of the protagonists. At times, they were describing their general feelings about an issue and I chose where in the narrative to insert those quotes; at other times, they were recalling their specific feelings during the moment described.

Prologue

For accounts of my personal experience at Brussels Airport during the bombing, see 'Eyewitness Accounts from Inside Brussels Airport', *TIME* magazine, 22 March 2016, and my piece on the first anniversary, 'Fear and Frustration Continue One Year After Belgium's Worst Terror Attack', *TIME* magazine, 22 March 2017.

Other details about the attackers and the timeline of the bombings are taken from multiple press reports at the time.

A Note to Readers

For further information on the demographics of Islamist extremists, see the paper published by the International Centre for Counter-Terrorism (ICCT) in February 2021, 'A Comparative Analysis of the Data on Western Foreign Fighters in Syria and Iraq: Who Went and Why?'. This shows the average age of male foreign fighters to be twenty-six and of female ISIS recruits to be twenty-one. There are fewer studies about the demographics of right-wing and left-wing extremists, but limited national studies show most as being in their twenties. A report by the Southern Poverty Law Center, 'The Alt-Right is Killing People' (February 2018), found the average age of white supremacists who carried out deadly attacks to be twenty-six.

1: Cathrine Moestue

The primary source for this chapter consists of interviews with Cathrine Moestue and family photographs provided by Cathrine. Some personal details have been changed to protect the identities of those involved. For corroboration and other perspectives, I also interviewed Cathrine's sister and Lisa I'Anson, Cathrine's best friend from boarding school in England.

A copy of the handwritten letter from Cornel quoted at the start of the chapter was provided by Cathrine.

A summary of Norway's immigration policy is from the Migration Policy Institute's March 2013 report, 'Immigration and National Identity in Norway'.

The descriptions of the Grove School (now called the Royal School) come from the school's brochure from the time, a copy of which Cathrine kept.

2: Peter Cytanovic

The primary source for this chapter consists of interviews with Peter Cytanovic. For corroboration and alternative perspectives, I interviewed his father – also called Peter Cytanovic – and had an email exchange with his mother, who did not wish to be named. Peter provided a copy of the photograph of his mother holding him, with the scar across her head from the brain surgery clearly visible.

For details on Ivy League colleges and their intake of lower-income students, see the September 2017 report by CNBC. com, 'Harvard's Incoming Freshman Class is One-third Legacy – Here's Why That's a Problem'.

For demographic details of the student body of the University of Nevada: Reno, see the *New York Times*' collation of data in the study of mobility by the Equality of Opportunity Project published on 18 January 2017 under the headline: 'Some Colleges Have More Students From the Top 1 Percent Than the Bottom 60. Find Yours'.

3: Hadiya Masieh

The primary source for this chapter consists of interviews with Hadiya Masieh.

For a good overview of the Ugandan Asian situation, see 'UK Did Not Want Ugandan Asians', BBC News, 1 January 2003.

There are innumerable accounts of how dehumanizing language facilitated the Rwandan genocide, but for an interesting look at the issue with an eye to the current situation, see 'In Rwanda, We Know All About Dehumanizing Language', Kennedy Ndahiro, *The Atlantic*, 13 April 2019.

4: Ibrahim Kamara

The primary source for this chapter consists of interviews with Ibrahim Kamara's mother, Khadijah Kamara. Ibrahim's story has been told in other media, and while this has created a wealth of secondary sources for this book to draw on, the tone of some of the coverage has been hostile. Most people I approached for an interview about Ibrahim for this book refused, apparently deterred by the proliferation of distortions in some of the coverage. However, one reporter has consistently excelled at capturing the nuances and wider implications of the story of the Brighton youngsters. *Guardian* journalist Mark Townsend wrote an excellent investigative piece in March 2016 titled 'From Brighton to the battlefield: how four young Britons were drawn to jihad'. He followed this up with an even more detailed account, *No Return: The True Story of How Martyrs Are Made*. Published in 2020, the book is a must-read forensic exposé of the failings of the British system.

For details of the brutality of the Sierra Leone conflict, I read an account by a former child soldier, titled 'Ex-child-soldier: "Shooting Became Just Like Drinking a Glass of Water"', published on the CNN website on 9 October 2012.

The Brighton *Evening Argus* published a story by Ben James on 6 October 2015, 'New Study Shows Brighton and Hove Has Some of the Most Deprived Areas in the Country'.

Details about the academic standards at Fairlight Primary School are taken from the 2004 report by Ofsted, the official British school inspection board. The details about Varndean School were also taken from its Ofsted report.

5: Mak Kapetanovic

The primary source for this chapter consists of interviews with Mak Kapetanovic.

6: Cathrine Moestue

The primary source for this chapter consists of interviews with Cathrine Moestue, and photographs provided by Cathrine. For corroboration and other perspectives, I also interviewed Christina – her best friend at the Charlie Rivel Entertainer Art School (now called the Eskilstuna Dance Academy) – and Lise, whose name has been changed to protect her identity.

For an insight into the similarities in the recruitment methods used by different cults and extremist groups, see the EU-based Radicalisation Awareness Network's April 2019 paper, 'Grooming for Terror – Manipulation and Control', and its June 2017 paper, 'Lessons from Adjacent Fields: Cults'.

7: Hadiya Masieh

The primary source for this chapter consists of interviews with Hadiya Masieh.

Multiple studies showed the rise in hate crimes against Muslims in Britain and America after the 9/11 attacks. British data shows that in the late 1990s, before the September 11 attacks, police in England and Wales recorded between 10,000 and 20,000 racially motivated attacks a year. The year following 9/11, that figure had soared to 54,000, and Muslims were disproportionately the victims. Today, more than 80,000 racist attacks are reported to the police each year. The figures can be found on the British government's 'historical crime data' database.

. For an insight into how political and foreign policy factors contribute to extremism in Muslim communities, see *Guest House for Young Widows* by Azadeh Moaveni, which follows a number of young Muslim women who joined ISIS.

There are multiple reports showing how trust in governments has been steadily declining. See, for example, 'Dissatisfaction with Democracy at Record High', BBC News, January 2020, and the April 2019 Pew Research Center paper, 'Public Trust in Government: 1958–2019'.

8: Tom Olsen

The primary source for this chapter consists of interviews with Tom Olsen, as well as interviews he gave to other media, and widely available photographs published of him during his years in the neo-Nazi movement.

9: Mak Kapetanovic

The primary source for this chapter consists of interviews with Mak Kapetanovic.

A good analysis of how Gamergate was the forerunner for the alt-right can be found in 'What Gamergate Should Have Taught Us about the "Alt-Right"' by Matt Lees (*Guardian*, 1 December 2016). Other sources for my analysis of 4chan were: 'Absolutely Everything You Need to Know to Understand 4chan', *Washington Post*, 25 September 2014; 'We Analyzed More Than 1 Million Comments on 4chan. Hate Speech There Has Spiked by 40% Since 2015', Rob Arthur, *Vice News*, 10 July 2019; '8chan, 8kun, 4chan, Endchan: What You Need to Know', Oscar Gonzalez, *CNet*, 7 November 2019; and an academic paper, 'The Web Centipede: Understanding How Web Communities Influence Each Other Through the Lens of Mainstream and Alternative News Sources', Savvas Zannettou *et al.*, *arXiv: 1705.06947*, 19 May 2017.

10: Ibrahim Kamara

The primary source for this chapter consists of interviews with Ibrahim Kamara's mother, Khadijah Kamara. Another key source is the Serious Case Review by the Brighton & Hove Local

Safeguarding Children Board, 27 July 2017. The report describes the radicalization of the Deghayes brothers at length, with some details on Ibrahim's situation too.

Information about Ibrahim's love of Manchester United and his popularity at school was contained in interviews with his brother and classmates published in 'Don't follow in my "brainwashed" son's footsteps', *Daily Mail*, 26 September 2014.

Khadijah makes a number of allegations about the lack of action by Sussex Police over her complaints of racism. I approached them for comment, but DCC Nev Kemp, who was the Brighton & Hove police chief at the time, refused two separate requests to be interviewed for this book, and a general enquiry to the Sussex Police press department went unanswered. It should be noted that the Serious Case Review corroborates the accusations of police inaction over racism and Islamophobia suffered by the Deghayes brothers.

Details of the friendship between Ibrahim and Amer Deghayes are contained in Mark Townsend's book, *No Return: The True Story of How Martyrs are Made*. I also contacted Beccy Smith, who ran the youth club Ibrahim and Amer attended. While she did not want to be interviewed, she confirmed the details in Mark Townsend's book.

Details of the Deghayes family's situation and the abuse they suffered are taken from the Serious Case Review.

Amer Deghayes spoke about his interest in the Channel 4 News foreign fighters' documentary in a CNN interview with Karl Penhaul, 'From Schoolbooks to Syria: How Four British Youths Turned to Jihad', 4 October 2014. The Channel 4 News documentary was aired in June 2013 and can be found online on the Channel 4 News website as well as on YouTube under the title 'Exclusive: The Jihadi Brit Who Fought and Died in Syria'. A *New York Times* article from 14 April 2015, 'Her Majesty's Jihadists' by Mary Anne Weaver, featured an interview with Amer's father, Abubaker Deghayes, who spoke about how the

Arab Spring radicalized his son. Townsend's *No Return* also goes into great detail about the effect the Syrian war had on Amer and Ibrahim.

For an account of the early adoption of social media by extreme Islamist groups, see 'Facebook, YouTube Aid in Al Qaeda's Spread, Study Says', *The Atlantic*, 8 February 2011.

11: Peter Cytanovic

The primary source for this chapter is an interview with Peter Cytanovic. For corroboration and an alternative perspective, I interviewed his father, who is also called Peter Cytanovic.

For an excellent analysis of how the YouTube algorithms work, see 'The Making of a YouTube Radical', Kevin Roose, *New York Times*, 8 June 2019.

The term 'cockroaches' was used to describe asylum seekers in a column in the *Sun*, a British tabloid, in April 2015. The US presidential hopeful Ben Carson compared Syrian refugees to 'rabid dogs' in November 2015. Hungary's president, Viktor Orbán, frequently uses the term 'aliens' to refer to people seeking asylum.

For a good overview of the debate at the time over the Confederate symbols, see '2 Years After S.C.'s Flag Came Down, Cities Grapple With Confederate Symbols', Sarah McCammon, NPR, 10 July 2017.

I used a variety of sources for the description of the Charlottesville rally. Peter's personal recollections form the basis of the account. I also reviewed the video footage of the night that is available on YouTube, accounts of the counter-protesters who formed a chain around the statue of Thomas Jefferson, and general press reports about the violence. In addition, I interviewed Samuel Corum, the photographer who took the famous photograph of Peter.

12: Shayne Hunter and Toby Cook

The primary sources for this chapter are interviews with Shayne Hunter and Toby Cook, and photographs and video clips provided by the two men.

Most of the incidents detailed in this chapter, including the Cronulla protests, were documented in video footage posted on YouTube by the opposing sides, and in articles published in Australian media at the time. See, for example, 'Anti-racism Activists Turn Violent at Cronulla Rally', Tim Elliott, *Sydney Morning Herald*, 12 December 2015.

There are many videos on YouTube of Toby and Shayne at various protests during the years they were active which corroborate their accounts.

Toby Cook provided a photograph of him posing with Pauline Hanson of the One Nation Party.

For an interesting look at the reciprocity between the far right and Islamist extremists, see *The Rage: The Vicious Circle of Islamist and Far-right Extremism* by Julia Ebner (IB Tauris, 2017).

13: Cathrine Moestue

The primary source for this chapter consists of interviews with Cathrine Moestue and photographs provided by Cathrine. For corroboration and other perspectives, I also interviewed her best friend at the Charlie Rivel Entertainer Art School, Christina, Cathrine's sister and Lise.

Cathrine provided copies of all the letters sent to her by Cornel.

There were a number of exposés of the cult deprogramming 'experts' of the 1970s and '80s. A good overview of the changing approach to helping people leave cults can be found in the Freedom of Mind Resource Center paper, 'Cult Deprogramming vs. Strategic Interactive Approach'.

Cathrine provided dozens of Norwegian and Swedish

newspaper clippings about the crime, which also detailed her situation. She also provided a copy of all the court documents detailing the trial of herself and Cornel. It should be noted that Cathrine was tried under the name Roxie Lenina, a name she had legally taken at Cornel's suggestion. This detail was omitted from the main text of the book to avoid creating confusion. Cornel's surname has been omitted from this book to protect surviving members of his family. His full name was, however, included in the court documents and in various media reports from that time.

14: Peter Cytanovic

The primary source for this chapter consists of interviews with Peter Cytanovic. I also interviewed Hawah Ahmad.

The interview Peter gave to KRNV can still be found on YouTube under the title 'Alt-Right Charlottesville Rally Participant Peter Cvjetanovic [*sic*] Interview' and on the Facebook feed of WGN TV under the title 'Peter Cvjetanovic [*sic*] speaks out after photos appeared of him attending a white nationalist rally in Charlottesville, Va.'. More than 1,800 people have commented on the latter. Many articles misspelled Peter's surname.

For articles exploring doxxing, see 'How "Doxxing" Became a Mainstream Tool in the Culture Wars', Nellie Bowles, *New York Times*, 30 August 2017, and 'White Supremacists Once Wore Hoods. Now, an Internet Mob Won't Let Them Stay Anonymous', PBS, 20 August 2017.

There were many press reports about Peter's attendance at UNR. See, for example, 'UNR Sticks by Stance Despite Petition Asking for Cvjetanovic's [*sic*] Expulsion', Natalie Bruzda, *Las Vegas Review-Journal*, 16 August 2017.

15: Ibrahim Kamara

The primary source for this chapter consists of interviews with Ibrahim Kamara's mother, Khadijah Kamara.

Details of the inaction of the Brighton authorities in response to the radicalization of four of its residents are in the Serious Case Review by the Brighton & Hove Local Safeguarding Children Board, published 27 July 2017.

I wrote an article about the emerging foreign-fighter phenomenon and the lack of coordination between different European nations: 'A Plot to Attack the Belgian Capital Stokes Fears Europe Will [Be] Targeted by Radicalised Fighters Returning from Syria' (Charlotte McDonald-Gibson, *Independent*, 19 January 2014). One of the most detailed reports into the problem at the time was the December 2013 research paper published by the International Centre for Counter-Terrorism in The Hague, 'Dealing with European Foreign Fighters in Syria: Governance Challenges & Legal Implications', by Edwin Bakker, Christophe Paulussen & Eva Entenmann.

The detail about Ibrahim writing a message for his mother comes from a CNN interview with Amer Deghayes by Karl Penhaul, 'From Schoolbooks to Syria: How Four British Youths Turned to Jihad' (4 October 2014). Details about Ibrahim's entry into Syria and the group's assault on Chalma mountain come from Mark Townsend's *No Return: The True Story of How Martyrs are Made*, and from a VICE News report, 'The Rise of British Jihadists in Syria', Nagieb Khaja (27 June 2014).

Details about Ibrahim trying to persuade other Muslims to travel to Syria come from a story published in the Brighton *Evening Argus* on 25 September 2014, 'Brighton Teenager Killed in Syria by US Air Strikes, Claim Western Fighters'.

16: Tom Olsen

The primary source for this chapter consists of interviews with Tom Olsen. Tom also provided photographs clearly showing himself in South Africa while dressed in skinhead attire. Norwegian press reports from the time also mention his flight to South Africa.

There was little coverage or analysis of white nationalist European fighters in South Africa, but an Associated Press story from 24 March 1994, 'German Killed in South Africa; Shady Links to Neo-Nazis at Home' by Larry Thorson, details one such case, while another enlightening article from the time is 'Foreign "Hooligans" Embarrass AWB' by Claus Stacker (*Mail & Guardian*, 17 June 1994).

I have never been to South Africa or Johannesburg, but I found some wonderful recollections of Rockey Street at the time, which complemented Tom's account of the area, in 'A Taste of Old Yeoville in Melville' by Dennis Webster (*New Frame*, 30 January 2019), and 'Street of a Past that Foretold a Future' by Nechama Brodie (*Mail & Guardian*, 10 August 2012).

17: Hadiya Masieh

The primary source for this chapter consists of interviews with Hadiya Masieh.

Many news reports dissected France's deradicalization scheme, including 'France's "Deradicalisation Gravy Train" Runs Out of Steam', Leela Jacinto, *France 24*, 1 August 2017, and 'France's Deradicalization Centers Seen as a "Total Fiasco"', James McAuley, *Washington Post*, 24 February 2017.

The case of the Dutch former extremist was recounted in 'Bilal L. turned out to be wolf in sheep's clothing', *De Telegraaf*, 23 August 2017.

I have published two articles on differing deradicalization and integration strategies in Belgium, drawing comparisons with the rest of Europe. One is a piece about Mechelen: 'Where Refugees Can Come Home', Charlotte McDonald-Gibson, *New York Times*, 3 December 2016. The other is a look into the case of Vilvoorde: 'The Former Neo-nazi Helping Returning ISIS Fighters Let Go of Hate', Charlotte McDonald-Gibson, *TIME* magazine, 16 February 2017.

18: Mak Kapetanovic

The primary source for this chapter consists of interviews with Mak Kapetanovic.

The figures about Donald Trump's allocation of counter-extremism funding can be found in 'Trump Officials Have Redirected Resources from Countering Far-right, Racism-fueled Domestic Terrorism', Molly O'Toole, *Los Angeles Times*, 5 August 2019.

The number of attacks by far-right extremists in the USA in comparison with those by Islamist extremists comes from a June 2017 analysis by the Center for Investigative Reporting.

For details on the New Zealand focus on Islamist terror at the expense of far-right threats, see 'NZ's Ardern Apologises as Report into Mosque Attack Faults Focus on Islamist Terror Risks', Praveen Menon, Reuters, 8 December 2020.

19: Cathrine Moestue

The primary source for this chapter consists of interviews with Cathrine Moestue and photographs provided by Cathrine. For corroboration and other perspectives, I also interviewed Lise and Haissam.

Press reports from Norway in the late 1990s and early 2000s show Cornel continuing to use the modelling agency scam in which he offers to take women's photographs for a fee.

Cornel died by suicide in the late 2010s. His death was

confirmed to me by Lise, who saw the documentation about his death and whose children by Cornel attended the funeral.

20: Shayne Hunter and Toby Cook

The primary sources for this chapter are interviews with Shayne Hunter and Toby Cook and photographs and video clips provided by the two men.

The Soufan Center, a US think tank, put out a research paper on the Azov Battalion in March 2019 entitled 'IntelBrief: The Transnational Network That Nobody is Talking About'. *TIME* magazine also quoted that think tank's founder, Ali Soufan, as saying that more than 17,000 foreign fighters went to Ukraine, in 'Like, Share, Recruit: How a White-Supremacist Militia Uses Facebook to Radicalize and Train New Members', Simon Shuster and Billy Perrigo, 7 January 2021. Most of those foreign recruits are believed to have been Russian, with 2,000 estimated to come from other nations.

For figures comparing deaths in the USA at the hands of far-left activists and far-right activists, see the analysis of various data in 'Anti-fascists Linked to Zero Murders in the US in 25 Years', Lois Beckett, *Guardian*, 27 July 2020. However, it is important to look at different perspectives, and the Global Terrorism Index puts out regular reports detailing violence linked to various ideologies around the world, demonstrating how the developing world suffers far more at the hands of extremism then anywhere in the West. The 2020 report by the EU policing agency Europol, meanwhile, shows that ethno-nationalist and separatist extremism is responsible for most violence in Europe. That report also showed a large increase in attacks related to left-wing ideologies.

The op-ed co-authored by Shayne, entitled 'I Established a Terror Movement in Australia, and I Quit', was published on news.com.au on 25 October 2017. It was deconstructed on the

ABC Media Watch blog on 30 October 2017, under the headline 'Confessions of a Homegrown "Terrorist"'.

21: Peter Cytanovic

The primary source for this chapter consists of interviews with Peter Cytanovic. I also interviewed Hawah Ahmad, Dr James Walters of the LSE Faith Centre, and Adam Solomons, the journalist who interviewed Peter for the piece in the *Beaver*.

A number of articles in both student and national newspapers detailed Peter's attendance at LSE and the campaign to have him expelled. These include '"White Nationalist" from Infamous Charlottesville Protest Now Reportedly Studying at LSE', Tom Barnes, *Independent*, 4 October 2018; and 'Face of Neo-Nazi Rally LSE Student "Regrets" Going and is "Sorry" for his Actions', Vaidehi Dhavde, *UCL Tab*, 13 October 2018.

The article about Peter appeared in the *Beaver* under the headline 'Exclusive Interview with Peter Cvjetanovic [*sic*]' (Adam Solomons, 23 June 2019).

22: Ibrahim Kamara

The primary source for this chapter consists of interviews with Ibrahim Kamara's mother, Khadijah Kamara.

The detail about the photograph of Ibrahim's body comes from a story in the *Guardian* headlined 'British Teenage Jihadi Believed to Have Been Killed in Syria' (Shiv Malik *et al.*, 24 September 2014).

The *Daily Mail* article that included allegations by Khadijah's neighbours was headlined 'Bewildered Fury of the Brighton Mum Whose Teenage Son Ran Off to Become a Jihadi' (David Jones, 27 September 2014).

To get an idea of the situation in Brighton, I interviewed Fiyaz Mughal of the community cohesion and anti-hate-crime group Faith Matters. He had been brought in by the Brighton authorities to consult on how relations with the Muslim community could be improved, and provided them with a detailed report and recommendations. He was not impressed by the progress made in Brighton since his report. I also spoke to a member of the Brighton & Hove Muslim Forum, who wished to remain anonymous. It is also worth noting that I grew up close to Brighton, went to college there, and lived there for many years, so I also drew upon my personal experiences of the city in writing these chapters.

Attempts to contact the council representative of the One Voice initiative were fruitless. The email address on the One Voice website returned a failure notice. When I managed to track down another email address of that individual, my email went unanswered.

The Brighton & Hove police chief at the time, DCC Nev Kemp, declined to be interviewed about how the force had responded to the radicalization of its citizens and what initiatives had been introduced to try and improve relations between different communities in Brighton.

23: Hadiya Masieh and Peter Cytanovic

The primary sources for this chapter are interviews with Hadiya Masieh and Peter Cytanovic.

Various reports show hate crime increasing after Brexit. Official figures show such offences doubled between 2012–13 and 2018. See the *Guardian* article, 'Hate Crime Surge Linked to Brexit and 2017 Terrorist Attacks' (Matthew Weaver, 16 October 2018).

The British government's evolving approach to deradicalization is detailed in 'Priti Patel's Plan to Tackle Radicalised Youth is So Flawed it's Mad, Says Study' (Mark Townsend, *Guardian*, 26 January 2020).

I wrote a detailed report for the *New York Times* on the fate of children taken to Islamic State territory, headlined 'What Should Europe Do With the Children of ISIS?' (Charlotte McDonald-Gibson, 23 July 2017). A more recent article on the BBC News website, 'IS Prisoner Issue a Ticking Timebomb for the West' (Frank Gardner, 24 July 2020), gives a good overview of the current situation.

For corroboration of Peter's accounts, I also interviewed Brad Galloway, the Canadian extremism researcher Peter worked with, and spoke to Peter's father about his feelings on his return.

The appearance of white nationalist messaging at UNR was detailed in 'UNR Students Voice Fear about Campus Climate After Racist, Discriminatory Images Appear at School' (*Nevada Independent*, 3 October 2019) and 'UNR Responds To White Supremacist Fliers On Campus' (Noah Glick, KUNR Public Radio, 10 September 2019).

Facebook did not respond to two press enquiries I made asking for further details about and explanation of Peter's removal from the platform.

For an excellent analysis of all the actions Facebook has and has not taken to moderate its content, see 'Facebook Is a Doomsday Machine' (Adrienne LaFrance, *The Atlantic*, 15 December 2020).

Epilogue

The primary source consists of interviews with Esa, whose surname I have withheld. It is worth noting that I did not omit Esa's story from the rest of the book because it did not completely conform to any overarching narrative, it was more that I felt I already had the right balance of different ideologies and his story did not add a particularly new angle.

Figures on the increase in depression during the pandemic come from the BBC News report, 'Depression Doubles during Coronavirus Pandemic' (Rachel Schraer, 18 August 2020).